Human Dignity

A dignidade não é uma coisa, mas muitas. O que importa é compreender como, na vida de um ser humano, estas muitas coisas se relacionam entre si. Se uma pessoa tenta dizer o que dela julga perceber, torna-se, involuntariamente, alguém que traça um extenso mapa da existência humana. A falta de modéstia que isto implica é inevitável, e portanto, assim espero, pode ser perdoada.

Pedro Vasco de Almeida Prado
Sobre o que é importante Lisboa, 1901

Dignity is not one thing, but many. What matters is understanding how these different things are interconnected in a person's life. When someone tries to express what he believes he understands of this matter, he will involuntarily end up drawing a sweeping map of human existence. The immodesty that lies in this is inevitable and hence, I hope, will be pardonable.

Pedro Vasco de Almeida Prado
On what is important Lisbon, 1901

Human Dignity

A Way of Living

Peter Bieri

Translated by Diana Siclovan

polity

First published in German as *Eine Art zu leben. Über die Vielfalt menschlicher Würde*
© Carl Hanser Verlag, Munich, 2013

This English edition © Polity Press, 2017

The translation of this work was funded by Geisteswissenschaften International –
Translation Funding for Humanities and Social Sciences from Germany, a joint
initiative of the Fritz Thyssen Foundation, the German Federal Foreign Office, the
collecting society VG WORT and the Börsenverein des Deutschen Buchhandels (German
Publishers & Booksellers Association).

Polity Press
65 Bridge Street
Cambridge CB2 1UR, UK

Polity Press
350 Main Street
Malden, MA 02148, USA

ISBN-13: 978-0-7456-8901-2

A catalogue record for this book is available from the British Library.

Library of Congress Cataloging-in-Publication Data
Names: Bieri, Peter, 1944- author.
Title: Human dignity : a way of living / Peter Bieri.
Other titles: Art zu leben. English
Description: English edition. | Malden, MA : Polity Press, 2016. | Includes
  bibliographical references.
Identifiers: LCCN 2016023506| ISBN 9780745689012 (hardback : alk. paper) | ISBN
  9780745689043 (mobi)
Subjects: LCSH: Respect for persons. | Conduct of life. | Dignity. | Philosophical
  anthropology. | Autonomy (Philosophy)
Classification: LCC BJ1533.R42 B5413 2016 | DDC 170/.44–dc23 LC record available
  at https://lccn.loc.gov/2016023506

Typeset in 10.5 on 12 pt Sabon
by Toppan Best-set Premedia Limited
Printed and bound in the UK by Clays Ltd, St Ives PLC

For further information on Polity, visit our website: politybooks.com

Contents

Introduction

Dignity as a Way of Living

Philosophy, as I understand it, is the attempt to bring conceptual clarity to important experiences of human life. In order to think and talk about these experiences, we have invented terms that are self-explanatory when used within their usual contexts. Sometimes, however, we wish to know more about what they actually mean, because something important is at stake – both in terms of understanding and of action. When we then take a step back from our linguistic habits and focus on the ideas themselves, we become confused because we realize that we did not at all understand what we were talking about the whole time. All of a sudden, the terms seem strange and mysterious.

This may happen to us with the concept of *dignity*. We know that human dignity is something important, that must not be violated. But what is it actually? What is it *exactly*? To gain clarity on this question, we can follow two different conceptual paths. The first regards dignity as a human *property*, as something that humans possess by virtue of being human. Then it is important to make sense of the nature of this property. We would not want to understand it as a natural, sensory property but as a special kind of property that is rather like a *right*: the right to be respected and treated in a certain way. We would regard it as a right that is immanent to every human being, that she carries within herself and that she cannot be robbed of, no matter how many horrible things are inflicted upon her. Some readings trace back this right and make sense of it in terms of our relationship with God as the creator.

In this book, I follow another path and take up a different perspective. Human dignity, as I understand and discuss it here, is a certain way of leading one's life. It is a pattern of thought, of experience and of action. Understanding this idea of dignity means envisioning this conceptual pattern and tracing it in our minds. For this, we do not need a metaphysical conception of the world. Instead, what we need is a keen and sharp look at the wide-ranging experiences that we seek to capture with the concept of dignity. What we have to do is to understand all these experiences in detail and ask ourselves how they are interconnected. We have to fathom the intuitive content of the experience of dignity.

There are three different dimensions to dignity as a way of living. The first is the way that I am treated by other people. They can treat me in such a way that my dignity remains intact, or they can destroy my dignity. Here dignity is something that is determined by others. To bring to mind this dimension, I can ask myself the following question: What can someone take away from another person when he wants to destroy his dignity? Or: What must one not take away from the other when he wants to protect his dignity? That way, I can gain an overview of the different facets of dignity in so far as it is dependent on others and clarify for myself how these facets are interconnected.

The second dimension also concerns other people in my life. But this time, it is not about how they treat *me*, but about how I treat *them*, and, more broadly, how I view them: what kind of *attitude* I have to them. It concerns what role, from my perspective, they play in my life. In this case, dignity is not something that is determined by others, but by me. The guiding question is: Which patterns of experience and conduct towards others allow me to *preserve* my dignity? And which actions and experiences cause me to *forfeit* it? In the first dimension, the responsibility for my dignity lies with others: it is their actions that either preserve or destroy it. In the second dimension, this responsibility lies exclusively with me: it is up to me whether or not I succeed in leading a dignified life.

In the third dimension, it is also me who decides about my dignity. It concerns the view that I have of myself. The question one needs to ask here is: Which ways of seeing, judging and treating myself let me experience dignity? And when do I feel as if I am forfeiting my dignity because of the way I behave towards myself?

How do other people treat me? How do I treat them? How do I relate to myself? Three questions, three dimensions of experience and three dimensions of analysis that all coalesce in the concept of dignity – this accounts for the *density* of this concept and its particular weight. Conceptually, it is possible to distinguish clearly between these three dimensions. However, they become intertwined in our experiences of the preservation, damage or loss of our dignity. Experiences in which our dignity is at stake often have this special complexity: the way that we relate to ourselves shapes our attitude to others, and this connection impinges on how and to what extent others can influence our dignity. Dignity is thus a multi-layered experience. Sometimes the layers overlap in such a way that they become indistinguishable as individual layers. The task of a conceptual representation such as this is to show them as separate experiences.

We experience the loss of our dignity as a horrible *defect*. It is not just *any* defect, that we can adjust to and from which we can keep an inner distance. It represents a stigma that can challenge our will to live, comparable only to great, irredeemable guilt. Through the loss of our dignity we are deprived of something without which life no longer seems worth living. This loss casts such a dark shadow over our life that we no longer actually live but only endure it. We feel that we cannot continue living with this defect. I wanted to find out: What does this great good of dignity consist in, and what makes the stigma of its loss so threatening?

This cannot mean that we should search for a *definition* of the concept of dignity: for necessary and sufficient conditions for someone's retention or loss of dignity. This is not what we want to find out. This is not the kind of precision and clarity we are in search of. What we want to comprehend are both the details and the entirety of the complex of experiences that we associate with the concept of dignity. I have found the following question helpful, which became the more pressing the longer I spent collecting these experiences: Why have we *invented* a dignified way of living? What is it an *answer* to? The idea that slowly emerged was that our lives as thinking, experiencing and acting beings are fragile and constantly under threat – from without and from within. A dignified way of living is the attempt to contain this threat. In our constantly endangered lives, it is important to *stand our ground* with confidence. What matters is that we do not let ourselves merely be swept along passively by bad experiences, but face them with a certain *fortitude*, saying: *I accept the challenge*. A dignified way of living is therefore not just *any* way of living, but the existential response to the existential experience of being under threat.

This book has therefore become a reflection on human life as such – an answer to the question: What kind of life do we humans actually live? What are its challenges? How can we best face up to them? I sometimes found the metaphor of *equilibrium* helpful. Some attempts to defy existential threats feel like the effort to retain our equilibrium in a testing force field. Losing and winning back dignity somewhat resembles losing and regaining equilibrium. Dignity that has been irredeemably lost is like an equilibrium that can never be restored. The concept of dignity stands for this special kind of equilibrium. This idea is essential. Without it, it we could not intellectually locate and articulate an important facet of our experience. It would be like having a conceptual blind spot in our mental field of vision.

The dignified way of living is not all of a piece. It has fissures and cracks, ambiguities and inconsistencies. Making sense of human dignity does not mean gilding and glossing over these imperfections. It means recognizing them and explaining them in their confusing logic. Individual experiences of dignity are not always unambiguous and seamless either. Different experiences can be in conflict with one another, giving rise to dilemmas of dignity. Our individual experiences are not crystalline – experiences with crystal clear, sharp contours. Our intuitions about preserved or lost dignity are often unclear and run at the edges – like watercolours before they dry.

I have no desire to present a *theory* of dignity. I am not sure that we need such a theory at all. I do not want to prescribe to anyone how she should think about this important dimension of her life. In general, my intention is not to be in the right about anything. The book is written in a tone of intellectual trial and error. My goal is not to prove anything, but to make certain things visible and comprehensible. This is about bringing to mind familiar experiences – and expressing them in the richest and most precise ways possible. My aim has been to talk about concrete people in concrete situations, in order then, in a final step, to arrive at a more abstract account. It is easy to get lost in this process, to become entangled in outlandish thoughts. I have tried to keep readers aware of this. And there is also an additional type of critical distancing at some points in the book: are we really certain, I ask myself there, if something is a real experience and not just a play on words, a verbal mirage? Something that we just tell ourselves? This doubt, like a will o' the wisp, is impossible ever to dismiss for certain.

Is it possible to conceive of conceptual stories about dignity that are different from my own? Perhaps in the framework of another culture? I would be surprised if there were an account that was *totally* different, that would contain *nothing* of what is discussed here, but a series of completely different experiences. Yet there might be variations: other emphases, other evaluations, other thematic connections that I did not recognize, as well as doubts about the links that I considered obvious.

Writing this book was like going on a conceptual journey that remained incomplete and that could be continued. With luck, this openness will transfer to the readers' experience, who might recall their own experiences and measure what they read against them. My aim in composing this text has been to involve readers in my train of thought, making them accomplices in this passionate search for clarity. I therefore hope that readers will not only be swept along and captivated by the ideas themselves, but also by the melody of these reflections.

'Nothing of what I've read was really new to me. It has brought many things back to me. But I'm glad that someone has found words for it and presented it coherently. And I'm also glad that he does not deny how much remains unclear and uncertain on the fringes of those thoughts.'

If this is the verdict of my readers, I shall consider the work a success.

1

Dignity as Autonomy

We want to determine our lives ourselves. We want to be able to decide for ourselves what we do and what we do not do. We do not want to be dependent on the power and will of others. We do not want to have to rely on others. We want to be independent and autonomous. All these words describe a fundamental need – one that we cannot imagine our lives without. There might be times when this need is thwarted, and those times can be long. Yet the need remains. It is the inner compass of our lives. Many human experiences of dignity arise from this need. Situations in which there is a lack of autonomy, in which there is dependence and powerlessness are situations in which we feel as if our dignity is being lost. Then we do all we can to overcome this dependence and powerlessness and to regain our lost autonomy. For we are certain: this is what dignity is founded on.

Yet no matter how simple and clear the words are that we use to explain and conjure up this autonomy, the experience in question is anything but simple and clear. It too is no unified, monolithic experience. To be autonomous – that can mean many and very different things. If we want to get to the bottom of the idea of human dignity by tracing the way of living that it is about, we have to bring to mind the diversity of experiences that lie behind the simple, suggestive words. We are not alone and cannot do everything alone. We depend on others in diverse ways and they depend on us. We have to rely on them. What part of this creates natural human relations that we do not want to be without? And what part do we experience as dependence that threatens our dignity?

Being a Subject

To do justice to this question we need a conceptual story that reminds us of what kind of beings we are, what type of autonomy we seek and why it matters so much to us. It must be a story about what it means to be a *subject*. Which faculties lead us to experience ourselves as subjects – as opposed to objects, items, things or mere bodies?

Each of us is a *centre of experience*. It feels a certain way to be a human. Humans are corporeal beings with an internal perspective, an inner world. It has several dimensions. The most basic is that of physical sensation. It includes a grasp of the body's position and its movements, but also typical bodily sensations like desire, pleasure and pain, heat and cold, dizziness and disgust, lightness and heaviness. In addition, there are our sensory experiences: what we see, hear, smell, taste and touch. A further layer of experience is formed by feelings, such as joy and fear, or envy and jealousy, sorrow and melancholy. The pattern of our desires is closely bound up with this. What we desire expresses how we feel. And our desires can be read from what we imagine, from our fantasies and our daydreams. This whole set of experiences has a temporal dimension. It is embedded in memories and in a conception of future life with its hopes and expectations. All of this generates the mental picture we make of the world: what we think and believe about it, what we consider true and false, justified and unjustified, reasonable and unreasonable.

This is thus one of the meanings of being a subject: in that sense, to be a centre of experience or, as one could also say, a being with *consciousness*. Our behaviour develops out of this experience. There is involuntary behaviour which is pure movement: a twitch, a cramp, a blink. It can have an experienced internal side and thus be sensed behaviour, but it does not *originate* in this experience and is not its *expression*. Only when behaviour is the expression of an experience is it *action*. Those experiences that stand behind the action and express themselves through it are the *motives* of the action. I do something because I feel and desire something, because I remember or imagine something, because I have thought about and believe in something. When this is the case, I am the *author* of my action, I am a *doer* who develops his doing out of his experience. And the motives that guide me give my action its *meaning*.

We can verbalize the motives of our action. We can find words for our experiences and say out of which thoughts, desires and feelings we act. This way we can *explain* our action, both to others and to ourselves. We can tell stories about our motives that concern individual acts or longer phases of our action. We are beings that can narrate their lives in that sense. A subject, one could say, is a centre of narrative gravity. We are the ones who our motive stories are about. These stories are recollections, stories about present experience and stories about what we imagine our future to be; stories about where we come from, how we became what we are and what we intend. Through such stories a *self-image* develops, an image of how we see ourselves.

It belongs to our experience as subjects to discover that in a life there are many more thoughts, feelings, fantasies and desires than the exterior biography shows. And also more than the inner, conscious biography shows. Over time, we learn that there is a dimension of motives for our actions that lies in the dark, and that a subject's life can be concerned with becoming aware of these motives. Not that individuals need to be ceaselessly preoccupied with this. There might also be good reasons to leave some things in the dark, even forever. But it is the mark of subjects that they know about the existence of unconscious, hidden motives and about the possibility of inwardly expanding the radius of self-understanding.

The self-image that we have as subjects is not only an image of how we *are*, but also an idea of what we *would like* and *ought* to be. To our faculties as subjects belongs the capacity to deal critically with ourselves and to ask ourselves whether we are content with our actions and experiences, whether we approve or reject them. It belongs to the nature of subjects that they can experience a conflict between what they are and what they want to be, and that they can see themselves as failures. Subjects are therefore beings that are capable of internal *censorship*, capable of *forbidding* themselves actions, but also mere thoughts, desires, feelings and fantasies. By virtue of this ability, they are beings who can *blame* themselves. Subjects can live in a state of inner conflict, and they can ask themselves whether they can *respect* themselves for what they do and experience, or whether they must *despise* themselves for it.

It is the mark of a subject that she can question herself in this way, instead of merely drifting through life. And it does not end with the question. Subjects can not only look after themselves in a critical manner, but also tactically take charge of themselves and *change* themselves in their actions and experiences in a desired direction. As we are not just the victims of blindly flowing experience, but can evaluate ourselves from a reflective distance, it is possible for us to envisage a new way of thinking, wishing and feeling and to take steps towards such a transformation. Then we are doing something *with ourselves* and *for ourselves*. As one could say, we are working on our mental *identity*.

We now have a first, still sketchy, picture of what it means to be a subject. In the course of this book this image will become increasingly more detailed, richer and denser. The experiences we have with our dignity are intimately linked with the experiences we have as subjects. When our dignity is in danger, it is often because our lives as subjects are in danger. If we trace the individual threats to and defences of our dignity, we will automatically penetrate deeper and deeper into the experiences that belong to us as subjects.

Being an End in Itself

As subjects we do not want only to be *used*. We do not want to be mere *means* to an end, which others set and which is their end and not ours. We want, one could say, to be regarded and treated as *ends in themselves*. When we are not so treated, this is not just unpleasant. It is much more. We feel violated or even destroyed as subjects. When this happens, we experience it as an attempt to take away our dignity. To the extent to which our dignity is dependent on how others treat us, it is founded on the expectation, the claim and the right to be not only treated as a means to an end, but as ends in ourselves.

While travelling, I passed by a fun fair and saw something that I would not have believed to be possible: a dwarf-tossing competition. A strong man grabbed one of the small people and tossed him as far as possible on a soft, bouncy mat. The man who was being tossed wore padded protective clothing with handles and a helmet. The gawping crowd clapped and hooted at every throw. The furthest throw was almost four metres. I learned that the man who was being tossed had been at the world championship in dwarf-tossing. For this had really taken place: a world championship in throwing humans. After my return I discovered that this issue had preoccupied the highest courts. In France the *Conseil d'Etat* had banned the practice of dwarf-tossing, and the UN Human Rights Committee had dismissed an appeal against this decision. In both cases, the justification had been that human dignity has to be protected.

This was also my spontaneous reaction at the fun fair: you cannot do this to a human being. It violates his dignity. 'Isn't this terrific?', the man next to me exclaimed at a particularly far throw. 'Repulsive', I said, 'intolerable!' 'But why', the man responded in an irritated manner, 'nobody forced him into this, he is getting paid and it's great fun!' 'It violates his *dignity*!', I said angrily. It was strange to utter this

solemn word in the midst of the hooting crowd – a bit like surfacing
out of the water and gasping for breath. 'Nonsense', the man said as
he turned to leave, 'what is *dignity* anyway?'

Dwarf-tossing is like shot-putting or hammer throwing. Bodies are
thrown and what matters is that they are thrown as far as possible.
The only thing that is important about the shot and the hammer is
that they are bodies – objects that have a mass and a weight. This
is also the case with the dwarf who is tossed. He is treated as a
mere body, as a *thing*. The moment he is being thrown, nothing else
matters: that he is a human being who can also move independently;
that he is a body with experience, for whom it feels a certain way to
be grabbed and thrown; that in the process he has feelings like powerlessness, repugnance or fear; that he has desires, for example that
this may end soon; that he might have his own views of the hooting
crowd, about the whole nature of the event and about his fate as a
small person. All of this is being blanked out by the throwers and
the audience. It is not of interest, quasi forgotten. And now we have
an initial explanation for the disgust one might feel at the event: the
human who is being tossed is deprived of his dignity, because it is
disregarded that he is also a *subject*. He is thereby reduced to a mere
object, a *thing*, and in this objectification lies the loss of dignity.

Yet this explanation does not go far enough. If a fire breaks out
in a cinema, everyone will try to make their way out without regard
for others. They will push other visitors aside, knock them over and
kick them. They will treat them like objects that are in the way, as if
they were clearing a mass out of the way. During a mass panic, the
individual no longer cares that others are also subjects with experiences like himself. This is cruel, but this is not the cruelty of stolen
dignity. When in this scenario a tall person grabs a small person and
tosses him away like an object in order to clear space, this is different
from dwarf-tossing at the fun fair. In what sense?

There is a difference in *situation*, that is matched by a difference
in *motivation*. The motivation of people trying to escape is blind
panic which only leaves room for the one thought: *getting out!* The
cruelty which reduces others to bodies that are in the way is not
deliberate and tactical. It is the blind cruelty of the will to survive.
'What else could I have done, my life was at stake!', the tall one will
say, who first grabbed and slung away a chair and then a person.
There is no such excuse at the fun fair. There humans are tossed for
mere pleasure. And if put this way, something else becomes apparent that makes this situation a degrading one. The pleasure of the
gawping and hooting crowd *consists* in experiencing how a human
is turned into a mere thing. They do not forget for a moment that
the object that is tossed is a person, a living being and a centre of

experience like them. If they forgot it, all the fun would be gone. That the person tossed for pleasure is deprived of their dignity therefore means that an individual who is clearly a subject is, without the need to do so and on purpose, treated like a mere object, a thing. This is one of the things that the judges who banned the event wanted to prevent.

The other thing that mattered to them was that the dwarf who is tossed is turned into a *plaything*. He is a thing with which one plays tossing games and organizes throwing competitions. He is considered and used as a means, an instrument to this end. During the competition he is *only* a plaything, *only* a means for the end of the competition and the entertainment of the audience. He himself does not at all appear in the game as someone who also *experiences* the situation. His perspective, his view of things, is treated as if it did not exist. This also happens when people are abused as human shields or walking bombs. They are, like the dwarf who is tossed, reduced to being bodies that are deployed for an end. The element of the game, of a spectacle and of entertainment might be missing here, but both cases have something crucial in common, namely that humans are used exclusively as a means to an end.

What the judges had in mind was an understanding of dignity that implies that humans, even when we regard and deploy them in a variety of ways as means and instruments in order to achieve an end, may not be *reduced* to this end, this function, either in the way they are viewed or in their treatment. Even when we have a purposeful, functional relation to them this may not be the *only* relation that leads us. In order to preserve their dignity, it must not be forgotten that the individuals *themselves* also matter. This is, the judges believed, precisely what disturbs and disgusts us about the dwarf-tossing. By using a person as a missile and a mere plaything, so that he himself no longer matters in any way, he is deprived of the most precious status that exists: the status as an end in itself.

Soldiers in war are also deprived of their dignity according to this understanding of the idea. They are sent to the front when it is known that they will be nothing but cannon fodder – human shields that run, fall and die, so that the others from the back ranks can attack better. Jakob von Gunten in Robert Walser's novel of the same name imagines what it would be like marching to Russia as a soldier under Napoleon: 'I would be only a little cog in the machine of a great design, not a person any more. I would know nothing of my parents any more, of relatives, songs, personal troubles or hopes, nothing of the meaning and magic of home any more. Soldierly discipline and patience would have made me into a firm and impenetrable, almost empty lump of body.'

Slaughterhouses

Visiting a slaughterhouse is distressing. Why? There are streams of blood and excrement, it reeks and one hears the fearful cries of the animals, which stay in the memory for a long time. A slaughterhouse is a factory of death. Thousands of animals are carted in in order to be mechanically killed and then processed into meat portions in a meat factory. Each of these animals, beyond being a living organism, is also a centre of experience. It senses its movements, feels hunger, thirst and pain, experiences pleasure and fear. Its experiences are simpler than ours, but they are experiences, and in this sense, such an animal is a subject. And now it is simply killed because we want to eat it. This thought alone is oppressive. 'But animals also eat each other!' But they do not establish killing factories with killing machines that are designed to execute as many animals as possible in the shortest possible time; to turn as large a number of animals as possible in the shortest possible time into saleable meat portions.

What disturbs us is not the killing alone. It is also the thought that the animals that end up here were *from the beginning* only bred, fed and cared for in order to be killed and turned into a product. It is the fact that these animals, who often grow up in a cramped and artificial environment, are at no moment in their lives treated as if they themselves – their lives and needs – mattered. From their conception to their death they are never anything other than the precursor to an edible supermarket product. They are things that are fed in order to then feed us. Nothing about the way they are treated gives them a chance to live as ends in themselves – the way we grant it to pets and as animals living in the wild are able to. When we leave the slaughterhouse, we not only feel sick because of the blood and the smell. It disgusts us because it makes us aware in a drastic way of something that we might well know already: that animals too can be treated in an undignified manner. And if we perceive it that way, this is because we apply the standard that we discussed earlier, namely that dignity consists in being treated not only as a means but also as an end in itself.

What If It is Voluntary?

In the evening after the event I met the star of the dwarf-tossing competition at his trailer.

'How can you bear this?', I asked.

'No problem', he said, 'it's a soft landing.'
'That's not what I mean', I said, 'I don't mean the risk.'
'What then?'
'Dignity.'
'What are you talking about?'
'I'm talking about the fact that when you're tossed, you're treated as just an object, as a thing.'
'Sometimes people toss children and they squeal with pleasure.'
'That's different. They're not treated as just things, but as human beings who are given *pleasure*. It's about them and what they *experience*.'
'Have you seen the boy who is catapulted with a swing to the very top of a human pyramid? After all, he's also being tossed and not for his pleasure.'
'He's *doing* something during it. He turns and paddles in a certain way. He spent a long time practising it. He demonstrates a skill. He's a performer.'
'There's a circus in the next town where a person is shot into the air through a gun barrel and then falls into a net.'
I had seen something like this when I was a child. At the time I had found it sensational and been completely absorbed by the thrill of the danger the man was putting himself in. Now I hesitated. Eventually I said:
'The man is not *tossed* by anyone. No one is *handling* him. He puts himself under the control of a machine.'
'And you have less of a problem with that? He's not *doing* anything either. Something is just *happening* to him, too.'
'That's true', I said, 'But you...you're being *grabbed*. It's obvious that you are being used, and that this is just about using you.'
'Using me? For what?'
'For entertainment. For fun.'
'When a clown trips someone, they're also being used to make the audience laugh. And actors also – '
'That's different. In that case, something is *acted out*. It's a shared performance to which everybody contributes something. You, by contrast, don't entertain through what you're doing, but through what is done to you. That way you become just a *plaything* for others.'
A dangerous gleam came into his eyes.
'Let me tell you something. When you look like me, it's damn difficult to make a living. Who are you to talk? You can choose among thousands of occupations. I can't. Who would employ a dwarf? And what's more, I *volunteered* to be in the show. *I* took the decision to

be tossed. Okay, you can say that I'm being used for the amusement of others. But I decided to *let* myself be used and be gaped at. It was my free decision. It was my free choice of career – even if you probably find this word ridiculous. And that's why you can't come along and blather on about lost dignity. Have you ever heard of Manuel? Manuel Wackenheim, the French dwarf? He went as far as the UN to fight for his right to be tossed in a circus. He lost. The judges said that it violates human dignity. I'm asking you, what about the dignity that lies in the freedom of choice?'

We will see later in this chapter how important the opportunity for free choice is to the experience of dignity as autonomy. When it is restricted or destroyed, dignity is in danger. Free choice is a *necessary* condition of dignity. Is it also a *sufficient* condition? The supreme court did not think so. Freedom of choice does not *in itself* confer dignity. We can freely choose to do something that violates our dignity, despite being voluntary. And this is why the court set a limit on freedom in this instance. One could say that the court deprived someone of his freedom in order to save his dignity. Underlying this is a conception of dignity that can be explained this way: although dignity is something that can also be determined individually, it is not *only* something that is under the control of individuals. There is also something greater, something objective about it that always affects individuals, but reaches beyond them. It characterizes an entire *way of living*. It is this entire way of living that is under threat when dwarfs are tossed – when human beings are degraded by being turned into objects and mere means. This way of living has to be protected by the legal system. Compared to an individual's freedom of choice, this way of living is the higher good. We are prohibited from wilfully gambling away our dignity.

The man I met at the trailer had not only spoken of his free choice but also of his difficulty in finding employment. What he said haunted me. During our conversation I had come dangerously close to claiming that he was, in terms of his employment, leading an undignified life. Nobody could accept being told that. It would amount to personal annihilation. This explained his irritation. He had then had recourse to a defence that drew out something important: our judgements about dignity do not only depend on the *action*, but also the *situation*. The more oppressive and the more hopeless a situation is, the greater our tolerance of lost dignity. It may be that a person is in distress and has no choice but to sell himself as a plaything. In that case, our judgement could be that he is robbed of his dignity not only through being treated as a mere thing and means, but also through being forced to gamble it away by selling himself. And that being the case, we can actually no longer say that he is gambling it away, for the gambling away of dignity requires freedom.

Humiliation as Demonstrated Powerlessness

When we are disregarded as subjects or misused as mere objects we feel *humiliated*. Humiliation is the experience of having our dignity taken away by someone else. What is at the core of this experience?

It is an experience of *powerlessness*. But what actually is powerlessness? The absence of power. But not *every* absence of power is what we call powerlessness. We do not have the power to alter planetary orbits, to turn water into wine or to cross the seas by foot. We know that we will never be able to do this, and yet we do not experience this as powerlessness. Powerlessness is the absence of a *specific* power: the power to be able to fulfil a *desire*. From an entirely formal point of view, the following applies: whenever we cannot fulfil one of our desires we are powerless. Yet the powerlessness we experience during an act of humiliation is a particular kind of powerlessness. It is the inability to fulfil a desire that is critical to our life.

It might be the desire for freedom of movement. That it cannot be fulfilled is the powerlessness of the paralysed, the captive or the individual in front of whose eyes a wall is built that will separate her from her family and prevent her from leaving the country. It might be the desire to have a certain career or occupation. That it cannot be fulfilled is the powerlessness of the unemployed. It might be the desire to buy oneself the necessaries of life and medicines. That it cannot be fulfilled is the powerlessness of the poor. It might be the vain desire to prevent suffering, for example when one has to look on impotently at a child drowning in the floods, at relatives being deported, at someone screaming in pain. And finally, powerlessness might consist in being forced by someone to act against desires that are part of our self-image, for example by betraying a friend, defiling a holy object or committing to a hated ideology.

An instance of powerlessness that merely *happens* to us is not of itself a humiliation. Earthquakes, famines and epidemics make us powerless but do not humiliate us. The powerlessness of humiliation is also not the kind of powerlessness that individuals can experience when their own abilities are not enough, for example when they fail to overcome an obstacle or to solve a problem. The powerlessness of humiliation has to do with other people. Viewed conceptually, humiliation requires a *perpetrator* and a *victim*. One person humiliates another. He humiliates him by bringing him into a position of powerlessness. This powerlessness is never unintended or unplanned. When I am knocked over and dragged along by a panicking crowd, it is powerlessness, but it is not humiliation. Humiliation only arises when one person *purposely* brings another into a position of powerlessness.

Merely making someone powerless is also not enough. When someone puts me in a position of powerlessness while acting in secret, so that I only suffer the pure result of her action, I do not experience it as humiliation. What matters is that I experience how the perpetrator *enacts* powerlessness, that she *demonstrates* to me how she renders me powerless. The experience of humiliation is thus an experience of powerlessness where its originator makes sure that I feel it as something that he does to me. Before my very eyes, he creates the wall that will destroy my life. He summons me to the boss's office where he fires me. He forces the Jews to clean the street with a toothbrush. Humiliation is demonstrated powerlessness. What belongs to it is *arbitrariness* as an expression of power – the conscious decision to perform an action despite having the option to refrain. The wall does not have to be built. The lay-off is humiliating because there is no compelling reason for it.

Yet humiliation is more than the naked demonstration of powerlessness. The person who humiliates me not only makes me feel that she is the originator of my powerlessness, but also that she *enjoys* and *savours* seeing me powerless. What is demonstrated is thus not only powerlessness but also its enjoyment. It is demonstrated by the individual who grins at the people standing by the window, powerless and desperate, while he puts stone after stone upon the wall. He makes sure his victims *see* him enjoying this demonstration. The experience of demonstrated powerlessness is bad enough. But what makes humiliation one of the most horrendous experiences that we know is this last element of having to experience how our powerlessness is enjoyed by its originator and how thoroughly he makes sure that we notice his enjoyment. You could see all of this in the pictures of American soldiers at Abu Ghraib prison relishing the sight of stacked up naked prisoners.

Escaping to an Inner Fortress

Dignity is the right not to be humiliated. What can I do if this right is violated? I cannot simply *endure* a humiliation. I cannot simply *persevere* through this terrible experience. But what can I do? I can *beg* and *plead* with the perpetrators not to do this to me – to tear down the wall or to rehire me. But this feels like being held aloft in the hands of a laughing giant. Begging only worsens the situation as it acknowledges the powerlessness. Every rejected plea is another experience of powerlessness that reinforces the previous ones.

We sometimes say that an individual who gives way to such hopeless pleading is humiliating himself, but this is actually wrong and even absurd. After all, he does not enjoy making himself powerless, and individuals generally do not cause their own powerlessness. Saying that he is humiliating himself is a misleading rendition of the idea that by begging and pleading, he affirms and reinforces his humiliation and thereby additionally gambles away his dignity.

What is the alternative? We need one, for mere endurance is impossible, as it would be unbearable. We need to somehow confront powerlessness, at least internally. And through our reaction we must avoid gambling away our dignity. After I had discussed with the dwarf the meaning of the verdict against his French colleague, I got up to leave. He then said:

'Nobody can take away my dignity – no matter what they do.'

'Doesn't it bother you that others are entertained by your appearance, and that tossing you further adds to their entertainment?'

'That's their problem, not mine.'

'But don't you feel humiliated?'

'I close my eyes and think of something nice. Afterwards it's like it didn't happen.'

Is it possible to save our dignity by escaping to an inner fortress during a humiliating situation, where others cannot reach us? This is the attempt to withdraw internally from the situation, evading our perpetrators' scornful, humiliating glances. We reject internally those who control us externally: 'You can't get me where I'm going! The person you're trying to humiliate is no longer here! No one will be home when you arrive with your humiliations and try to gloat over my powerlessness! I've disappeared inside and now your humiliating gestures can't touch me.' Lip service might be the model here: one performs what looks like a meaningful deed, but which is in reality nothing but an empty, automatic movement, from which one as an experiencing subject has withdrawn a long time ago. I could try this strategy when, surrounded by the others' scornful laughter, I am forced to clean the street with a toothbrush – vacant movement as the last defence of dignity. Or is this a self-delusion, essential to our emotional survival, but unable to prevent the loss of dignity? I return to this in Chapter 5.

Having Rights

Rights are a bulwark against dependence that is caused by arbitrary action. They therefore contribute to our experience of dignity as autonomy. People with rights can make demands. They do not need to *ask* to do something or to have something done for them. They can *claim* or *sue for* it. They are not dependent on anyone's goodwill. They cannot be shoved around like those without rights. When I have a right to something, it means that others have a duty to do or to abstain from doing something for me. My legal position provides me with autonomy in the sense that it offers protection against arbitrariness.

Rights are a bulwark against powerlessness as they give me the power to stand my ground. They are therefore also a bulwark against humiliation. They narrow the scope of those who want to demonstrate my powerlessness to me and enjoy seeing me powerless. I can take legal action when I am feeling powerless. If a court declares that I am right and I have been able to hold my ground, I feel as if my dignity has been restored or affirmed. The previous humiliation has been repealed.

I come home and see a gang of people who are about to clear out and destroy my house. They roar with delight on seeing my impotence, and this is humiliating. In a society without rights this deprives me of my dignity and there is nothing to be done against this powerlessness. As a subject with rights, by contrast, I have this dignity: I can call the police to put an end to the powerlessness. I have a right to it and in this right lies my dignity. This dignity accrues to me through the acknowledgement that I am a subject with rights. And when I am annihilated as a legal subject, I am deprived or robbed of my dignity.

Being Patronized

When we demand to be treated as autonomous human beings, we claim that we are *mature* and responsible for ourselves. When someone contests this by nannying us and making decisions over our head, we feel *disfranchised* and *patronized*. We experience a loss of *authority* over our life, of the power to decide freely and act independently. Others now determine what we may want and do, and this can mean humiliation and endanger our dignity.

Yet dignity is not always under threat when we are patronized. It depends on *who* takes away that authority and autonomy and for what *reasons*. The worst case is that of a despot. He and his clique, the party, force upon us an entire way of living that runs counter to our thinking, desires and conduct. We are made compliant through threats, surveillance, blackmail and torture and are forced to surrender authority over our lives completely. Under the rule of such total arbitrariness, someone else decides where we should live, where we should work and even whom we should love and marry. Our speech is also controlled, and ideally the despot would even like to dominate our inner lives, our thoughts, feelings and desires.

This happens in the world of George Orwell's *Nineteen Eighty-Four*. 'The party seeks power entirely for its own sake', O'Brien, the chief torturer says to his victim Winston. 'Power is not a means, it is an end.' The paternalistic treatment and oppression of citizens does not in the slightest serve their wellbeing, their benefit or their protection. They are not for a single moment viewed and treated as ends in themselves, but are nothing but playthings of power. And they are humiliated. O'Brien again and again relishes the powerlessness that he inflicts on Winston and makes sure that Winston sees his enjoyment. He is not only a monster because he does not shy away from any kind of physical cruelty, but also – and especially – because he makes Winston see his own powerlessness. He is a master in the art of humiliation.

Of course, not every state intervention in our life is a paternalistic act that violates our dignity. Laws passed by parliaments are often commands and prohibitions that narrow our freedom. They diminish individual authority and, in that sense, laws are paternalistic – we can no longer do everything we want to do. This ranges from issues of transport, over property and commerce to laws that prohibit crimes. We are required to wear helmets and safety belts, banned from smoking in certain places, from dealing drugs, from entering or interfering with others' property, from purposely hurting or killing people. The reason we accept these things is because – overall – they protect our dignity. This does not represent a submission to despotic power, but a renunciation of freedom for the benefit of society. The idea is that we sacrifice freedom for the common good, which also benefits individuals. Because of this logic, we are expected to accept these paternalistic laws. What is crucial is that such laws should be explained to us in every single case and that we can *follow* their logic. This is respectful of our dignity as subjects, of us as thinking, comprehending beings who refuse to accept incomprehensible, blind impositions. We might see individual cases differently, doubt the alleged evidence and question the conclusiveness of the arguments. But as long as we have the freedom to have our views heard and to be involved in the discussion, our dignity is not violated. It is only violated when we are silenced. Only then are paternalistic actions an experience of powerlessness and humiliation.

I once flew to Teheran to attend a book fair. As we were landing, the pilot made an announcement. 'I would like to remind all women on board that they are required to wear a headscarf on leaving the plane', he said. 'This also applies to foreign visitors.' I knew about this rule and yet I could not believe this was really possible – a state that prescribes what people have to wear. At the fair I was introduced to my translator. I wanted to shake her hand, but it remained concealed by her black dress. 'It is not permitted for a strange man to shake a woman's hand', I was told. Later on I happened to be walking next to a female stranger in the street. A revolutionary guard jumped out of an archway and grabbed by arm. 'You not go with woman!', he said. I explained that I had not been walking *with* the woman, but accidentally happened to be walking *next* to her. 'You not go with woman!', he repeated. I rebooked my flight and went home early. When I turned on the television that night, I saw a report about women in Saudi Arabia who are not allowed to drive cars and may only travel with a male guardian.

A few days later, a law was implemented in France that prohibits women from wearing religious headscarves and burkas in public. 'This is intolerably paternalistic!', a woman said to the camera. 'Telling us how to dress! I feel violated in my dignity!' 'France is a secular state and does not tolerate symbols of religious oppression in its public sphere', a government representative said. 'But I *don't* feel oppressed! I *want* to wear the veil!', the women exclaimed, 'It's part of my religious dignity!' 'The state sees this differently', the man said, 'it has to protect the constitution by defending the principle of secularism and prohibiting its violation.' 'I feel *humiliated* when you force me to take off my scarf!', the woman screamed. 'I feel so *powerless*!'

Transparency in the goals and reasons behind paternalistic laws or campaigns is what guarantees dignity. This has been pre-eminently captured by Wilhelm von Humboldt: 'The only method of instruction, perhaps, of which the State can avail itself consists in its declaring the best course to be pursued as though it were the results of its investigations. But where it coerces the citizens by some compulsory agreement, directly by law or indirectly in some way, or by its authority, by rewards, and other encouragements attractive to him, or lastly, merely by arguments, it will always deviate very far from the best system of instruction. For this unquestionably consists in proposing, as it were, all possible solutions of the problem in question, so that the citizen may select, according to his own judgement, the course which seems to him the most appropriate; or, still better, so as to enable him to discover the solution for himself, from a careful consideration of all the objections.'

'I can't believe you don't have referendums out there!', my cousin Hans from Bern said when I last saw him. 'Why would you want to live in a country like that! You can vote for your members of parliament, but that's all. Then they make the decisions for you. You essentially *hand over* your authority. You *give it up*! The rest is pure paternalism. You sit in front of the TV and watch how they make decisions on things that concern your life – your life! You have given up your authority over those things. What an absurdity! I'm so glad it's different here. Here, I can be involved up to the very end. I might eventually lose, because the majority is against me, but I was still able to vote and have an influence, even when it wasn't enough in the end.'

'Complex things need to be decided', I said. 'Without any expert knowledge and special expertise you can't reach a balanced verdict. It's not enough to debate these things in the pub. And such pub talk is also dangerous, dominated as it is by slogans, half-truths and dark, irrational emotions – a dubious kind of authority. If I leave these things to the members of parliament, the ministers and the cabinet, I do it in the hope and with the trust that they will make their choices with more consideration and rationality than if each of us decided spontaneously, according to his gut feeling. And by the way, Germany has had horrible experiences with direct democracy. That's why it has decided against it. It's possible for a nation to be completely swept away by a flood of indoctrination, bias and blind emotion. And the individual's authority is swept away with it, without his even noticing it. That's what I call unmitigated paternalism.'

'It's quite naive just to hope and trust. Politicians have no idea either! And what about their motives? Aren't they just as murky and irrational as ours? No, no, I tell you – never give up your control of the important things in life. Don't volunteer to be patronized. That's stupid. And *undignified*!'

'That's an abuse of the term', I said coolly. Our parting was icy. A few days later I received a postcard from Hans. ' "Undignified" – maybe I went too far', he wrote. 'When I look at some of the things that have happened here recently – I'm no longer *entirely* sure about it.' 'When I look at some of the things that happened *here* recently', I wrote back, 'I'm no longer *entirely* sure either.'

Caring Paternalism

Individuals can also patronize other individuals. Whether or not this endangers their dignity again depends on the intention behind the action and whether the infringement of freedom appears comprehensible and justified. In this case, it also depends on the will and the intentions of the person for whom decisions are made.

It may be that she does not yet *have* a will on the point at issue. This is the case with children who do not yet have either the maturity or authority to make their own decisions on such serious matters as the choice of a school or the treatment of an illness. Then either the parents or a legal guardian make the decision. As young children we are glad about this. The issue is too big for us, we are not up to it and feel overwhelmed when we are left alone with it. Let us imagine my parents failed to get me vaccinated. 'But you pulled such a face', they say. 'Why didn't you *insist* on it?', I say when the disease breaks out. 'Against your will?' 'Yes, of course. I wasn't able to judge for myself!' This is how we can end up *blaming* someone for not patronizing us.

While children sometimes do not *yet* have a will and authority that need to be respected, people who are senile or have dementia may *no longer* have such a will and authority. Then others have to make decisions for them, for example on where they may or may not go, what they should eat and which medicines they need to take. When children do not yet have authority, this does not create problems for dignity, as they are on their way to developing such authority. But when authority wanes with old age, it is hurtful, both to those affected by it and to us who have to watch it. We treat these elderly people gently and try to help them preserve their dignity. But this dignity is no longer their former dignity, which was founded on autonomy. I return to this distinction in the last chapter.

Sometimes there is a firm will, but we do not *know* it and cannot enquire about it either. Then we also need to make decisions over someone's head and, in that sense, patronize them. This is the case when there is an accident, a stroke, an unexpected turn during an operation or when someone falls into a coma. In these situations, doctors decide *on behalf* of the patient. If they do it right, they do not thereby violate the patient's dignity. What they must do is put themselves in the patient's position and ask themselves what their will would be. They might make mistakes. Perhaps I would have preferred to die of the tumour that was discovered during the operation, rather than live with the disability that was caused by cutting it out. Yet there was no way for the doctor to know this, and even though I am unhappy about her decision, I will not seriously resent her for it. And I certainly will not accuse her of having insulted me in my dignity. I will only make such an accusation if I learn that, although it looked hopeless, she cut out the tumour because it would enable her to make progress with her scientific research. Now I know that I was a guinea pig and that through her patronizing treatment, I was used as a mere means.

Such situations are especially tricky when we believe that we can make decisions *against someone's known will* without damaging their dignity – because we want to prevent something bad from happening and avoid suffering. We follow the formula: take away freedom to avert suffering. Being led by this goal – we think – prevents us from humiliating those affected by our paternalistic actions. We think that although they will inevitably experience it as powerlessness, they will not see it as powerlessness that we desire, intend and enjoy, but will recognize that what we impose upon them is the lesser evil. This is already our hope with minor paternalistic acts towards children and teenagers. We do not let them watch as much television as they would like, take away their violent computer games, do not allow them to drink alcohol or drive a car – although there is nothing they would rather do. We do not prohibit them from doing these things because we enjoy patronizing them, but out of a desire to protect them.

Sometimes we also act in this spirit towards adults and when much more serious issues are at stake. A doctor may conceal a shocking diagnosis from a patient and his relatives may support him in doing so. 'It would be such a burden on him – it would make everything even worse', they might say. 'Isn't it better for him to live a bit longer without having to worry about it?' 'You treated me like a *child*!' I will respond when they can no longer keep it from me. I will feel the kind of resentment that only occurs when someone's dignity, in the sense of autonomy, has been violated. The relatives will be offended by my resentment and say: 'But we had only *good* intentions!' 'Good intentions? What's that supposed to mean? How can you have good intentions towards someone when you don't take him seriously and have so little confidence in him? You have deprived me of something very important: the possibility of coming to terms with my fate and preparing for death fully consciously and independently, when I am not yet beset by weakness and pain. How could you steal this authority from me? How could you possible think you have a right to this? That's inexcusable!'

Or could I imagine saying: 'Although I feel betrayed and patronized, somehow I'm also glad. Had I known about it, I would have decided against doing some things that were important to me. Knowing about such a tumour, you wouldn't make a voyage on the Trans-Siberian Railway, would you?'

A situation that is problematic in a different way is when we take away pills from someone because we are concerned he might use them to end his life. While in the case of the concealed diagnosis we interfered with someone's *knowledge*, now we interfere with the realization of a plan, with an *action*. 'What were you thinking, taking the stuff away from me? It's *my* life and *I* alone decide about it!' 'Sure. But I thought that it might be imprudent, unnecessary and premature if you do this now. I hoped you might still find another way. I wanted to protect you – from yourself.' 'How could you presume to take that decision? This is not about how *you* see it, but only about how *I* see it. Nobody but *me* has authority over my life. I will now leave – forever. And don't you dare involve yourself again in my life – or in my death!'

And yet, perhaps one day I will receive a postcard that will say: 'I'm glad that you took the stuff away from me. But I can't live with you any more. Something has been broken. I know that you acted because you care for me, but still. P.S. I have collected enough pills again, and this time no one will take them away from me – no one.'

Yet another and even more complicated situation arises when such caring paternalism has to cross ideological barriers. There are religious communities that consider blood transfusions wrong and would condemn and exclude a member who has received one. A child is brought to the hospital by her parents. There is no doubt that she will die unless she has a transfusion. This is out of the question, the parents explain. 'Exchanging blood – that means meddling with God's work. It means damnation.' A strange struggle ensues between two conflicting acts of paternalism: on the one hand, the parents' wish to protect their child from damnation; on the other, the doctor's desire to save the child's life.

'Why would you believe that you're right *on such a matter*?', the parents ask. 'Damnation is worse than death. You can't inflict that upon our child. We have to protect her against your interference!' The idea of damnation means nothing to the doctor, who only has one thing on his mind: if he does not override the parents' will, the child will die. Nevertheless, he might hesitate. 'After all, it's their child and not mine,' he might think. 'She's a part of their life, not mine. Does this biological and psychological closeness, this proximity to her life, not give the parents an authority over the child's fate that is superior to my authority as a doctor? And does this greater authority not mean that I have to defer my judgement to theirs, no matter how much I'm against it? After all, we also grant parents such supreme authority in questions related to the upbringing of children, which are also very important. Isn't what I plan to do perhaps a dubious act of paternalism?'

Respect for Alterity and Conviction

In the end, the doctor has the parents removed from the room by force and carries out the transfusion. 'I *couldn't* act differently, I *had* to do it', he says afterwards. Before, he had another conversation with himself: 'The worldviews we hold are historically and geographically contingent. It is this insight that creates true tolerance. This is the view I usually also support. Why do I not act in accordance with it *now*?' Yet this inner monologue could not change his first impulse, which was to save the child's life. He had the feeling that if he did not follow his convictions in this case, he could not live with himself. 'How will I be able to sleep at night if I knowingly let this child die, just because her parents have this absurd idea of damnation?'

Later, when everything is over, the doctor searches for some conceptual clarity. 'You cannot refrain from doing what you believe is right, just because others consider it wrong', he tells himself. Why exactly is this the case? If I have the abstract, theoretical knowledge that my view – like all views – has traces of historical contingency, this does not change the fact that I consider it to be the *right* view and not just one possibility among numerous others, each of which I could adopt and act upon with equal force and conviction at any given moment. Otherwise I *would not* hold it, for believing in something means considering it to be *right*. That means that it was a question of my *seriousness* and also of my *authenticity* that despite considering it, I ultimately could *not* say to myself: 'Well, perhaps the other view is right after all. Perhaps the child's life and health are indeed worth less than her salvation in the afterlife.' Where would one be without this seriousness and authenticity when dealing with the important things in life? Is this not also a question of dignity?

These are the reflections the doctor will recall when he faces his next dilemma of caring paternalism. A woman in labour is admitted to the hospital. An examination reveals that the child's position makes a natural birth impossible. 'We have to carry out a Caesarean', he says to the woman. She comes from a remote village in a country with a powerful clergy. 'Under no circumstances!', the woman says, and the doctor learns that in the region she is from and will shortly return to such a procedure is considered sacrilegious, a violation of divine order. She would be condemned by the church and ostracized by her husband and the fellow villagers. It would be hell for her. The doctor explains that without the procedure, her child will die for certain and her life will also be in danger. 'That is still better than damnation and rejection!', the woman exclaims.

I imagine being in the doctor's position. Time is running out, but I want legal reassurance and call a lawyer. 'As you will know', the lawyer says, 'surgical procedures are considered bodily injury, but are justifiable with the patient's active consent. Consent is not subject to the standards of rational action, but may be denied on the basis of the patient's personal standards. That means that a Caesarean carried out against the patient's will is an act of unlawful bodily harm. But in your case, I wouldn't be too worried. You can use your freedom of conscience as grounds for exculpation. You can't be expected willingly to let the woman and child die, especially as you were on emergency duty and were surprised by the situation, so you couldn't have planned in advance to refuse to carry out such treatments.'

This helps, but not in every respect. This situation is more complicated than the refusal of the blood transfusion. In both cases, a child's life is at stake. But here, the child, although it is about to be born, is still a foetus and in a certain sense part of the mother's body over which she has authority. The procedure is therefore a paternalistic act towards the woman, which goes even further than in the earlier case – her body is cut open against her declared will. Furthermore, she expresses a clear choice: she would prefer death to exclusion. If I insist on the procedure, it would be like saying to her: '*You* don't get to decide this, *I* do, and I say: better exclusion than death.' *Am I allowed* to do this? Is this not a glaring violation of the woman's dignity and of her independence and autonomy? 'With all due respect to your seriousness and authenticity,' someone might say to me, 'here, in this particular case, another person's autonomy limits your commitment to your convictions. To put it another way: it's her dignity against yours.'

What am I to do? Something I definitely have to do is find out how unambiguous and firm the woman's will is. How articulate is she? How well can she explain it? Has she truly understood my explanation of the risk she faces? Am I certain that no misunderstanding is involved? How coherent is what she says? Is she, perhaps, primarily afraid of the operation? Perhaps she has a mistaken idea of what it is like? Does she perhaps feel threatened by the dramatic nature of the situation, the time pressure or the presence of someone she is afraid of and on whom she is dependent?

I send away the husband and the priest. I leave the woman alone for a while. I come back and look her in the eyes. 'No', she says, 'The scars. They would reject me. It would be hell.'

What might happen now?

I insist on the operation and go ahead with it. She holds a healthy child in her arms and the scar heals well. But she refuses to speak a word to me. This changes after a few days. 'I will stand up to them. If necessary, I will run away with the child. Away from the village, from their paternalistic rules. I am glad that we are both alive, the child and I. Thank you.'

But things might also turn out differently. She never speaks to me again and returns to the village. I also go there, in secret, incognito. She lives alone in the last house, more of a hut than a proper house. She and the child both look as if they have been starving and have also experienced other hardships – you can read the consequences of rejection in their faces. She seems to have lost all of her dignity. 'You have ruined my life', she might say to me. When she was discharged from the hospital, I had said to her silent, impassive face: 'I had no choice.' Had I been too preoccupied with *myself* and my emotions, despite the fact that this was solely about *her*? Can commitment to one's convictions be a mask for reckless self-centredness?

Reflections such as these might well lead me to decide against operating. The child dies, but I manage to save the woman. She cries for the dead child and is distraught because she will never be able to have children again. But she is at peace with herself. 'Thank you', she says when she is discharged. 'For saving my life. But especially for having respected my wishes. I'm sure it wasn't easy for you.' I visit her in the village, where everybody knows what she has been through. She is a well-respected woman, who carries her misfortune with dignity. What are my feelings? I imagine how much she could have been spared through the operation, how much more she could have of life. 'I know', she says, 'this is how *you* see it.'

But maybe the woman will one day come back and confront me, because she has changed her mind. 'Why didn't you ignore my foolish views, despite knowing what great suffering they would lead to? How can you call it "respect" when what you're respecting is obvious folly, leading to suffering and death? Why didn't you *save* me from it?'

'Well', I say, 'it was your wish, and my respect was not respect for folly, but respect for your competence and your desire to determine your own life. At that moment, this was what your dignity consisted in and I had to protect it. Respect for self-determination cannot be respect with the caveat that the will in question has to be identical with the will that we, the others, would have under the same circumstances. If my respect had this silent caveat, it wouldn't be real respect for a *different will* and therefore no true respect at all. It would instead be a paternalistic act and thus a violation of dignity. My respect – which was genuine – was also shaped and carried by the realization that I was *convinced* that you didn't have the right will and weren't making the right decision, because it would – as

I saw it – bring so much suffering. But I was also aware that we cannot speak of *knowledge* in relation to this issue. We aren't talking about *facts*, that someone can either know or not know, as in the usual case of knowledge. This is about *evaluations*, about someone's views on what is *important*, more important than other things, that are less important. And what could true respect for another human being consist in if not in recognizing what she considers important, no matter how much it differs from what we, the others, consider important? Your views have changed. But at the time, you considered the other thing to be more important. What else should I have done, other than respect the judgement that was valid at the given moment? After all, you would also like me to respect your *current* judgement, although we both know that such judgements can change with time.'

'But didn't you realize that I wasn't truly *free* in my judgement? That I was thinking and feeling the way I did because I was living in a state of dependence – on the opinions of my husband, the prejudices of the village and the judgement of the priests. And that I was afraid of all these things and, at the time, not yet in a position to oppose them and make myself independent of them? You must have known that the views I was referring to had been imposed on me – by men who were concerned with their power and their position and not at all with my interest. And if you indeed knew this, why didn't you – so to speak – side *with* me *against* myself, by protecting me against the others' assaults, as I wasn't able to do it myself?'

'Against your declared will? How can you defend and protect someone against her declared will? Is this not an assault in itself, a paternalistic act that is always prohibited because it violates dignity?'

'You know perfectly well that a person's views that cause suffering will inevitably shift and change through the experience of such suffering.'

'No, you can't know this because whether suffering is at all perceived as suffering depends on judgement. And that's why judgement also determines if the experience will later change the whole framework of the judgement and perhaps go beyond it completely. When a judgement leads to suffering never being experienced as suffering, this transformation doesn't take place. Suffering that is not experienced as such therefore *is* no suffering, because *suffering* is a subjective category. It is not objective, but bound to experience. If we don't take experiences into account, we lose the entire category of suffering. It was impossible for me to anticipate how your thinking and feeling would change once you had to continue living in the village as a mother in mourning and a childless woman. I couldn't have anticipated that your grief and despair would turn against those who had previously enslaved you with their views and prohibitions. And that's why the kind of substitutional acting that you have in mind and the absence of which you bitterly reproach me with, would have appeared to me as an assault, a violation of your autonomy and your dignity.'

Thus situations can arise in which there is a conflict between different experiences of dignity. It might be that for reasons of dignity I follow my convictions and put them into action, even when this means patronizing someone else whose dignity is thereby compromised. Conversely, it can also be the case that in order to protect someone else's dignity, in the sense of autonomy, I become unfaithful to myself and jeopardize my own dignity, in so far as it relies on my conviction and authenticity. The fact that there can be such dilemmas in regard to questions of dignity is connected to something I spoke of in the Introduction: neither the experience of dignity, nor the way of living that belongs to it and through which it expresses itself, are all of a piece.

Dependence: Asking and Begging

Willy Loman, the protagonist in Arthur Miller's *Death of a Salesman*, is sixty years old, unsuccessful and tired. 'He used to be able to make six, seven calls a day in Boston', says his wife Linda, 'Now he takes the valises out of the car and puts them back and takes them out again and he's exhausted... He drives seven hundred miles, and when he gets there no one knows him any more.' Loman cannot go on any longer and goes to see Howard, his boss, to ask for a post that does not involve travel.

What sort of situation are we in when we have to *ask for* something? What experiences can result from it? And what do they have to do with dignity?

Requesting something means articulating a desire and asking for someone's assistance in realizing it. Requests thus create situations in which we receive *help*. This involves admitting a lack of autonomy in a certain matter and that we are *dependent* and *reliant* on others. It is not within our own power, but that of another individual, to satisfy our need. Loman cannot transfer himself to a post that does not require travel, only Howard can. Howard has power over him, and this situation therefore from the beginning contains the danger of making Loman feel powerless.

Being dependent on help does not in itself constitute a threat to dignity. Otherwise dignity would only exist for the strong who never need anyone's help. What then determines it if being in need of help threatens dignity?

One aspect of it is the *nature of the relationship* between me, the petitioner, and the person who can either fulfil or reject my request. It is straightforward when the helper is a stranger, merely an administrator of state help, for example an official at the social welfare centre. Having to sit in a shabby corridor and hold a number is oppressive. But it is important to be precise with the description of our emotions: having to sit there *hurts*. Perhaps I used to work as an engineer or a director of a company, or I am an associate professor with a long list of publications – and now I sit here and have to request social assistance. I am hurt in my *pride* and in my *vanity*. 'This is so humiliating and degrading!', I might say and get drunk on these words because they allow me to experience soothing self-pity and relief through indignation. But these words are *wrong*. Nobody is presenting me as impotent, nobody has an interest in making me feel my powerlessness. The man behind the desk, whom I later have to sit across from, cannot arbitrarily humiliate me. I do not have to accept it if he says to me: 'Oh, it's you again!' It is not at his discretion whether or not I receive assistance. I have a *claim* to it and he *has* to grant it. My dignity in the relationship with him lies in my legal status as a citizen of this country.

He might send me off to clean a park, where I find myself one morning, rake in hand. I see my former colleagues drive to work in shiny cars, eat lunch in expensive restaurants. They greet me affably from afar. What precisely are my feelings? There is, of course, envy and disappointment, perhaps also resentfulness and anger, as I feel that the others are obviously less capable than me, the whole situation is unfair and I quarrel with the circumstances. But this has nothing to do with losing my dignity. 'This is beneath my dignity', I might say and consider withdrawing my claim for state assistance. Yet despite being a common turn of phrase, this expression is misleading. It is true that raking does not match my abilities. I am punching beneath my weight, so to speak, and this hurts. And when this continues for a long time, I might be overcome with despair, as I experience this type of work as alienating. This constitutes great misfortune, but it is not an experience of lost dignity. And this is because no one is plunging me into powerlessness through his power and arbitrariness, while grinning and making sure that I see his enjoyment.

The relationship between Loman and his boss Howard is of a totally different kind. It is entirely at Howard's discretion to grant or reject Loman's request. He has the power, and Loman has no way to make a claim. When Loman enters the room, Howard is busy connecting his new wire-recording machine, which was all the rage at the time and a status symbol for those at the top.

Howard: Hello, Willy, come in.
Loman: Like to have a little talk with you, Howard.
Howard: Sorry to keep you waiting. I'll be with you in a minute.
Loman: What's that, Howard?
Howard: Didn't you ever see one of these? Wire recorder.
Loman: Oh. Can we talk a minute?
Howard: Records things. Just got delivered yesterday. Been driving me crazy.

Howard plays the machine, one can hear his children's voices and he gives them his full attention. Willy, who has already twice articulated his request to have a conversation, is only the audience for a performance of this miracle device and is otherwise not present. In the midst of the girl's whistling coming out of the machine, Loman launches a third attempt:

Loman: Like to ask you a little favour if you...

And a fourth attempt:

Loman: That is a wonderful machine. Can we...

The fact that Howard ignores all three attempts is a humiliation because it demonstrates power: 'My amazing machine and I come first...' And it is a demonstration of Loman's powerlessness: 'You can try this as many times as you like – only I decide when we will discuss your request.'

Having to wait until the other has time is not in itself a humiliation. It is not humiliating when there are understandable reasons for the delay that are either directly visible or that we can guess from the situation, for example when one has to wait at a government bureau, for the doctor or the handyman. I experience dependence, but it is not accompanied by a demonstration of power, by arbitrary action that I have to endure powerlessly. Above all, there is no demonstration of an enjoyment of powerlessness. Even when negligence or plain laziness cause the wait, this does not yet lead to an experience of humiliation, only to frustration and anger. What is needed is purposeful arbitrariness, for example when a nurse makes me wait because she is visibly conducting a private phone conversation; or an officer at the government bureau who comes out of his room, locks up and smokes a cigarette outside while my time runs out; or security officers at the airport who, for no reason, make me take off my shoes to send through the scanner. The message is: 'You are dependent on my will.' That is what turns normal anger into the kind of fury that rises up when someone – for no reason and while clearly enjoying it – demonstrates our powerlessness to us. I saw a person who, driven by this fury, boarded the plane without wearing shoes. His body language showed that it was a question of dignity for him. A fellow passenger went up to him and congratulated him – nobody found it ridiculous.

The arbitrariness of Howard's behaviour is obvious. The wire recorder could wait, and by playing it, he shows off his power to do whatever he likes. What is perfidious about the scene is that he demonstrates a form of amusement that Loman would never be able to afford. To this, he adds mockery: 'They're only a hundred and a half. You can't do without it.' When Bobby Fischer competed against Boris Spassky for the world chess championship in Reykjavik in 1972, a Ferrari was on display in a shop window. Fischer's people found out that Spassky spent a lot of time every day standing in front of the shop window. Fischer bought the car and arrived in it for the game.

Loman's request for a conversation becomes *begging*. When does asking for something turn into begging?

It has to do with *repetition*. A single request was not enough. Loman had to repeat it. But it is not only the temporal aspect of the repetition – the repeated request; the second request and each that follows is also experienced differently because is it overshadowed by the memory that the previous one remained unanswered. The need for repetition is experienced by Loman as powerlessness, as humiliation: Howard makes him feel that their relationship is not one in which one single request would be enough, and that he has the power to ignore every new request. The transition from asking to begging occurs again after Loman finally manages to express his request for a job change.

> Loman: Well, to tell you the truth, Howard. I've come to the decision
>   that I'd rather not travel any more.

'Come to the decision': He wants to make it seem as if *he* decided about himself and his future work, as if his autonomy was not under threat. This is why he does not formulate it as a request, but as an announcement. Choosing the words of free choice is a pathetic, helpless attempt to deny his dependence and counter an impending humiliation. Howard explains that there is no in-house post available. If Loman now still continues to press his case, the announcement will inevitably become a request.

What makes requests dangerous is that their justification unavoidably involves admitting neediness and revealing weakness. In other contexts, a person might speak of her weaknesses motivated by the intimacy of a relationship. Such revelations can lead to even deeper feelings that would not develop if she did not allow the other person this insight. This is the case when Loman says to his wife: 'I'm tired to death. I couldn't make it. I just couldn't make it, Linda...I suddenly couldn't drive any more. The car kept going off on to the shoulder, y'know?...Suddenly I realize I'm goin' sixty miles an hour and I don't remember the last five minutes...' This admission of weakness does not endanger Loman's dignity because he is confessing it to his wife – he does it voluntarily, inspired by the intimacy of their relationship, not strategically in order to achieve a goal and not because he is forced to. What makes voicing requests difficult is not only the admission of weakness, but also that one does not speak of it voluntarily, but is forced to do so because of a predicament. Our reluctance to do this is demonstrated by the fact that we sometimes prefer to leave our desires unsatisfied rather than reveal our weaknesses to others. Illiterate people, for example, often forego many opportunities in their lives just to avoid asking for help.

This is connected to the second answer to our question about when being in need of help threatens our dignity. It not only depends on the nature of the relationship, but also on our *own attitude* to the weakness. Loman sees his exhaustion and lack of success as *defects*. This puts him in a predicament. In order to reach his goal, he has to address what he regards as his greatest possible defect, his lack of success. It would have been easier for him if he had never been enslaved to the so-called American Dream. 'Well', he could say to himself then, 'it's going downhill. But is it surprising, for a salesman of my age? Howard is an arse who cares only for success and money. Let's see if he'll help me. If not, I'll have a problem. But it will only be a financial problem, not a problem of my dignity. *He*'ll be the one with the problem of dignity. If he throws out someone who's been plodding for him his entire life, he's an undignified lump.'

It now all depends on how much Loman has to reveal of himself in pleading his case. He starts with a remark about his family situation that does not yet express any sentiment of weakness or despair.

Loman: I tell ya, Howard. The kids are all grown up, y'know. I don't need much any more. If I could take home – well, sixty-five dollars a week, I could swing it.

Howard: Yeah, but Willy, see I –

It did not help. Loman feels that he now has to escalate matters to another level, the level of emotions. This is a level that has so far

never played a role in his relationship with Howard. And he esca-
lates to it not because things between them have naturally progressed
towards greater intimacy, but because he has to achieve something
– as a means to an end. This step is humiliating for Loman, because
he takes it out of powerlessness.

> Loman: I tell ya why, Howard. Speaking frankly and between the
>   two of us, y'know – I'm just a little tired.

Why is this oppressive? What is happening here that should not be
happening? Loman is trying to give his admission of weakness a
veneer of worth, a certain dignity. He is presenting his trust and his
openness as something valuable to Howard, as a new, more intimate
definition of their relationship. This is oppressive because we know
that there is nothing Howard wants less. And above all, it is oppressive because it is clear that Loman also knows this – and does it
anyway. It is a paradoxical act, because it uses trust and openness
as instruments to achieve something with a person who from the
very beginning denies this kind of intimacy. Used this way, trust and
openness are destroyed. They are undermined by their utility. Loman
tries to haggle with his own weakness. He does it out of despair, but
even so, he is about to forfeit his dignity in the shape of something
we will discuss in Chapter 5 – his self-respect.

There really is no post for him, Howard repeats.

> Loman: All I need to set my table is fifty dollars a week.

If thus far we have been able to speak of a request, now it has clearly
become begging. Loman then tells Howard, who is not interested in
hearing it, about a legendary salesman, his role model, who inspired
him to become a salesman himself. Today, he says towards the end
of his story, everything is different. And then he utters the desperate
words:

> Loman: They don't know me any more.
> Howard: That's just the thing, Willy.
> Loman: If I had forty dollars a week – that's all I'd need. Forty
>   dollars, Howard.
> Howard: Kid, I can't take blood from a stone…

He cannot go lower than that. Not only because Loman certainly
could not survive on an even lower salary, but also because at some
point, every act of begging reaches an end, a point at which it would
not be possible to continue with any remaining self-respect. What else
can Loman do? He can turn to a moral attack:

Loman: I put thirty-four years into this firm, Howard, and now I
         can't pay my insurance. You can't eat the orange and throw
         the peel away – a man is not a piece of fruit!

There is also something oppressive about this. But what? It is the fact
that the viewer knows that Howard is not the kind of man who might
be moved by such an outburst or appeal. The feeling of oppression is
further heightened because we know that Loman also knows this. His
words therefore have no real audience. It is as if he were addressing
an empty room. It is in fact worse than if he was screaming these
words into an empty room, for there they would not be met with a
humiliating human silence.

Begging for Feelings

When we feel lonely we might want to say to someone: 'Why do you
no longer feel anything for me?' Not only: 'Why don't you *show* me
your feeling?' But: 'Why don't you *have* feelings for me?' This is not
meant to be an accusation, but comes out of a desperate desire to
escape loneliness.

This is an impossible request. We cannot determine our feelings
that way. We do not have control over them and cannot command
them. Feelings are not at our disposal. This is therefore worse than
a request for work, food or shelter, which can be granted if someone
wishes to do so. The request that another feel something makes such
feelings even less likely – everybody knows that. Those who still
beg for feelings deny this insight. Loneliness and despair do not in
themselves endanger dignity and nor does expressing these feelings.
If there is a threat to dignity here, it lies in the act of begging, of
which the beggar knows deep down that it is asking for something
impossible. Through this begging he experiences and demonstrates
dependence and powerlessness, which questions his overall existence
as an autonomous person – under another person's gaze.

I imagine a couple: Bernard and Sarah Winter. On a Sunday night,
Sarah drives her husband to the hospital. It is a silent journey. Bernard
understands his own silence – it is due to the anxiety he feels at the
thought of what lies ahead of him – but he does not know why Sarah
is silent. It hurts that she is silent and that he cannot read why. Now
they enter the hospital room where he will spend the coming weeks.
It is bleak, functional, clinical and smells of disinfectant. Sarah walks
in behind Bernard. He senses her fright, her repulsion, her silent
relief at the thought that it is not she who will have to stay here. She

leaves the door ajar, to serve as an escape route. He wishes she would shut the door and help him unpack, help him – with her words and her glances – make the room more bearable, less like a cell. But she leaves her coat on and stays where she is, already partly turned to the door.

'Ok, then', she says, putting her hand on the door latch. 'Can't you stay a little longer?', he asks, startled at the faltering sound of his own voice.

This question does not yet forfeit his dignity. He only expresses a desire and with it, a range of emotions: fear of loneliness and abandonment, the alienness of the clinical, grey environment, his illness. These are weaknesses, but showing weakness is not in itself a threat to dignity, as dignity cannot mean never admitting weakness. It is still possible that Bernard's admission of weakness and his desire for Sarah to stay longer might resonate with her and make her want to stay with him.

But things happen differently. 'I have to leave early tomorrow morning', she says as she opens the door even further.

'Please', Bernard says with a hoarse voice, 'this is so…and it's only 7 o'clock.'

The first time, it was a request, now it is already pleading. As before, it is an admission of weakness, a cry for help: 'I do not yet have the strength to be here by myself.' The message of her reaction is: 'My desire to leave is stronger and more important than your desire for me to stay.' The only way he can perceive this is: 'My desires and I are not important enough to her. She does not have the feelings for me that I wish she had.'

If Sarah now shut the door and sat on the bed in her coat, it would no longer help Bernard because she would do it like someone who throws alms in a beggar's hat. It is clear that she actually, in the sense of spontaneous desire, does not want to stay. If she does it anyway, it will be a forced duty: 'I'm his wife, after all.' And perhaps she might also think: 'The poor guy really has a lot ahead of him.'

'It's better if you leave now', Bernard might say, 'I'll be fine on my own.'

He stands under the door and watches her walk down the corridor without turning around. If only I had not begged, he might think. Does it make a difference whether his next thought is: 'I'm not worth the few extra minutes in this bleak room' or whether it is 'She was petrified. The room probably reminded her of her own traumatic experience at the hospital'? Does it make a difference for his dignity?

Inner Autonomy: Thought

We do not only want to be autonomous towards the outside world and it is not only dependence on other people, like that experienced by Willy Loman and Bernard Winter, that can threaten our dignity. There is also a need for *inner* autonomy, for the power to determine our feelings and desires through our thoughts and in that sense be independent and not reliant on others. When we fail to have this kind of autonomy, we can also perceive it as threat to our dignity. What does this inner autonomy consist in?

It cannot consist in never being influenced by other people. Being autonomous in our inner world does not mean being entirely closed to the outside, indifferent and insensitive to external influences, as if we were living on an island or inside a bunker. How we live and experience our lives, including our inner lives, is influenced by others in a multitude of ways, and we want it to be that way, as it allows us to develop and evolve. As we will see in the next chapter, mutual influences are an important part of genuine human encounters, which are also a form of dignity.

What then is the difference between independence and a lack of inner autonomy that constitutes a problem for one's dignity? The difference has to do with what makes us subjects: we do not have to let our life, including our inner life, simply *happen*. We do not need to be just *swept along* by what is happening to us internally. We can thematize our inner action, question it and *tend* to it.

The scope of our intervention and the nature of the autonomy that we gain depend on the nature of our inner events. A first form of autonomy can be autonomy of *thought*. A lot of what we think, believe and say initially comes about through imitation and habit. Something was said to us, we parroted it and found that it worked – it fits in with the others' talk. Autonomy of thought, belonging to a dignified way of living, manifests itself in a special alertness towards what we think and say. 'What *exactly* does that mean?' and 'How do we actually *know* that?', are the two questions in which this alertness expresses itself. Part of being autonomous is that these questions become second nature to us. They are motivated by the realization that a lot of what sounds meaningful is actually without meaning; that a lot of what looks like a thought is not really one; that we have not examined the origins of much of what we habitually think and believe; and that what looks like a valuable idea is perhaps just a cheap phrase. Autonomy means being sceptical towards empty words and glossy slogans. It means being unrelenting and passionate in our search for conceptual clarity. Those who have this kind of autonomy wish to get an orientation in their thoughts and feel the need to scrutinize their convictions. They have, in this broad sense, the need to form their own opinions. They are alert towards attempts to seduce and dupe them with slogans and empty words. They do not let anyone patronize them in what they consider to be meaningful and true. They are not fooled – by pub talk, newspapers, politicians, their family or the clan. They will trust their own minds, their own justifications and proofs, their own experiences. They will direct their thoughts themselves.

The counter-figure to those who are intellectually autonomous is the follower, the obedient servant of the ideas and slogans of others. An intellectual floater, he lives off habitual views, slogans and rhetorical lumps that whizz over his internal stage and find their way out in blurry sentences. He does not know the difference between chatter and thought. The desire for clarification, examination and correction is alien to him. He says what is expected of him at the pub, in the election campaign or in a talk show. He is an ideal party follower. It is boring listening to his predictable phrases. His babble is an undignified spectacle.

We react sensitively when someone tries to interfere with our intellectual autonomy and make us repeat babble, because this is not only irritating but also a threat to our dignity. Orwell describes the destruction of this kind of dignity in *Nineteen Eighty-Four*. 'Whatever the Party holds to be the truth, *is* truth', O'Brien says to Winston. He holds up four fingers and asks Winston how many fingers he sees. 'Four', Winston says. 'And if the Party says that is it not four but five – then how many?' 'Four.' O'Brien tortures him until this basic form of intellectual autonomy – the trust in one's perception and the elementary knowledge of numbers – is destroyed. 'How can I help it?', Winston calls out desperately. 'How can I help seeing what is in front of my eyes? Two and two are four.' 'Sometimes, Winston. Sometimes they are five. Sometimes they are three. Sometimes they are all of them at once. You must try harder.' He intensifies Winston's pain. 'How many fingers, Winston?' 'Four. I suppose there are four. I would see five if I could. I am trying to see five.' 'Which do you wish: to persuade me that you see five, or really to see them?' 'Really to see them.' And then O'Brien says words whose cruelty cannot be surpassed, for they are nothing less than a manifesto for the destruction of dignity through the annihilation of intellectual autonomy: 'When you finally surrender to us, it must be of your own free will. We do not destroy the heretic because he resists us: so long as he resists us we never destroy him. We convert him, we capture his inner mind, we reshape him... We bring him over to our side, not in appearance, but genuinely, heart and soul. We make him one of ourselves before we kill him. It is intolerable to us that an erroneous thought should exist anywhere in the world, however secret and powerless it may be.'

Victims of torture, who have been in show trials and were forced to make false confessions and ideological kowtows, say that the worst part of their experience was not the pain and not even mutilation. It was the attack on their dignity as independently thinking beings. Lip service was their only salvation, and this is the escape route from which O'Brien tries to cut off Winston.

The dignity of inner autonomy is not conditional upon its successful realization, but on an awareness of the goal and the attempt to reach it. Those who fail at being autonomous because they lack conceptual clarity and have stumbled do not lack dignity. One can easily take a wrong turn and get lost intellectually. One can easily be overburdened. This does not undermine dignity. Dignity is only forfeited when we either lose sight of the principle of autonomy, or when it is absent from the beginning. A failed attempt is not undignified. What is undignified is not attempting it all. Worst of all is the individual who despises the very ideal of intellectual autonomy – we would call him a bullshitter. We will encounter him again in Chapter 4.

Inner Autonomy: Wanting and Deciding

Another form of inner autonomy is the ability to determine one's own will. At each point in time, we have several desires that are in conflict with one another and cannot all result in action. The desires that become effective constitute the will. By thinking and weighing up, we influence our desires, making some effective and others not. This is the freedom of decision. It lies in our ability to use autonomous thought to wish what we consider to be right. Influencing our own will through independent reflection is what we call making decisions. We are autonomous in our desires because we can influence our will through autonomous thoughts and decisions.

The degree to which we direct our desires and actions through independent thinking also determines the openness of our future. This openness is an important aspect of the experience of inner autonomy. Of course, other people often decide what happens around and to us, and in that sense we are dependent instead of autonomous. Others can obstruct our future through their tyrannical actions – for example by building a wall. But when we have to decide what, under given circumstances, we wish and want to do, there is this openness: we can wish different things and decide to do different things. The past does not determine and constrict us irreversibly. It does not turn us into stone creatures. We can *distance* ourselves from our past experiences and desires. We can *change*. This experience of having an open future is the temporal manifestation of inner autonomy.

We can further explain this form of autonomy by thinking about the opposite experience and realizing how the feeling of lost dignity accompanies it. This would be the experience that thoughts and judgement have no impact on our will, gliding off it without any effect: that the will takes its course unalterably and unstoppably. It would be the experience of *inner compulsion*, such as we experience it with addictions that make us lose our inner autonomy. I decide that the drinking or gambling or my destructive work mania must stop and that I do not want to continue living like this. The powerlessness that is created by inner compulsion consists in that this decision is futile; that I cannot steer my will and, against my better judgement, it remains in control of me. The addict's reflections run on empty, he is spinning his wheels. 'I can't do anything against it', the alcoholic who is battling his addiction without avail says, 'I simply can't control this damn desire to drink.' She is not the king of her own castle, not the author, but the plaything of her addicted will. In such cases, we sometimes speak of a weakness of the will, meaning that the addict does not have the strength to beat the addiction and give authority to her insightful will.

Because the compulsive will cannot be controlled, it remains incorrigible through experience, appearing like a uniform, monotone will. The autonomy of my thoughts and my experiences should have the potential to shape my will, but it does not. The will that lacks autonomy can also be described as alien, as I do not experience it as something that belongs to me. It grows inside me like a foreign body. And this strangeness can also be perceived as impotence. The compulsive will is stronger than me; it creeps over me like an internal landslide. The future of my will and my decisions is not open because I am not at the driving wheel. I cannot interfere and make the will follow a different direction. The compulsive will unrelentingly and with an iron uniformity continues to carry me in the same direction. It is as if I am fossilized in my desires and the future will be exactly like the past.

This is an experience of dependence and of a lack of inner freedom. It is accompanied by the feeling that one's own dignity is in danger. What perhaps most bothers the alcoholic is the fact that her dignity, which was founded on her previous independence and strength of will, unstoppably decays. What I have said about independent thought also applies here: the dignity of inner autonomy is not conditional upon success but on an awareness of the goal and effort. Those who temporarily fail to achieve autonomy of will do not lack dignity. Everybody can be caught up by addiction or another adverse will. This alone does not undermine dignity. It is only forfeited when we lose sight of autonomy as a goal, when we no longer want to tend to it. We have an expression for this that is as terrible as it is accurate: 'He has given up on himself.'

Inner Autonomy: Emotions

What can it mean to be autonomous in our emotions? Autonomous in our fear, anger, hate and jealousy? Does the idea of autonomy even make sense here? We cannot simply turn emotions on and off. They are not at our free disposal. Being autonomous here thus cannot mean deciding when to have which emotions. But what else can it mean?

We can ask ourselves if our emotions are *appropriate* to the situation, whether they *fit* the situation and its history. We do not want to be determined and swept along by emotions that lack any basis in reality. This would make them seem like a prison. Do I really have a reason to be afraid of being fired, of an infection or of an earthquake? Am I a victim of scaremongering? Is my irrepressible anger or my hate directed at the right person? Is this emotion even appropriate? Or is this perhaps, when examined closely, not actually anyone's fault? And in the case of my jealousy: am I really being cheated on, or do I only imagine it? Such questions allow us to counter emotional dependence in the sense of *delusion*: we do not want to be the victims of a series of erroneous emotions. Perhaps we can also speak of an *authority* over emotions: we want to be certain that our emotional reaction is appropriate. We can do something for this authority that rests upon our autonomy of judgement: gain assurance on the true or erroneous causes of our emotions.

When the verdict changes, the emotion itself is also likely to change. Fear or envy disappear when we recognize their cause as illusory. In that sense, we can influence emotions and demonstrate autonomy towards them. Yet sometimes, something analogous occurs to the weakness of the will that we discussed earlier. The realizations that we reach vanish in the face of the all-consuming emotion, in the same way that the addict's rational judgement succumbs to his compulsive desires. The emotion thus becomes alien to us; it seems not properly to belong to us and can lead to an experience of powerlessness. This is the case with unfounded, recalcitrant fears such as a fear of flying, claustrophobia, of spiders, of water or a generalized anxiety that prevents us from leaving the house. We might bear hatred towards an individual or a group without being able to discern the cause of it. We can also be afflicted by disproportionate anger or by jealousy that we have long ago determined to be baseless. Here, we could also speak of authority. Our understanding fails to gain authority over the forces of emotion. We experience this as lacking autonomy.

But autonomy and authority towards our emotions is not limited to exerting influence through insight. This is also about *control*. How far is our dignity dependent on having our emotions under control? A person might let his raw emotions be in control out of pure convenience, for example when he lets himself go under the influence of alcohol or as part of a bragging group ritual. When we see such behaviour, we find it undignified. But there are also explosions of fear, anger and hate and also jealousy that do not endanger one's dignity. The enormous pressure of a situation can make a loss of control appear understandable, even unavoidable – it would be extraordinary, even unhuman, if nothing exploded under such circumstances. Such emotions make me appear authentic, as the person I am. Autonomy and its dignity lie in the overpowering force.

Authenticity does not necessarily have to show itself through overpowering emotions. It can also be the case that I deliberately *decide* to give myself over to an emotion. My autonomy then lies in my decision that only by not curbing and suppressing this fear or anger, I can be myself and evolve. Dignity can thus be the courage to show emotions that I can identify with. And I will not let anyone else dictate these emotions.

Inner Autonomy: Self-Image and Censorship

As subjects, we are beings with a self-image – an idea of who we are and how we would like to be. This is accompanied by a tendency not to let all of our thoughts, desires and emotions enter our actions, and some of them we even bar from experience. Subjects are thus beings who can censor and control themselves in their impulses. Therein they possess a form of inner authority. This is another dimension in which there can be either autonomy or dependence, dignity or indignity.

The self-images and censoring tendencies that we carry with us have their origin in our upbringing and the habit of imitation. Others suggested and demonstrated certain behaviour to us and we imitated it in a process that essentially internalized the dictates of external authorities – that of parents, teachers, religious leaders or institutions. Inner authority thus originated as internalized external authority – in that sense, we all start out in a state of dependency: this internalized authority is overpowering and uncontrollable, especially because it is not conscious and therefore not recognized as authority. It operates behind our backs.

Yet we are capable of becoming autonomous and self-determined. This first means becoming conscious of the suppressed desires and emotions. It means learning to notice their presence and recognizing the routine with which we censor feelings such as desire and longings, fear, envy and jealousy, and also forbidden anger; for example towards our life partner, our own children or religious authorities. As a second step, then, it means re-evaluating these desires and emotions in the light of our own judgement. The censorship is loosened and our inner world becomes more open to the dark side: we admit erotic desires, previously forbidden fears, anger and outrage towards parents and superiors, cravings for recognition and applause, for exuberant emotions and transcendental experiences. We make our own rules about what is allowed and what is prohibited. It is important that we gain such an overview of the inherited self-image, developed through osmosis, and then review and reshape it. Developing a new authority on these matters is also an educational process. We learn that in other parts of the world, in other cultures, other standards and norms apply, and we can ask ourselves how we stand towards this fact. Unlike in the beginning, our authority is no longer blind.

Autonomy in relation to our self-image and its censorship is also connected to the openness of our future: I am not doomed to defer to an inner censorship that owes its existence to the accidental influences of external authorities. I can open my future by loosening the previous censorship and making new types of experience possible. I thus gain a new lease on life. My dignity also lies in this kind of autonomy, and again it lies less in succeeding than in trying.

Someone can lose her dignity by delegating this censorship to an external authority, an institution or a leader, giving up all independent judgement and submitting entirely to theirs. She thereby forfeits all authority over her life. As long as she was the censoring authority herself, the conflict between censorship and impulse happened within her. Now it is experienced as a conflict between the leader and her. This means self-inflicted incapacitation with a complete loss of dignity. Its survivors report of many disastrous and tragic consequences: impotence, suppressed revolt and blind obedience. Many say that the worst part was the loss of autonomy in their own judgement, which they experienced as a loss of dignity. They say it was as if they had not even been there the whole time.

Humiliation Through Serfdom

When we do not succeed in channelling our desires through judgement, controlling unloved emotions and directing our inner censorship ourselves, we experience powerlessness. Sometimes we also speak of humiliation. 'It's so *humiliating* that I can't do this!', the addict might say. But according to our understanding, his powerlessness is not in itself humiliating. There is no one who enjoys making the addict feel his powerlessness. A condition of inner bondage only becomes a humiliation when it makes us *dependent* on someone else. Then there is not only our inability to combat a compulsive desire but also dependence on the will and caprice of the person who can satisfy it. The drug addict is not only powerless in the face of his addiction, but is also in the hands of the drug dealer and his good will. When pathological fear makes me incapable of leaving the house by myself, I not only feel powerless because I cannot control this fear, but also because I am dependent on an assistant and her moods. The humiliation is complete when my dependence is taken advantage of and gloated over. The drug dealer humiliates me when, in order to raise the price, he shows me the package with the white powder, grins and pulls it back when I try to reach for it. My assistant can humiliate me by making me wait arbitrarily or by suddenly running away on the street, watching me stiffen with fear. Perhaps this will also make the price for her services go up.

We call dependence that is caused by inner compulsion *serfdom*. I need another person to satisfy a desire that I am trying to combat in vain. It is a form of external serfdom caused by internal serfdom. The other controls me like a puppet by playing with my rejected, but unconquered impulses. One could say that he is consuming my lack of freedom. And a serf is always vulnerable to extortion: no matter how high the amount demanded, the serf can never be rid of his master.

The drug dealer and the assistant are interchangeable. In this case, I am only a slave to someone because of his or her *function*, because of his or her ability to help me satisfy my desire. It could also be a different individual. But one can also be a serf to a *specific* person. It is her and only her for whom I have that overpowering, obsessive lust. One could say that I am a *slave* to her. She can do whatever she wants with me. My inner servitude gives her limitless power over me and therein lies the loss of my dignity.

This is the case when the college professor Humbert Humbert in Vladimir Nabokov's novel *Lolita* spends many months touring America aimlessly. His only goal is to satisfy his lust for the girl, for which he puts up with her boundless moodiness and the endless extortion of pocket money. This is a story about the loss of dignity through serfdom.

Such a story is also told by Heinrich Mann in his book *Small Town Tyrant*. The prim and dusty school teacher Gaubage, who has dedicated his life to writing a treatise about Homer's use of particles, falls for the cabaret artist Rosa Fröhlich. She can treat him however she pleases. He allows all of her humiliations and even enjoys them. 'She was now impatient and now friendly with him, and it lifted him beyond his accustomed self when she showed dependence upon their friendship unconsciously. He was much less embarrassed when she scolded him. So she would sometimes sit sentimentally, a little piece of needlework in her hand, and wearing the expression that it was proper to put on when talking to a man who was "serious". But soon – and this was a relief to him – she would push him off his chair as if he had been a bundle of old clothes. Once she slapped his face, but she quickly put her hand to her nose and said: "You're greasy." He reddened helplessly, but she went on quickly: "The man paints his face! So that's how he learned to do it so quickly! He taught himself on his own face. Oh you – Old Garbage!" He looked furious; "Yes, you are – Old Garbage!" And she danced around him. He broke into a laugh. It was a shock to him, but not a disagreeable one; on the contrary, he was rather glad.' It seems an absurd and pointless gesture when Gaubage says that whether or not he has forfeited his dignity is 'a matter for myself alone to decide'. His serfdom has already subverted his well-ordered life. He writes love letters on the back of his sheets on Homer: 'He saw even his work undermined by her, his thoughts absorbed by her, his whole life come to an end through her.'

In Humbert Humbert's and Professor Gaubage's experience of serfdom, a conflict between inner censorship and uncontrollable impulses remains noticeable. Their condition of serfdom leaves censorship intact as an internal institution. In both cases, there is a flaring struggle against the impulse, and in this struggle lies a remainder of dignity. As long as the struggle continues, their dignity is not completely extinct.

In a different, all-embracing form of serfdom it is lost completely. In this case, the censoring institution has been shifted to an external authority, for example a cult leader. This kind of serfdom is particularly vicious because I do not even realize that I have fallen into it. I have submitted myself to the leader. There are no more internal conflicts and not even the possibility for them. The leader no longer has to break any censorship in me. I willingly follow him as the one with total authority. This is my serfdom.

Humbert Humbert and Professor Gaubage can still *experience* their humiliation because there is a position of independent censorship within them. When I have lost myself to a cult leader, I am the victim of a particularly gruesome form of humiliation. It is all-encompassing and completely swallows me, but I cannot recognize and experience it because there is no longer a difference between what I desire and what the leader wants. The leader thus cannot be experienced as someone who demonstrates my powerlessness to me and humiliates me. The humiliation can only be experienced in retrospect, when I become aware of the appalling extent of my previous incapacitation.

Autonomy Through Self-Knowledge

The need for inner autonomy is connected to the need for self-knowledge, that is the need to understand why my experiences are the way that they are. These two needs are interconnected because a lack of inner autonomy is commonly accompanied by the inability to *understand* why I have certain compulsive thoughts, strange emotions and a stubborn will that I cannot control. I feel that I lack understanding of how they occurred in my life history and in what tricky ways they protrude into my present. Only this kind of knowledge could succeed in giving me back my lost autonomy and inner authority.

For that, it can be helpful to realize that in our life, there are many more thoughts, feelings, memories, fantasies and desires than it seems. We are only familiar with one part of our inner world, while another part lies in the dark. When we are plagued by experiences that we do not understand, the decisive step might be to search for their origins in the less conscious areas of our emotional life. It is important to uncover the sub-streams of emotion, desire and imagination that determine our life without us knowing it. If we succeed, unconscious emotional events turn into conscious experience. Part of this process is a growing alertness towards the inner world, a verbal articulation of it and a biographical understanding that allows the hidden logic and dynamic of repressed and covered-up motives to come to light. At the end of this process, I gain a better knowledge of my inner world. And it does not stop with just knowledge. Growing self-knowledge can lead to liberating changes and to greater inner autonomy. The compulsive desires and the incomprehensible, uncontrollable emotions are, after I have explained them to myself, easier to contain and might perhaps even dissolve entirely. They become superfluous. Many experiences that earlier appeared like foreign bodies lose their strangeness through growing understanding and can be recognized as a part of the person – they can be *appropriated* and made into an explicit part of one's emotional identity. This appropriation means that they no longer threaten my inner autonomy.

When we thus succeed in inwardly expanding our radius of self-understanding, we reduce the risk of powerlessness and humiliation. It is now harder for me to become a victim of dependence, blackmail and serfdom. The inner compulsions, from which the external enslavement arose, could only last as long as their motivating forces lay in the dark. When I bring them in front of me and understand them in their context, their power dwindles. I win back my inner authority and with it, my dignity.

Needing Therapy

I might reach an emotional dead end in my life. Conflicts with family, children, my partner, perhaps also with colleagues at work grow more and more oppressive, while I have fewer and fewer friends. Before, I was able to talk about it and life would somehow move on. But for some time now, talking has not helped. Words only express the conflicts and intensify them. I no longer know what to do. I feel it, and people also tell me that I need help – I need therapy. This thought signifies a break and is a shock. I hesitate. Which feelings lie at the ground of this hesitation? And what do they have to do with dignity?

Needing therapy means that I cannot cope alone. This violates my need for autonomy. But what kind of autonomy? Did I have this autonomy before I needed therapy? Does this autonomy even *exist*?

What this crisis endangers is the idea that I can control and adjust everything about my inner life myself. I wish I could be the all-powerful scriptwriter and director of my inner life and write the life-long drama of my emotions all by myself. Of course I know that this drama also relies on external influences – by the world, by other people. But how I react to it intellectually and practically is determined by me alone, and for that I need no crutches and no helpers. I might sometimes be overwhelmed by things that I cannot immediately bring under control. But in the end, I can handle them on my own.

It would be *insulting* to have to admit to oneself that this is no longer the case. It is a greater insult than having to ask for other types of help, such as money or other support. It makes me think that I would rather claim social assistance or beg on the street than see a therapist. For all this would only affect external things, leaving me reassured that I remain autonomous where it really matters – in my inner world. It would not only be a lack of autonomy, a lack of emotional autarchy that I would have to admit by going to the therapist. I would also have to recognize my lack of self-knowledge. I would have to admit that I live in ignorance in a sense, lost in the most important of all countries: my own life.

Feeling insulted in such situations is perhaps unavoidable. But what can be avoided is the misapprehension that this is humiliating and constitutes a loss of dignity. I will show my weakness and powerlessness in front of the therapist. I will admit them for the first time there, also to myself. But nobody is turning this into a humiliation that would take away my dignity. An individual who humiliates me demonstrates my powerlessness and enjoys it. The therapist teaches me to see my weakness, but she already considers this a first step towards overcoming powerlessness.

In fact, the opposite is therefore true: working with a therapist lessens my powerlessness and helps me win back my lost dignity by acquiring self-knowledge. It liberates me from unfree desires, emotions and actions. Dignity in the sense of self-determination grows and is consolidated. And dignity also grows in another sense, which we will discuss in the fourth chapter: I learn to see through lifelong deceptions and self-delusions and to be more honest with myself. Going to see a therapist is thus an expression of dignity, while refusing to do so is a sign of false pride, a pride that misapprehends damaged vanity as a loss of dignity. 'False' is the right word here, as it is a veritable *error*.

In a practice shared by several therapists, there might be encounters between patients in the waiting room. People who require this kind of help sit across from each other and now they know this fact about each other. They have admitted their emotional need, their lost autonomy and their lack of knowledge about themselves. As a result, there might be a certain self-consciousness in the air, which does not occur in other doctors' practices. Physical health problems are not a cause for self-consciousness, at least not of this kind. Being physically ill is not insulting and does not question my emotional autonomy. The glances exchanged between patients in a therapist's waiting room are special. They can be shy and evasive. 'What we have in common is that we are in emotional distress and can no longer help ourselves;

but it is easiest if we keep it to ourselves, even though we now happen to be sitting here together for a few minutes.' But it might also be that their glances express openness: 'It's hard no longer being able to cope alone, isn't it? I'm glad to see that others are in the same situation. Somehow it makes it easier.' Or perhaps the glances might even say: 'So, we've both taken this step – we can be proud of this, because we've taken responsibility for ourselves.'

Suddenly a neighbour or colleague comes in. 'You too?', I say. 'Just a consultation, a few hours...', the colleague responds. 'Oh, really? I would like to do this for a couple of years', I say.

Having to rely on medication for one's emotional equilibrium can also be experienced as humiliating. But this is wrong. It is indeed oppressive and brings a loss of independence, because I have to remember to take the pills and must not forget my prescriptions. There are also the pharmacist's glances, real or imagined. But dignity is not endangered. Everything that happens to us on an emotional level is connected to physical events. This is something we take for granted when we drink coffee or wine. Why then is it so offensive when the brain needs chemical support? 'A metabolic disorder, like diabetes.' 'Yes, but...' 'But *what?*'

One day I saw my neighbour pick up psychoactive drugs at the pharmacy. He saw that I saw him and looked down in shame. 'Those damn metabolic disorders!', I said. 'Simply ridiculous! One day, it's the liver that plays up, then the brain, then...' He looked with bewilderment into my laughing face. Then we laughed together and went for a coffee – something we have been doing more often since. An essential part of human dignity is the realization that all inner autonomy is fragile, as if built on sand. This realization can create a precious feeling of solidarity.

Dignity Through Work

In Tunisia, where fifty percent of people are unemployed, there are banners saying: *Pas de dignité sans emploi! No dignity without work!* These desperate words are instantly compelling. But what exactly is the connection between work and dignity?

A person who loses her work might feel that this also brings her dignity into danger. She has to clear out her office, her desk, her locker, give in the keys, badges, work clothes. She stands in front of the factory gate, the shop, the office building and looks over, think-ing: 'I'm no longer a part of this.' 'I've got a line of people to see this morning', Howard says to Willy Loman after firing him. 'Sit down, take five minutes, and pull yourself together, and then go home, will ya? I need the office, Willy. Oh, yeah. Whenever you can this week, stop by and drop off the samples.' Loman feels many different emotions: fear of no longer being able to pay the bills, anger at Howard's callousness, the oppressive feeling of no longer knowing what to do with his time, shame towards Linda and towards his neighbours, who see him in the garden at an unusual time. The feeling that his dignity is in danger is different from all these other emotions. What is this special feeling about?

What Loman loses is his *independence*. He can no longer earn his living. He is dependent on help, perhaps on welfare, perhaps on Linda who has a cleaning job. Work creates dignity in the sense of financial independence. In that sense, any work is better than none, even when it consists in cleaning public toilets. From the day someone earns his own money, he acquires a new sense of himself, he walks differently in the world. And it is no coincidence that the Tunisian banners speak of *emploi*, actual employment and not simply *travail*, work. What matters is not just doing any work, but having *paid* work – in order not to live in dependence and constant gratitude; in order to be, at least in relation to money, the master of one's life.

Yet independence is not the only thing we seek when we want work. It is also about the experience of being proud of an achievement. It is about the feeling of being *worth* something through this achievement. When Loman gives back the valise with the samples and creeps home, he will feel as if he is no longer worth anything. He will read this in the neighbours' eyes, and he will also feel it of himself. This experience is separate from the money issue. Let us imagine that Loman and Linda have inherited some money. 'It doesn't matter', Linda says when Loman is fired, 'we don't need the money.' Of course this makes things easier, but being fired still hurts Loman, as what it takes away from him is *recognition* – the possibility of receiving the appreciation of others and thereby having a sense for his own worth. This is what it is also about when someone wants to work in order to be part of a community and contribute something to a project: the wish for such belonging is the wish to be needed and recognized through one's achievement as a valuable member of the community. This is also an experience of dignity.

Work not only contributes to our dignity through autonomy and recognition, but also gives us the opportunity to develop our skills and *evolve* holistically as people. There are types of work that allow us to be completely at ease with ourselves, as if at play. This is work that allows us to have our own say. At the other end of the scale lies work that we experience as *drudgery*. We are forced to do it, either because we have been ordered to do so, as in a labour camp, or because it is the only option we have to earn a living. In such cases, what we do remains external to us. It is, as we say, *alienated* labour, that is work in which and through which we became alien to ourselves. What does that mean?

There are some instances of alienation that destroy dignity and some that merely make us unhappy. It might be that the work does not match my skills and training, perhaps obtained during a lengthy apprenticeship that required effort and sacrifice – for example, when an engineer has to work as a floor tiler or truck driver, or when a doctor can only find employment as a nurse, or when someone who has a degree in music finds himself playing piano in a bar, or when a nursery teacher cleans toilets. Does this affect one's dignity? Only when appropriate work is available and some person is trying to humiliate me by forcing me to do the low-status work. In this case, it is not the work itself that hurts my dignity, but the act of humiliation.

Low-grade work is alienated and alienating. When it continues for a long time, I lose my skills and the feeling of satisfaction that goes along with appropriate work. There is no possibility of development. But the experience of alienation in this sense is not yet an experience of lost dignity. It is insulting, it is frustrating. But it does not have to break someone in his dignity. At the opera I happened to stop by the man who keeps the urinals clean. Our eyes met. 'Tedious work, isn't it', I said. 'Got to be done', he said and smiled. The confident smile followed me to the car park, where a stuck-up twit in a fur collar was acting up because someone had touched his Jaguar, leaving a hardly visibly scratch. How undignified he seemed compared to the man by the urinals!

Yet alienation can go so far that dignity comes under threat. Perhaps I have to toil for so long every day that I only get a couple of hours' sleep and have to hastily gulp down my meal. I lose myself because, beyond the drudgery, there is no scope for my own life. There is not scope for me and my needs, including my need to take care of myself, understand myself and develop an idea of my life – the things that make me a subject. Then the alienation becomes degrading. I am a mere machine and, out of pure exhaustion, I am about to lose myself as a subject.

Work can also alienate me from myself in another way: by forcing me to do things that contradict my self-image and destroy my identity. I might be forced to make weapons, drugs or dangerous medicine. I know these things will destroy countless human lives. Or I might be forced to take part in human experiments, chop down forests for pure profit or teach a stupid and dangerous ideology. This is a type of alienation that destroys my dignity. Imagine two people next to each other: on the one hand, the doctor in the white coat who is forced to take part in human experiments or the teacher who has to teach ideas he does not believe in. They drive home after work to a comfortable flat. On the other hand, the public toilet attendant who lives in a noisy, damp room. Both perform alienating work. In one of the cases, dignity is also destroyed, in the other, it is not.

There is yet another way in which work can alienate me from myself and thus damage my dignity – when it is *meaningless* work, as in the case of the Jews who were forced to clean the street with a toothbrush. Or let us assume that instead of sending off unemployed people to clean parks, the social welfare department forces them to compile a statistic about the dogs in the park: How many dogs come to the park? Which breeds? How often do they urinate or defecate? And this goes on for weeks and months on end.

Money

In Alfred Andersch's novel, *The Redhead*, the main character, Franziska, escapes a humiliating affair and goes to Venice with only a few thousand lire in her pocket. She cannot resist the temptation to drink tea in a luxury hotel. Afterwards she addresses the head porter: 'May I speak to you for a moment? I should like some advice from you.' 'If I can give you any?' 'I'm an interpreter. Italian, English, French, German. I also do shorthand typing and all kinds of secretarial work. Do you think I can get a job? Either with you or somewhere else in Venice?' 'Not with us. Not in any hotel, in winter, in Venice.' 'I see. Haven't you any vacancies on the inside staff?' 'What do you mean by inside staff?' 'I mean I can also make beds and tidy rooms, anything.' 'No. Even if we were short of domestic staff we shouldn't engage someone like you.' She watched him as he opened a drawer beside him. 'You had expenses here,' she heard him say. 'Permit the hotel to reimburse you.' He passed her a one-thousand lire note. 'Dismay turned her face crimson', Andersch writes.

The porter's gesture is a humiliation, a demonstration of powerlessness, because it says: you cannot even afford a tea with us. You are poor and dependent, almost a beggar.

Having no money means a loss of autonomy. It means powerlessness and dependence. And this deficit brings with it the constant danger of humiliation. Money means external autonomy – which Franziska and Willy Loman no longer have. There is an aspect to this type of autonomy which is of particular significance for the experience of dignity: you can say whatever you want. Inversely, few things make us as open to coercion as money: 'If you don't..., I'll stop paying you.' When such coercion forces me to hide and warp in what I think and feel, it can give rise to a suffocating endangerment of my dignity. We often have this oppressive feeling when a representative of an institution, a company or a political party steps to the microphone. We know that they *have* to say what they say – otherwise they will lose their jobs. It might happen that shortly after, one of them steps to the microphone for a different institution and says the opposite – now he is blackmailed by another source of money. We feel that this is worse than having to clean toilets, because in those cases, the lack of autonomy and dependence have reached the inside, infiltrating the people's words, claims and in the end even their convictions – for money. This is the poison that destroys dignity. It can make some people physically sick.

As dependence through money can also poison us internally, we avoid taking on debts. Debt is fine in business, but not in private. The poison comes from feeling obliged to someone. It inhibits us, curtailing our freedom to say and do everything we want. It might even take away our emotional freedom. 'Did you forget that you owe me money? That I bailed you out?' This is the question we now constantly dread.

Why can money destroy love and friendship? Because the emotions that belong to them presuppose symmetry, an encounter of autonomous individuals. These emotions are tainted when money endangers this equilibrium by creating dependence and constraint.

This constantly lurking danger makes it difficult to offer, lend or gift money. It is dangerous territory, because it is always connected to the thought: the other person cannot cope alone – and she knows that we think that of her. How do I prevent her from feeling violated in her dignity? Of course I will avoid every word and gesture of humiliation. But is this enough? 'But it's only money!' This is not enough either and can cause the opposite. Why is it easier to hand someone the keys and title to a derelict car than to give her a sum of money?

Excessive generosity can also bring someone's dignity in danger because it belittles him and erodes the pride of his own effort. There is a destructive kind of generosity. It can be offensive because it boasts: 'Look at what I can afford!' While this is merely unpleasant, there are also situations that affect a person's dignity: 'Look how little you are compared to me! What a shrimp.' You will then toss the money down the drain, go home and enjoy a lunch of leftover lentil soup.

Money is also a threat to dignity when it is given as a substitute for attention, sympathy or affection. Then it is cheap money. Max

Frisch reports in his work *Montauk*: 'A painter who likes his wine but has little luck in selling his paintings celebrated his sixtieth birthday, and I sent him sixty bottles of his favourite wine. He told me later that he had smashed or given away every one of them. I had been abroad, and so I could not attend the opening of his show, but I had not even bothered to write him a letter. Sixty bottles! Thrown at you by a millionaire in passing as if it were nothing. I can understand his rage. If I had not had money, I still might not have written him a letter; but that would not have hurt his feelings.'

And there is yet another connection between money and dignity. When money, beyond being a means of exchange, becomes an end in itself, a fetish, it feels as if there is a lack of dignity. This is especially highlighted in quarrels about money. There are many arguments about money of course, because money represents independence, freedom and convenience. But there are also quarrels about money that seem to be about something other than what you can buy with it. Such arguments can be especially stubborn and acrimonious, and they can seem mysterious, for they appear to be only about this one thing: *money.*

2

Dignity as Encounter

Dignity is not only founded on a person's ability to determine her life and therefore her autonomy. It is also founded on the nature of her relationships with other people: on how she encounters them and how they encounter her. This might sound self-evident, yet is only so if we allow ourselves to be led by familiar phrases, assuming that familiarity equals understanding. If we pause, take a step back from these commonplace phrases and ask ourselves what they mean exactly, we realize how much there is to query and clarify. For what actually is an *encounter* between people?

When Subjects Encounter Each Other

A meeting between human beings is a meeting between subjects, as we defined them at the beginning of Chapter 1. What does this mean for the nature of their encounter? How do subjects confront one another? What kinds of relationships can develop between them?

Every person is, as we have said, a centre of experience. This is what we instinctively assume when we meet someone. This spontaneous assumption characterizes every encounter we have with a subject, distinguishing it from an encounter with a mere thing. We also make the, similarly natural and obvious, assumption that the other person's experiences express themselves in his actions. We view him as the author of actions that are motivated by his experiences. This assumption prescribes an initial pattern for our encounters: we regard the other person's actions as meaningful deeds, which we can understand by ascribing certain motives to them. In that sense, too, we regard the other as a being similar to us, for we also follow this pattern of comprehension: we explain what we do by saying what we experience.

We need not only *infer* the motives of another person's actions. She might also *tell* us her own stories about them. We may thus comprehend her as her motive stories' centre of gravity: as a subject, she is the one around whom these stories always revolve. Through these stories, she explains to us how she became who she is and what she plans for the future. We sometimes listen to these stories as if they were neutral reports on a lived past, on experiences of the present and on a planned future. Yet with time we have learned that these reports often express a *self-image* rather than *facts*: that the voice of internal censorship speaks through these stories, and that they are intended to make a person appear in a certain light in front of others. There are many elements of invention in these stories, making every self-image a construct of dubious veracity, full of errors, self-persuasion and self-delusion.

When we encounter others, we thus know that what they tell us is not a genuine representation of their experienced reality, but a presentation of motives that has been repeatedly fractured by the interests of their internal censorship and self-image. This makes every encounter an uncertain, open and flexible experience. This is especially so because we know that others, just like us, have many motives that lie in the dark and remain inaccessible to conscious experience, sometimes forever. Many elements of an encounter between human beings indeed take place on this unconscious level.

When two people become acquainted with each other's motive stories, it is as though they become *entangled* with one another: they acquire meaning for each other and the encounter affects them both. There are various ways in which they can become entwined in their experiences. First, they can become entwined in thought: we reflect on the other person's thoughts and about what he might think about our thoughts. This creates, one could say, an intellectual *intimacy* between us. We can also become entangled in our feelings and desires: we fear the other person's fear, in which the fear of our own fear resonates. Our desires are fuelled by the other's desires, which are in turn directed at our desires. And perhaps we wish that the other might have desires referring to our desires. The more our experiences thus become entangled with another person's, the greater the emotional intimacy between us. It can be the intimacy of friends or enemies. This intimacy is the substance of which encounters between subjects are made.

Intellectual and other entanglements that subjects experience also provide the basis for their ability to *communicate*. I do not engage in communication simply by sending out signs and messages – they might remain unheard. Others have to receive and understand my message. For that, it is not enough for them to recognize an intention behind it. They must also understand that the intention is specifically directed at them and their thoughts: they must be able to see that I what I want them to recognize in the sign and in the message is my desire to communicate something to them. Only then will they understand that I have *said* something to them. Encounters thus do not take place because people talk to each other. The opposite is true: people can only talk to one another because they can encounter each other – because they can experience the kind of entanglement that makes true communication possible.

As subjects, we can also become entangled with another person in a different way: by imagining what it would be like to be in her position. We do not just have to listen to her story from a neutral distance. We can attempt to *re-enact* it and ask ourselves what we would experience in such a situation. Would we also feel fear, envy or jealousy? Would we also feel the impulse to run away, attack or hide? There will be things that we cannot comprehend and that form a border of unfamiliarity. We can also never be certain if the other would really experience the situation in the same way. Yet by using our social imagination to empathize with others, we allow, through this kind of understanding, the rise of additional intimacy in our encounters.

Commitment and Distancing

When we encounter someone, we often spontaneously *respond* to him in our actions and experiences: what he does and experiences makes a difference to us; the meeting affects and changes us. This raises the temperature of the encounter. When we experience such a response, we also react to it. We play back the inner changes that we experience, allowing them to affect the other in turn. In that sense, we become *involved* in the other person's life. This creates the heat of mutuality and constitutes a *committed* encounter.

A committed encounter involves an experience of *closeness*: we are not left cold by what the other does and goes through – we are not indifferent to it. This does not just have to be about pleasant, amicable things. There are committed encounters in anger and hatred: for example when I fight with a rude neighbour or passionately hate my boss. This creates closeness, even when it is hostile closeness. In addition, there are all the fervent entanglements of lust, desire and longing, the manifold shapes and shades of empathy, in both joy and misery. What this is always about is taking the other person *seriously* in her experiences and actions. Given the closeness and temperature of the relationship, I also *expect* and *claim* certain reactions from the other. Committed encounters therefore often bring disappointment: sometimes the other person's responses do not match the expectations that, from my perspective, define our encounter. This creates feelings of hurt, anger, irritation and hate. They arise from the commitment and are evidence for the perceived closeness. There would be no accusations without commitment.

When expectations and possible accusations stop, the relationship as a committed encounter also stops. We can call what remains a *distanced* encounter. We have countless encounters of this kind: in the street, on the bus, while shopping or at government offices. These are encounters with strangers. Our lives do not touch internally. This distance does not threaten our dignity because distance is all there ever was. Our dignity is only in danger when distance in an encounter occurs in consequence of a painful retreat from previous commitment.

There are different steps to such a retreat, that also vary in cruelty. The first step: I no longer react externally. This can be a prudent, tactical move, that I might take in order to protect myself, for example from anger or accusation: I play dead. The passionate entanglement is dissolved, the normal flow of behaviour is interrupted. The relationship's breath is visibly taken away. One variant of this is irony and sarcasm: I continue to act, yet no longer as a prisoner of commitment, but merely like a seeming bystander who comments on things with faked amusement. All of this is still compatible with my internal reactions remaining as before. I pretend, bluff and act as if I am uninvolved. I do this to show strength or, paradoxically, in order to attack the other. This might make him angry and perhaps also make him feel powerless: 'What an evil provocation!' But his dignity is not in danger because he can read from the situation that, behind the façade, I am still committed to him.

The next step constitutes a more dramatic break: I no longer respond internally either. My emotions remain silent – no more anger, fury, disappointment or resentment. This is only possible through an internal retreat: it is cruel because it dismisses the other person as a *partner*. I still talk to him and, in that sense, remain entangled with him. But the entanglement has thinned and become more abstract as it has lost the dimension of felt response. 'Just let him talk!' The involvement and entanglement that used to define the commitment between us has disappeared from the relationship. It is like a change of perspective: I now see the other person completely differently. I still take him seriously in the sense that I *reckon* with him: he is still present with his competency, for example as a smart opponent – but *only* in this way. Beyond that, I have terminated the encounter. I got out.

The other person can experience this as an attack on his dignity. He is still treated as an autonomous being – this facet of his dignity remains untouched. But his dignity as a partner in an encounter has been taken away from him. I have not forgotten that he is still a centre of experience, a subject. But I no longer relate to him as someone to whose experience I could respond. He is pushed back, in his actions and in his emotions. His help and generosity, offering and sacrifice no longer receive an answer, and even his feelings find no response. He will experience it as shadow boxing. Affection, compassion, grief and anger are no longer returned. I let him feel that they are unwanted and that I am merely annoyed by the need for closeness that he expresses through these emotions. There are still conversations between us, exchanges of information that settle practical things. But I no longer address him as a being with emotions. And as part of my retreat, I have also abandoned the effort to empathize with him, depriving him of the dignity of a person who can take such empathy for granted. This feels like inner frost.

When I am myself the victim of such distancing, the new gaze of the others makes me shiver. It is like the gaze of behavioural scientists: cold, analytical and uninvolved. I am not only frightened by their terrifying lack of commitment, but also because I feel as if my experiences simply *congeal* under these alienating looks. These looks cannot extinguish me as a centre of experience – even as the object of an indifferent gaze, I remain a subject. But when I feel their cold looks, once but no longer committed, it is as if my existence as a subject is in imminent danger of being transformed into objective, reified existence. I know that it is impossible, but this knowledge cannot take away the terrifying threat contained in this gaze.

When someone distances herself from me in such a way, she thereby cannot help but demonstrate my powerlessness to me. I cannot *force* the other to resume the commitment. She is slipping away from me, the relationship is slipping away from me, and there is nothing I can do about it. Every attempt to enforce commitment pushes her even further away and makes me feel like a fool. Every effort to resume an emotional connection is ignored, treated as if it never even took place. It is like the powerlessness experienced by someone who shouts into a dead phone line: 'Can anybody hear me?!' This feeling of powerlessness might lead to me to beg for commitment. This would not be begging for *specific* emotions, like those Bernard Winter begs for at the hospital after his wife just drops him off. Rather it is the relationship, the commitment *as a whole* that I would be begging for. The risk of forfeiting my dignity is even greater than for Bernard Winter.

Destroying a relationship by distancing oneself is inevitably a demonstration of powerlessness and thus the starting point of a humiliation. It can happen in a triumphant manner or be accompanied by regret. I might enjoy pushing another person into alienation because I feel anger or have a desire for revenge. I can also show her that I enjoy it. I look at her triumphantly: 'Look, it's no longer how it used to be – I am no longer touched or moved by what you do and feel. I feel indifferent to you – and I'm so glad about it! I want you to see my indifference!' This is humiliation in the full sense of demonstrated and enjoyed powerlessness. Alternatively, I may say to the other person: 'I can't go on any longer. I have to protect myself from you and stop responding to you internally. You leave me only this one choice: to become cold and indifferent.' This message leaves the other feeling powerless and also humiliated in the sense of rejection. Yet he is spared the annihilation of his dignity through a triumphant enjoyment of his impotence.

There is yet another level of retreat from a committed encounter: looking at another as we look at a *sick person*. I continue to see him as a centre of experience, and in that sense he remains a subject to me. But other features of a subject, as we have described it, are absent: coherence of thought and feeling, the comprehensibility of action, a recognizable self-image, the ability to use understanding and judgement to review one's identity. This is the reason for my retreat. It is no longer possible for me to see the other as an actor, as the author of coherent deeds. Instead, he has become the site of rather mysterious internal events. The bizarre nature of his behaviour has forced me into this change of perspective, as a true encounter is now impossible. There is nothing left for me to expect and claim from the relationship. He is, in the full sense no longer autonomous.

It is hard to describe what this means for his dignity. The implications are still clearest for me. Although I now see the other with cold, medical objectivity I have to make sure that I do not write him off forever and that I regain a committed perspective on our relationship when he finds his personal coherence again. My own dignity then demands that I give him back his dignity as an autonomous person. But what might it look like for him? It might be that he gradually loses distance to himself, as well as his entire mental coherence, as the consequence of being poisoned by drugs, so that when others meet him they might assume he has dementia or a mental illness. All he now encounters are the doctors' curious, alienating looks. As he has not experienced a full-blown breakdown, but just the onset of a confusing cloudiness he has not lost his sense of dignity – this is how deeply rooted this feeling is in us. Because of this, he must find it devastating to be treated as if he had lost all autonomy and coherence forever. 'I am a pure happening for them, a trickle of awkward sensations', his feelings will tell him. What will it look like inside him once the drugs have taken away even this perception?

The transitions between these distancing steps are fluid and there might be fluctuations. 'You need therapy', I might one day say to another person with whom I used to live in great intimacy. 'You need help, a type of help that I can't provide. Without it, you won't beat your addiction.' This is a dangerous moment and humiliation is not far away. What I am saying is this: 'I want to continue living with you and I want our encounter to continue evolving. I don't want to end our shared life, and I am not abandoning you and retreating into indifference.' This is commitment. But at the same time, there is distancing: 'I'm at my wit's end and exhausted. I need a break. Someone who can provide professional help must take over.' And I might add: 'Dignity demands this – the dignity of insight, your dignity, the dignity of our relationship.' Then I hope that this will not be perceived as a humiliation that means the end of our relationship.

Recognition

'I put thirty-four years into this firm, Howard, and now I can't pay my insurance. You can't eat the orange and throw the peel away – a man is not a piece of fruit!' These are the words that Willy Loman, the salesman, spews at his boss when he fires him. He is angry, and his anger arises from his fear of a future without money. But even more this anger is triggered by the experience that, after having done so much for the firm, he is simply thrown out. 'He opens up unheard-of territories for their trademark, and now in his old age they take his salary away', says his wife Linda. Loman is outraged because he is plunged into poverty. Yet behind this outrage, there is even deeper outrage at the lack of recognition. 'He's not to be allowed to fall into his grave like an old dog. Attention, attention must be finally paid to such a person', says Linda. Miller uses the word *attention*. This is of course partly what this is about: given his lifelong effort, Loman cannot simply be ignored and forgotten. He deserves attention and appreciation for what he has achieved. One could say: he deserves our *esteem* or our *respect*. Yet there is also a stronger and richer term for this: *recognition*. What exactly is it?

It begins with *noticing* what someone has achieved. These can be professional achievements, as in Loman's case. But they can also be other types of accomplishments, for example raising children wisely and with dedication, keeping one's composure while living though an illness, a loss or imprisonment, embarking on a difficult maturing process. Recognition, in the first instance, means seeing this achievement and weighing it appropriately. The opposite would be to look away and ignore the achievement, or disregard it. 'You just drove around for a couple of years, so what?', Howard might say.

Yet just being noticed is not enough. Recognition is not an attitude that remains internal. It is a *demonstrated* attitude that others are meant to know about. We may not only deny recognition to someone by closing our eyes but also by pretending that we did not see his achievement. 'Well, it must have been tough for him travelling so much for all these years . . . ', Howard might later say to a secretary who overheard his conversation with Loman. 'That's what you should have told him in person', she might respond. Recognition is thus not only an attitude, but a *manifested* attitude that *reaches* the other person.

In order to feel recognized, it is not only the fact that my effort has been noticed that has to reach me. What I want to know is that my effort is *appreciated*. 'Fine', Howard might say to Loman, 'you drove around a lot, but wasn't it fun? Others have to do much worse types of work, so what are you complaining about?' Or someone might say about a volunteer of the fire department: 'He's doing it for fun and for his own pleasure.' Recognition is appreciation. Its enemy is disregard.

But even demonstrated appreciation is not yet enough to bring full recognition. The recognition must make a difference to one's *behaviour*. For example, I might be offered a higher salary – salary negotiations are always also about recognition. Or I might get an award. Or something might change about the tone of the encounter, the words, gestures, the entire interaction. Correspondingly, when there is a lack of recognition, someone might say something nice to me but nothing really changes – I remain at the bottom. 'I know that you're doing a great job, driving around so much', Howard might say, 'but I can't offer you more money. And now, if you'd excuse me, I have to attend to this miraculous wire-recorder . . . '

When recognition does not find expression in action it does not have the effect of true recognition: it does not change the overall nature of the encounter, both in its external style and also on an emotional level, by showing me a new type of behaviour. For this is what recognition is about – making encounters richer and deeper. This is its contribution to our dignity.

'You can't eat the orange and throw the peel away – a man is not a piece of fruit!' These are Loman's indignant words. His indignation is directed at a form of humiliation that we have not discussed so far: a refusal of recognition that can also revoke earlier recognition. When we are humiliated, we feel powerless. The powerlessness that we experience lies, as we have said, in our inability to fulfil a desire that is critical to our life. This might be the desire for recognition. It might be crucial to someone's life to gain the recognition of a teacher, boss or one's life partner. When it stays unmet, it can cause serious inner damage. Humiliation is the demonstration of powerlessness where its originator makes sure that we feel it as something that he does to us and that he enjoys. This is the case when Loman has to beg Howard. Howard refuses a true encounter by refusing recognition to Loman, and he lets him feel his powerlessness when he plays with the wire-recorder. 'They're only a hundred and a half. You can't do without it.' The mockery makes the humiliation complete.

It could have been even worse. Instead of just denying him respect and recognition, Howard could have shown *contempt*. This is not just a lack of recognition and attention, but more. It is an explicit *denial* of respect, a refusal of recognition that is stressed and emphasized. It is a demonstrated lack of recognition. While Loman is still within earshot, Howard might say to his secretary: 'What a whining shrimp. Hasn't been bringing in any money for years. It was high time to get rid of him.' This would be the complete annihilation of Loman's dignity, in so far as it depends on Howard.

Equal Rights

The experience of dignity that is not dependent on us but on how others treat us has a lot to do with equal rights: with the experience of having the same rights as everyone else and not being treated differently from them in important matters. When rights that are valid for others are denied to us, there is no mere irritation. We are violated in our dignity and feel a kind of resentment that is particular to these situations. This happens, for example, under apartheid regimes: when members of a certain race or tribe cannot vote, cannot attend all schools, take all buses or go to all restaurants. This is also the case with other types of discrimination, for example when someone is not allowed to do certain things because of his or her gender or sexual orientation, or when one does not receive equal pay for equal labour.

Rights, as we said earlier, are a bulwark against dependence caused by another person's arbitrary actions. In this sense, rights contribute to our autonomy and dignity. Rights are also a bulwark against impotence: they give me the power to hold my ground. This is why they are a bulwark against humiliation. They narrow the scope for those who want to demonstrate and enjoy my powerlessness. When someone is denied these rights because he is not recognized as a legal subject, he has a particularly strong experience of powerlessness. Even when he does not actually want the things that he is denied a right to, the awareness of the discrimination against him constitutes a threat to his dignity.

Our sensitivity with respect to unequal treatment is not just restricted to formal rights. It is present in all contexts where justice in the sense of equal treatment is at stake. Whether it is about a symmetrical distribution of goods and opportunities, or about receiving what we have earned: our dignity is at stake when things are not handled neutrally and according to the rules. The anger of those who go to the barricades to protest against injustice is not simply the anger of the disappointed and frustrated. It the anger of people who sense that one of their lives' most important elements is in danger: their dignity in the sense of fair recognition.

Putting Someone on Display

When, as in the case of dwarf-tossing, I grab and throw a person or use his body as a protective shield, a resistant piece of material, no encounter takes place between us. In order to encounter a person – in this weighty sense of the term – I have to meet him as a subject: as a being who, like me, has his own perspective on the world and therefore, like me, wishes to be regarded as an end in itself. Such an encounter is characterized by reciprocity and symmetry: we mutually regard and recognize each other as subjects. This is what is missing with the dwarf-tossing, or with any other treatment that turns a person into a mere plaything or generally a mere means. This is what the judges aimed at when they prohibited this kind of show: they saw it as their duty to protect a dignified way of living, in which humans encounter each other as subjects and may not demote each other to missiles or to mere things in general.

When dwarfs are tossed for entertainment at the fun fair, they are put on display. Being put on display in this sense is different from performing in front of an audience. When an actor or performer appears in front of an audience, he is also stared at. But unlike with dwarf-tossing, his dignity is not in danger. Why?

It has to do with several things. One is that the actor or performer is *doing* something, while something is just *done* to the dwarf. A performer *shows himself*, while the dwarf is *shown*, and one could also say: he is *displayed*, as though in a shop window. Another part of it is the fact that the actors and performers do not *just* show themselves by appearing in front of people. They show themselves as part of a *performance* that expresses their *skills*. They show them-selves as acting, capable subjects who can do something and demon-strate it to an audience. The people offer respectful, admiring looks, to which the performers respond with a gesture of gratitude. This entanglement of looks and gestures creates an encounter. And there is even an encounter when someone is booed and responds to the audience with an expression of anger, indignation and contempt. The fact that an encounter takes place prevents the person who shows himself from feeling as though he is merely on display and thus vio-lated in his dignity. The dwarf, by contrast, is merely *inspected*, as a human toy and curious missile. He is not demonstrating anything to the audience when he is tossed. It is the person who tosses him who shows off a skill. Accordingly, the looks received by the dwarf do not contain admiration, but are just the looks of people gloating over a curiosity. Being a mere object and mere instrument of others' amuse-ment – this is what endangers his dignity.

Dignity is additionally endangered by the fact that the others not only gloat over the throw, but also that the person who is being thrown has an unusual body shape. Fewer people would come to watch if children, with their normal height, were tossed. What is displayed and gloated over is not only a spectacle where humans are tossed, but specifically the tossing of a person whose appearance is so unusual that it might be perceived as a *defect*. This defect is not just an additional source of entertainment. The event relies on the fact that this person is thrown *because* of this defect. This gives the event and the loss of dignity that takes place an additional dimension of cruelty.

At a different fun fair, which I visited as a child, there were tents in which people with deformities put themselves on display: the fat Bertha, a woman of an unbelievable size; a man whose hands had six fingers; Siamese twins. There was a peculiar silence in those tents. I believe it was two different things that left the audience speechless:

on the one hand, it was the repulsive deformations themselves; on the other hand, it was the fact that they were put on display for money. 'How can they allow this?', my mother asked afterwards. 'And we went inside and looked at them!', I said.

Those who decide to go to see the fat Bertha do so out of a craving for sensation. The audience's gawping looks are what takes away the woman's dignity: she is stared at as a monstrous thing, an astonishing pile of human flesh. The situation is different when people with deformations are shown in medical lectures. There will also be an element of sensationalism there, but the set-up in the lecture theatre is different from the one at the fun fair. These demonstrations serve the purpose of learning and training, making students familiar with medical phenomena, which are presented as illnesses that need to be treated and suffering that needs to be alleviated. This is also how the situation is explained to the patients, and officially nobody is forced to show himself and his defect to hundreds of viewers. Nevertheless, some patients experience it as a threat to their dignity. 'I was just a *demonstration object!*', a crippled man said to the professor afterwards. 'It was for a good cause', was his answer. 'But still', the man said, 'all those looks!' Another time, a woman with terribly swollen limbs and discoloured skin with warty growths was shown to the students in order to familiarize them with the condition of elephantiasis. The professor had just begun to speak when the woman got up and lugged herself out of the lecture hall. The room was eerily silent, the only sound was the woman's slurring steps. The lecture was not continued. After she was discharged from hospital, the woman no longer left her house. Some time later, she applied to an organization to be granted assisted suicide. She always felt so *on display*, she said – even when no one was present.

Human subjects are also presented and displayed in psychiatric lectures, in this case because of their psychological defects. They are used, for example, to demonstrate the behaviour of a person who has lost his spatial or temporal orientation or his intellectual and emotional coherence. They are asked catch questions, led into traps and subjected to tricks. Under the students' gaze, their suffering becomes a classifiable *defect*. Here too, dignity is endangered through display – one can read it in the patients' faces. It is interesting to notice how the atmosphere in a lecture theatre changes when the lecturer succeeds in showing the patient as a person. This can be achieved by involving him in a conversation about his illness, which shows that he is not just a sick body but a person who has learned to deal competently with his suffering. This also makes the looks the patient throws into the audience much more open and freer – he is ready for an encounter. His looks allow the students to ask him questions. I have met patients who became lecturers on their condition and would correct the professor when subjective symptoms were discussed. One of them, who was suffering from a psychotic illness, made a proper career out of his role as a case patient. With him, every appearance in a lecture theatre immediately became an encounter with the audience. There was laughter, and he was having the most fun of all. An exposition turned into an encounter. The danger of stolen dignity was thwarted.

Sex Objects

In the early 1980s, a man in north-west Germany applied for a licence to run a peep show. Naked women on a rotating stage should present themselves to the audience. Those watching would sit in individual booths, invisible to the women. By tossing coins into a machine they would get to see the women's naked bodies for a limited amount of time. The proposition was considered unethical and rejected: it was deemed immoral because it degraded women to mere objects of anonymous voyeurism. The man filed a lawsuit against the decision and initially prevailed: the women, it was said, were not required to perform any sexual acts; the viewers were anonymous, and no looks could be exchanged – that is why the women's dignity was not violated. But in the end, the supreme court reached a different verdict: 'Human dignity is violated when an individual is degraded to an object.' The court argued that although those visiting a strip club also did so out of a voyeuristic desire, the dancers there retained the possibility of remaining subjects because they could exchange looks with the audience and in that sense take part in an encounter. In the peep show, by contrast, the women were assigned a 'degrading object-like role'. The court statement said that 'the unilateral visual contact emphasizes the reifying isolation of the women who are displayed as sex objects' and that this 'depersonalized commercialization of women' turned them into mere 'objects for sexual stimulation'.

It is interesting to compare the two verdicts: they are, as far as their understanding of dignity is concerned, completely opposite. For the judge who wanted to permit the peep show, the voyeurs' anonymity and the impossibility of any kind of encounter with the women on the rotating stage offered protection for their dignity. For the judge at the supreme court, this was precisely what was scandalous about the idea. He found that this arrangement degraded the women to mere things, instruments for sexual pleasure. The first judge was ultimately merely concerned with peace and wanted to avoid causing a stir. Only the second judge actually addressed the topic of dignity. He applied exactly the standard that we have been using: that dignity consists in not reducing a person to a thing or mere object.

We can ask ourselves if actors in pornographic films are better or worse off than the women at the peep show. Are they better off because they at least do something, albeit not something very skilful? Or are they worse off because they not only put themselves on display with their nakedness, but also with their sexual pleasure, be it real or simulated?

Human Commodity

When you walk along one of the canals in Amsterdam, you suddenly find yourself standing in front of shop windows where women in lingerie offer themselves up for sale. You may feel as in the case of dwarf-tossing: you cannot believe this is really happening. Why?

It is because of the shop windows. They turn the women into pure commodities, who are also displayed *as* commodities – as something that may be inspected, about whose price one can enquire and that one eventually purchases. It is like buying a cow at the cattle market, a slave at the slave market or a doll in a toy shop. Only here, it is a human doll who you pay in order to do whatever you want to it and with whom you can amuse yourself at your leisure. The fact that you only hire this human doll for a limited amount of time does not improve matters. Sitting in a shop window as a sex object is degrading, even more so than being on the stage in a peep show. Now it is not just the few individuals in the cabins who know that the woman has become a commodity. Everyone in the street, in the entire city knows it. And this commodity may not only be gawked at by the voyeurs, but can also be *consumed* through touching and penetration.

The women do not wear price tags, although this would be appropriate. As I was walking along the canal, it was suddenly invaded by a horde of tourists. They asked the women for their prices, compared and shouted the numbers to each other. The women on display were treated and traded as *interchangeable* commodities. Although not everyone would take every woman, it was ultimately the *price* that determined whether or not the customer made the purchase. It had nothing to do with the women as humans and unique individuals – with who they were and what they were like apart from their flesh.

Each time a tourist entered to ask for the price, a shop bell would ring. It was ghastly. I fell asleep on my flight back. When I woke up I wondered if it had all just been a dream.

Neglect

'One learns very little here, there is a shortage of teachers, and none of us boys of the Benjamenta Institute will come to anything, that is to say, we shall all be something small and subordinate later in life.' This is the opening of Robert Walser's novel *Jakob von Gunten*. Jakob, a student at the Institute, speaks to the Principal upon his arrival. 'Herr Benjamenta asked me what I wanted. I told him quietly that I wanted to become his pupil. At this, he fell silent and read newspapers.'

There are words that are spoken in vain: nobody is there or they do not reach the other person. Here, it is different: it is impossible that Herr Benjamenta has not heard Jakob's words, but still it is as though Jakob had not said anything. The words are treated as if they had not been spoken. And these are after all not insignificant words, that do not express an insignificant desire. It is the same as if someone silently reached for the newspaper after being told: 'I'm leaving you, I can't live with you any more', or 'I want to spend my life with you and have children with you', or 'I want to start a business with you.'

The Principal treats Jakob as if he were invisible. There was a dark-skinned boy named Rabah at my school. He was the brightest and fastest in the year. The teacher consistently ignored him. Rabah would raise his arm until it hurt, but the teacher would not let him speak. He was not counted during assembly. The others avoided him, as if he were an object, a mere obstacle. He tried to break through this exclusion by saying the answer faster than everyone else. He was sent outside. When he got up and went to the door, he grinned: he had been spoken to – he had won.

The theft of someone's dignity through denigrating him to a mere object consists in the refusal of an encounter: there is no mutual recognition as subjects who have the right to be treated as ends in themselves. This is what Herr Benjamenta and the racist teacher do: they deny an encounter to someone in front of them. This time, however, the encounter is not denied through objectification, by making the other a toy or object, but by pretending he does not even exist. He is being *ignored*. The destruction of dignity, unlike earlier, consists not in *abusing* someone, but in *neglecting* him.

Talk To Me!

One can also neglect another person by talking *about* him instead of talking *to* him. This also amounts to the denial of an encounter.

'Is this the liver cirrhosis case?', the doctor asks his assistant after stepping to my hospital bed without greeting me.

'Pancreas', says the assistant.

The doctor leans over the medical file the assistant is holding. His cheek brushes her hair.

'He's been here for a while.'

'When can I go home?', I ask the doctor.

'He's not ready yet', the doctor says to the assistant while looking at the file.

'What's the matter with me?', I ask.

'We have to keep him under observation for some time', the doctor says to the assistant.

'Professor Müller, I'd like to know: What is the *matter* with me?', I say, annoyed.

'A complicated case', the professor says, looking at the file again.

'Damn it, will you *talk* to me!', I yell. 'Talk *to* me! Talk to *me!*'

'Why are patients always so short-tempered?', says the professor, shaking his head and exchanging a smile with the assistant.

This is when I throw a glass at him. It smashes against the wall.

The doctor takes the assistant's arm.

'Just ignore him. How about going for a coffee?'

Laughing at Someone

Willy Loman is not only humiliated because he is fired. He also experiences a different threat to his dignity: 'You know, the trouble is, Linda, people don't seem to take to me. I know it when I walk in. They seem to laugh at me. I don't know the reason for it, but they just pass me by. I'm not noticed. I'm fat. I'm very – foolish to look at, Linda. I didn't tell you, but Christmas-time I happened to be calling on F. H. Stewarts, the salesman I know, as I was going in to see the buyer I heard him say something about – walrus. And I – I cracked him right across the face. I won't take that. I simply will not take that. But they do laugh at me. I know that.'

What is it: *laughing* at someone? It is not the same as laughing at something funny that someone does. This becomes clear when the comic effect is on purpose, for example when someone pulls a funny face, trips up like a clown or tells a joke. Then we laugh about a specific *action* rather than the *person*. This distinction is also present when something is not intended to be funny, as is for example the case with an amusing slip of the tongue, when someone slips on ice or when there is a funny mix-up – here laughter is also just directed at an *episode*. However, when we laugh at someone, we laugh about the *entire* person. This might be prompted by a failed performance, for instance when someone sings with a croaking voice or, like in Loman's case, by a peculiar appearance. These are in themselves also just details. Yet what is crucial is that when we laugh at someone, we include the whole person in it: as if the entire person were as ludicrous as these details. For those who laugh at Loman, he is a walrus and therefore overall a laughable person – no matter what else he might be.

Laughing at someone in such a way is a blatant way of not taking him seriously. We withdraw attention and recognition from him. We thus deprive him of something that I did not mention when I spoke of recognition earlier and that I would like to add now: his *authority*. Recognizing someone for something involves granting him authority in it: the right to be heard in his judgement and respected in his actions. By laughing at someone, I am effectively saying: 'What you do and say no longer has any importance or meaning for me.' This devalues the entire person. It makes him a figure of fun, an object of ridicule.

Laughter creates *powerlessness*: there is no defence against a laughter that makes me a figure of fun. Whatever I might do, it would only be included in the laughter and ridicule or might even set off new laughter, which would make things worse. Nothing I can do can force the others to stop laughing at me and to take me seriously. Every attempt to be taken seriously is *devalued* in advance. And, of course, those who laugh at me enjoy my powerlessness and let me feel their enjoyment: it is a clear case of humiliation. Loman defends himself by smashing the other salesman's face. This does not help. On the contrary, this only shows the others how deeply hurt he is – a fact that they will gloat over. 'Looks like I really hit the mark there!', the salesman will say, while laughingly wiping off the blood. And others will join him in laughing.

Are humour and self-mockery of any help? They might help protect my dignity when the others' laughter is only directed at a mishap and not the entire person: I simply join them in laughing about it. This is perceived as sovereignty: 'He doesn't take himself too seriously', they might think. Laughing together averts the danger of being devalued as a person. I summon the necessary distance to myself and join the others' mockery – I win. I sense that the worst reaction would be to feel insulted. 'When I wanted to get in the car this morning, I accidentally slid beneath it!', Loman might say. Could this turn the tide to his advantage?

Self-mockery is more effective than punching someone, which only underlines one's impotence. But when the others are determined to laugh at my entire person, it reaches its limits. Perhaps I ran for an office for which I was totally unqualified or put myself forward for a prize that I am not nearly good enough for. Now the others laugh at me as a windbag who greatly overestimated his abilities. I could take the bull by the horns and say: 'I guess I'm quite a windbag, huh? Perhaps I should go for the Nobel Prize!' By saying this, I distance myself from the person they are making fun of, who did not have such distance to himself. Through self-mockery I have become a person who can be taken seriously again because of his ability for self-criticism. I try to join in with the others' laughter – but at that moment, it stops. Their silence makes clear that they have no respect left for me as a person.

Being laughed at can give rise to hatred and a desire for revenge. The laughter does not need to be loud or blatant. A hint might be enough. Nicolas Sarkozy, for example, had a veteran French news presenter fired because he had said in an interview that in pictures taken at summits, Sarkozy always gives the impression of being a little boy, excited to be part of the big boys' club.

Denying Explanation

'Someone must have been slandering Joseph K., for without having done anything wrong he was arrested one fine morning.' This is how Franz Kafka's unfinished novel *The Trial* commences – with an incomprehensible event: an innocent person is arrested. When K. wakes up, he realizes that Anna who normally brings him his breakfast did not come. 'This had never happened before.' K. rings the bell. 'At once there was a knock at the door and a man entered whom he had never seen before in the dwelling. "Who are you?" asked K., half raising himself in bed. But the man ignored the question, as though his appearance needed no explanation, and merely said: "Did you ring?" "Anna is to bring me my breakfast," said K., and then with silent intensity studied the fellow, trying to make out who he could be. The man did not submit to this scrutiny for very long, but turned to the door and opened it slightly so as to report to someone who was evidently standing just behind it: "He says Anna is to bring him his breakfast." A short guffaw from the next door came in answer; one could not tell from the sound whether it was produced by several individuals or merely by one. Although the strange man could not have learned anything from it that he did not know already, he now said to K., as if passing on a statement: "It can't be done."'

The story of Joseph K. is a story of powerlessness. Because this powerlessness is purposely deployed by others, who let K. feel their power and enjoy seeing how K. notices them savouring his powerlessness, it is also a story of humiliation. This powerlessness neither consists, as in Jakob von Gunten's case, in being neglected, nor in that others talk about K. instead of talking to him. There are also elements of this kind of powerlessness, but they are not at the core of the experience. This is a new type of experience: humiliation through being denied the opportunity to *understand* one's own situation.

'Who could these men be? What were they talking about? What authority could they represent? K. lived in a country with a legal constitution, there was universal peace, all the laws were in force; who dared seize him in his own dwelling?' Because he wants to know and understand what sort of situation he is in and hear the reasons for what they are doing to him, K. confronts the intruders: 'Who accuses me? What authority is conducting these proceedings? Are you officers of the Law? None of you has a uniform.' This is a humiliating nightmare because K. never receives an answer to these questions. And that is not all. His experience of powerlessness continues in that the information he receives defies all rules of sense and meaning. 'You are only under arrest, nothing more', he is told. This horrible announcement is accompanied by the remark that this is not at all a reason for despair. The disturbing contradictions continue: ' "You'll be going to the bank now, I suppose?" "To the bank?" asked K. "I thought I was under arrest? How can I go to the bank if I am under arrest?" "Ah, I see," said the Inspector, "You have misunderstood me. You are under arrest, certainly, but that need not hinder you from going about your business. You won't be hampered in carrying on in the ordinary course of your life."'

This is a humiliating situation for Joseph K. in which others are trampling over his dignity. It begins with the fact that he is not *informed* about the circumstances: the men do not tell him who they are and who has sent them. This is demonstrated powerlessness. Every situation in which we lack the necessary information to orient ourselves is connected to an experience of powerlessness: when I get lost and do not know where I am; when I wake up from a coma and do not know what day it is; when someone stands by my hospital bed and I do not know who he is. A lack of information, however, is not in itself a humiliation. It only becomes one when we find out that this information is being consciously *withheld* from us.

'What is the diagnosis?', I ask the doctor. He browses through his papers and looks at the screen. 'What is it?', I repeat. 'I can't tell you', the doctor says. 'But this is about *my illness*! This is about *me*!' 'It's better for you not to know.' 'That's up to *me* to decide, not *you*!', I yell, getting up and grabbing the medical file. It would be similar if a police officer refused to tell me the cause for my arrest: I would try to snatch the arrest warrant from his hand.

What lies behind my angry reaction is not just confusion because of my lack of knowledge, but also outrage at the fact that I am consciously *left in the dark*. This can also happen during smaller incidents: our train is stopped between stations in the middle of nowhere, and for hours nobody tells us why we are being delayed and when the journey will continue. This is not simply frustrating because the lack of information prevents us from dealing with the situation appropriately. We also feel neglected and violated in our right to be treated as subjects and independent persons – and this is a question of our dignity.

This also happens when it is not just about information, but about an *explanation* and *understanding* – not only about *what* is happening, but *why* it is happening. K.'s powerlessness and humiliation throughout the book above all consist in that many things are said and done to him that he is unable to understand because they are not explained to him. Up to the end, he does not find out why he is arrested, tried and executed. He is violated in his dignity as a human being who has the desire to know what is happening to him. The mysterious mastermind behind K.'s arrest and trial carries this violation to the extreme by also denying him the common meaning of words and alienating him from his own speech: he cannot understand what it means to be 'under arrest' if he may continue living his life as before.

Again, this is not just about *lacking* an explanation. The humiliation lies in the fact that the explanation is *withheld*. When a drug does not work and the doctor cannot explain it either, my dignity is not in danger. It is only in danger when he knows why it does not work but refuses to tell me. It can also be about less important things. My internet connection is not working. I call the provider and a lady in a sickeningly sweet voice tells me: 'There's sure to be a reason for it. Have a nice day!' I ask the train conductor why we have been stuck for a half an hour. 'Wouldn't you like to know?', he responds with a grin. 'They're really messing us around here!', says a fellow passenger. This is not just annoyance in the usual sense, that I for example feel when someone runs into me or mugs me. Although this is not a big issue, perhaps just a trifle: we wish to be taken *seriously* as individuals who want to know what is happening. There is an announcement that the journey cannot be continued 'for operational reasons'. 'They treat you like a piece of shit here!', someone yells. He is not just referring to the lack of politeness and general lack of respect. What he means is the lack of respect for rational, intelligent beings who want to hear reasons and understand.

Dignity in this sense is of course especially endangered when things that are of great significance for our life are at stake: our health or rights, for instance. In such cases, a denial of information and explanation is often accompanied by a refused *justification* for an action that affects me. This happens to Jakob von Gunten: 'Then the Principal inquired, in his imperious voice, if I had any money with me, and I said that I had. "Give it to me, then. Quickly!" he commanded. The money was pocketed, and there was silence. Then I found the heroic courage to ask, quietly, for a receipt, but I was given the following answer: "Rascals like you don't get receipts!" '

Being caught up in a hospital's bureaucratic machine is horrible for many reasons. One of the most important is that patients are often deprived of their dignity of knowledge and understanding, because they do not receive an explanation for what is done to them. One day I woke up in the hospital, realizing that my bed was no longer in my room but had been pushed to the corridor.

'Why am I here?', I asked the nurse.

'Because you're ill', she replied.

'But why am I here on the corridor and not in my room?'

'You're ill.'

'And why are you connecting me to a drip? I've never had this before.'

'You're ill.'

I then had only one impulse: to run away – and to hell with the therapy! Any illness, any amount of pain was better than this treatment. At the café, I felt better than in a long time. 'I ordered Perrier water – why did you bring me a San Pellegrino?', I asked the waitress. 'I was just about to explain: We're out of Perrier. Would you like anything else? Shall I bring you the menu?' This made me feel even better. I lit a cigarette. The pain came back after a while. I still thought that my escape had been the right thing to do.

When we are condemned, moved or dismissed without reason, it feels like a violation of our dignity. We also feel this way when something changes about our relationship with others, something that concerns our feelings. When someone terminates a friendship, dumps me or all of a sudden treats me with contempt I want to know why. When someone who used to be a part of my life disappears without a word, it is doubly hurtful: because of her absence, and also because of her silence – it makes me feel violated in my right to an explanation. Feelings are not blind dispositions or uncontrollable internal turbulences. They are embedded in our general desire to understand our lives. A person who disrespects this through an action that affects my inner life violates my dignity. She leaves me behind in a state of powerlessness. This is the powerlessness of humiliation.

The story of Josef K. is a story of annihilation. It is also a physical annihilation, as he is executed. But above all, it is a personal annihilation that lies in the annihilation of this man's dignity. It is a particular kind of dignity that is destroyed: the dignity that lies in the right to know what is happening with one's own life.

Manipulation

Others cannot only take away our dignity by using, patronizing or neglecting us. They can also endanger our dignity by *manipulating* us. What does that mean?

Manipulation is a particular way of influencing a person. Stepping in front of someone, touching her, showing or telling her something: these are all instances where we influence a person and effect change in her experiences and actions. What makes manipulative influence special? Why does it undermine a person's dignity?

In Claude Sautet's film *Max et le ferrailleurs*, a police inspector named Max seduces a gang of scrap dealers and petty criminals into robbing a bank. Max, who comes from a wealthy family, was originally a judge. One time, he had to acquit someone for lack of evidence, although he was absolutely convinced of his guilt. This is something he could not come to terms with, and he decided to become a police inspector in order one day to be able to catch a criminal on the spot.

There was recently a series of bank robberies, but each time Max fell for false information and arrived late. 'I look like a complete idiot again', he says. His colleagues laugh about him. This is when he decides to help things along. Making it look like a coincidence, he meets up with an old acquaintance from the army, Abel, who together with a group of other failed characters scrapes by through selling scrap metal. After the meeting, Max tells his boss that he knows of an amateur who is planning a big job. 'What kind of job?' 'I don't know', says Max. 'And neither does he. I just know that he's planning it.' And later he adds: 'I want a smooth, clean crime with a minimal risk for us. We could lend a hand, couldn't we?'

Max becomes acquainted with Lilli, Abel's girlfriend, who works as a prostitute and is the star of the group. As the next step in his plan, he rents a flat where he regularly meets with Lilli. He pays her handsomely, but does not want anything from her. They play cards, he photographs her, they play, talk and laugh. He pretends to be Felix, the owner of a small bank that, once or twice a month, after the wholesale meat dealers drop by, has a lot of money in the building. 'You must make it by the time you're forty', he says. 'You need luck', Lilli says. 'Luck? You need to take matters into your own hands', says Max. He passes her a bunch of money. 'Help yourself. Take as much as you like.' He reads her a fake newspaper article about a friend whose bank was robbed. 'It's not a big deal', he says, 'Banks are insured.'

His plan works out. 'I can't go on like this', Lilli say to Abel. 'The money is at the bank', he defends himself. 'Why don't you rob one then?', she says. She thinks of Felix and talks to Abel about the alleged bank owner and the large sums of money that the meat dealers deposit with him. One day, Max calls her: he has to move their next meeting because the meat dealers are coming. He tells her the date. She passes it on to Abel. He and his gang rob the bank. Max and his colleagues are waiting and arrest all of them. Max has his smooth, clean crime. He is finally able to catch someone in the act.

Deception

Max *uses* Lilli and the guys from the gang: they serve as an instrument for him, allowing him finally to succeed as a police inspector. Yet this is different from the other example of using someone that we discussed earlier: unlike the dwarf-tossing, Max does not make Lilli a mere thing. Although he pays her, he does not use her as a sex object or turn her into a commodity. What is clever about the story is that Max uses a woman who is accustomed to being exploited as a sex object in a much subtler way, giving her the impression that she is not being used at all. He talks to her about all kinds of things, including personal issues from both of their lives. They laugh together like two people who simply enjoy each other's company. For Lilli, it looks as if there is an encounter between her and Felix: a symmetrical relationship in which they both see and recognize each other as sub-jects, as beings who are not just means to an end but ends in themselves.

But all of this is part of Max's plan and a mere pretence: all he wants is to get Lilli to convince the other gang members to rob his fake bank. In the end, Lilli is nothing but a transmitter of specific information, a mere switching centre, a kind of relay. What she is by herself, independent of this role, must not be of interest to Max – it would endanger his plan.

The plan indeed comes under threat when the simulated encounter almost becomes a real one for Max, too. In order to prevent this, he puts up a fight with Lilli. 'You don't need to pay me any more, if you like', Lilli says one day. 'I just want to see you, without money.' 'I don't think that would be right', Max says defensively. 'You think you know me, but you don't know me at all, Lilli!' He gets angry: 'You don't *know* me!' He also has to struggle with himself: he delays the alleged visit of the invented meat dealers, and when she finds out the date, he has to force himself not to warn her.

After the act and Abel's arrest, they sit across each other. Lilli believes to have Felix, the banker, in front of her – the person she took advantage of. 'It was me. I told them…', she begins. 'I know', he interrupts her. 'I know it because my name isn't Felix. And I'm not a banker either. I'm a police inspector. *A police inspector.*' Stunned and incredulous, Lilli shakes her head and breaks down.

The truth is a great humiliation for her: she has been the powerless plaything of Max's strategizing. By telling her who he really is, he lets her see her own powerlessness. In order to make it a humiliation in the fullest sense, he would also have to grin on seeing her break down. This is not what happens in the film because the fake encoun-ter with Lilli was about to turn into a genuine one. Max does not know where to look; he is also about to lose the ground under his feet. One can sense that he is experiencing a loss of dignity that is of a particular kind and that we will discuss in Chapter 4: the loss of dignity experienced by swindlers and forgers.

He cannot protect Lilli from the humiliation that lies in becoming aware of her powerlessness. Because he cannot offer her this protec-tion, he at least tries to save her from being arrested for her complicity in the crime. When his colleague tries to arrest her, he shoots him. He catches Lilli's eye from the police car: it is an exchange of looks between two people who have lost their dignity for different reasons and in different ways.

How can we describe Lilli's horror on finding out the truth? What exactly scares her so much?

'You *used* me all the way through', she might say to Max, 'you *manipulated* me like a *puppet*. You took away my dignity.'

'This is not what it's been like', Max might try to defend himself. 'A puppet is controlled externally, someone pulls the strings, it doesn't have any emotions, it doesn't think, feel, want or decide anything. That's not what it was like for you. You had the possibility of reacting with your own thoughts and emotions to what I was doing and saying to you. You had the ability to think and judge. You eventually decided to convince Abel to commit the robbery and tell him the date. Nobody *forced* you to do it. *You wanted it yourself!* Nobody took away your freedom of decision. Unlike a puppet that is controlled by others, you were in control of yourself. You were free in what you did and what you wanted. It was your own reflection that determined your will. I watched you call Abel from the café: you hesitated, but you did it anyway. It was your free choice. You can't compare yourself to a puppet. And that's why you can't claim that I took away your dignity.'

'But still: this entire time, you were just coldly *watching* me, like a scientist who studies insects. And you were *calculating* my behaviour. I was nothing but a *piece* in your plan, your strategy. It was not for a single moment about *me*. This is also how you can steal a person's dignity.'

But Max also has a defence ready against this accusation: 'I admit I was calculating. But we constantly do that to a lot of different people without causing damage to their dignity. Businessmen try to analyse their customers, politicians their voters, athletes their opponents. Does that steal their dignity? Is a game of chess undignified, just because the two players are constantly calculating each other's moves? We also analyse people who are close to us, in the sense that we try to predict their actions based on what we know about their thoughts, feelings and desires. This is what I was doing with you. And instead of being bad and undignified, this is actually good: *we have* to be intelligible for one another to be able to live together.'

Lilli was neither able to reach her goal by using the metaphor of a puppet, nor by accusing Max of calculating, strategic behaviour. These were not yet the decisive features of the idea of manipulation, and they are not at the core of our intuitive feeling that Max has damaged Lilli's dignity. Lilli's next attempt gets closer:

'You led me into a *trap*. You *lied* to me and you *deceived* me. You trapped me in your illusory world: the world of Felix, his apartment, his wealth, his bank and the large deposits. None of it was true. Deceiving and misleading someone in such a way is manipulation. It makes the person who has been deceived a powerless victim, who can only notice her powerlessness in retrospect.'

'In football, the penalty-taker deceives the goal keeper by sending him to the wrong corner. Every chess player sets traps. Advertising and election campaigns are full of lies and deception. My little tale was harmless in comparison. There was certainly no injured dignity.'

'Of course there was. Football and chess are games – such ploys are allowed and even part of the allure. Advertising and election campaigns are different – there we resent the deception, our resentment being in proportion to the significance of the issue. When after being wooed with peace, social justice and prosperity, the government ends up leading us into a war – we are outraged. And this outrage is not only caused by the suffering we have to endure, but also by the fact that we feel manipulated and thus injured in our dignity. We have been completely misled: in what we believed, felt and wanted. We do not merely feel manipulated in a single aspect, but as *entire persons*. And this was also the case with what you call your 'little tale': you manipulated me in what I believed, what I felt and what I desired. You manipulated me as a *whole person*. The self-determination and freedom of choice that you ascribed to me earlier: What are they worth if one is entangled in a web of lies and deception?'

Lilli here touches on a connection that we will discuss in Chapter 4: the connection between dignity and truthfulness. Why is it not merely annoying and hurtful when we are lied to and deceived about important things? Why do we in addition also feel injured in our dignity? It has to do with the fact that these false convictions, delusive feelings and imaginary desires all *lead to nothing*: we lose our anchoring in reality, tumble without realizing it and only realize in retrospect that we have not been taken *seriously*. We have been of no *meaning* and *weight* as a person to the other.

Encounters that are based on lies and deception are not *genuine* encounters and in fact not even encounters at all. The deceiving partner not only lies to us about matters of fact, but also about the fact that he regards and recognizes us as equals. The feigned symmetry and mutuality also turn out to be a fata morgana. 'It has never been about *me* and it has also never been about *us*', Lilli might say. 'What a dirty, undignified cheat you are!' You can also read this accusation in the looks she throws at Max in the police car, together with astonishment at his deed – a deed that shows that there was a kind of genuine encounter after all or at least the openness to one.

Seduction

'You wanted it yourself!', Max says to Lilli. 'Yes, but you *seduced* me to it!', Lilli might respond. This is a new accusation and a new reading of manipulation: manipulating a person by seducing her into something. When Max seduces Lilli into making the bank robbery happen, it is part of his deceptive ploy. Nevertheless, the seduction is different from the deception. One can seduce another person without deceiving her. What is seduction and why can it endanger dignity?

It has to do with an aspect of our self-image and internal censorship that I have not yet described. Our image of ourselves and the judging, censoring perspective that belongs to it are not detached from and untouched by the rest of our experiences. They emerge from this stream of experience in the course of a life story under a variety of influences and can also be changed by it again. There is no other position outside all this action, no space reserved for a cool, silent director who sits in the dark, pulling the strings in our mental drama. What we are is entirely determined by our experiences and actions, via the perspective of our self-image and the complex interaction between the two.

We understand this and therefore know that we do not have full control over what happens to us. We know that our inner world can rebelliously and uncontrollably refuse censorship; we know how unstable, corrupt and fragile self-images are; we have experienced moving far away from previous experiences and self-images over time, without always being in control. And still: we claim a certain *authority* with regard to our ability to change. This is no imaginary authority that operates from an internal high seat. Rather, this authority lies in that things within us do not change entirely without our cooperation. When previous censorship is loosened, giving space to desires that used to be banned, we do not want this to happen behind our backs and without our knowledge. We want to be *there* when it happens. We do not want the censorship to loosen itself, setting things in motion like a landslide. We want to be able to feel that it is *we* who loosen it: that we notice this internal transformation, form a judgement about it and, if necessary, halt it. This is also the case when the issue is not censorship through our self-image, but a transformation of the self-image itself. We know that this also involves forces that we cannot control. Yet we would find it disturbing if we did not feel that we were also participating in this process. Our self-image, with its evaluating perspective, is something that has emerged

from a reflective, critical distance to ourselves. We also want to preserve this inner distance when we change our perspective on ourselves. Here too, we want to be *there* when it happens. And here too,
it is about having certain authority: we want to be *heard* on this issue,
which is in a way our most important issue. When someone endangers this authority, he endangers our dignity.

The deceptive drama in which Max involves Lilli brings many
things into motion within her. So far, she has been the star, the queen
among a group of people who had resigned themselves to a small
life. She lives with Abel, but earns her own money on the streets. 'I'm
independent, monsieur', she says angrily when Max asks her about
a pimp. She later also says: 'My job is as worthy as yours.' And then
Felix, the banker, comes along and encourages her to take as much
money from him as she likes; Felix, who is so different from Abel
and the other guys at the scrap yard; a man who took matters into
his own hands and became rich; an energetic man, so different from
Abel, who has no perspective and spends most of his time lying on
the bed, smoking; a man who also seems to have an interest in her
and her expectations of life, albeit in a very different way from her
customers, which is somewhat mysterious. All of this rouses desires
in Lilli: for more money and independence, perhaps also for a different man and a different life in general. And in the end, these desires
translate into her wish for Abel to rob Felix's bank. Previously censored wishes and feelings now pass censorship. Lilli's self-image has
changed.

She speaks – as we have imagined it – of a *seduction*. What can
she mean by that? We could put Max's ploy aside and imagine that
he really is Felix, the bank owner. It might be that, as far as Lilli's
growing desires are concerned, he has no particular intentions and is
not following a plan. He lets her see the large sums of money, talks
about the wholesale meat dealers and the insurance, and apart from
that just plays and chats with Lilli – everything is as it happens in
the film, just without the lies and a plan. Then we could not call what
happens a seduction. One might want to say that meeting Felix is a
seduction for Lilli, or also that she is allowing herself to be seduced
by the circumstances. But it would be wrong to accuse Felix of seducing her.

Seduction, in the strict sense of the term, requires *intention*: the
resolution to change someone's inner balance of forces that is created
by latent desires and internal censorship; or to shake up her self-
image, leading her to do something that she would have previously
found unimaginable. Seduction is an attack on someone's inner
balance that is maintained by the self-image.

Let us assume Felix has such an intention. Felix sees how Lilli pretends – in front of others and herself – that she is content with what she has. But he also senses that this contentment is just a pretence and that Lilli is actually fed up with prostitution and the life in the scrap yard. To seduce someone, one has to draw on a lingering desire. Felix draws on Lilli's silent dissatisfaction. His intention could be to scare a bank manager whom he hates and despises. Or perhaps he is just curious and wants to see how far Lilli will go. In both cases, his intention is *selfish*: it is not about her, but about him.

Lilli could say to Felix, the real bank owner, what she also says to Max: 'You have used me.' Could she also accuse him of having damaged her dignity? If my conceptual account is correct and dignity is grounded in what I called personal authority, Lilli cannot make this claim. Felix has not taken this authority away from her. Lilli was fully conscious and present when things began to change in her – she was there. She had the possibility of *pausing* and *reflecting* on what she wanted. When she moved between the gang and Felix, she was able to feel how all of a sudden, she found Abel's passivity more annoying than before and how she became increasingly disgusted with her customers. She started imagining certain things and she was aware of those dreams. She was up to date about her own development and could decide herself how far she wanted to allow it to go: how far she wanted to loosen the censorship and let her self-image change. Seduction took place because Felix, purposefully and for selfish reasons, created the possibility for internal transformation in Lilli. But there was no destruction of the internal, critical objectivity *vis-à-vis* herself and of her authority. That is why we can say that her dignity has remained intact.

There are cases of seduction that are different, namely where the seducer systematically sets in motion an inner dynamic, suspending a person's internal censorship and altering her self-image unrecognizably. Let us imagine that Felix does not seduce Lilli, but Abel, who in the film has spent ten years in the foreign legion for alleged manslaughter. Perhaps Felix senses this man's hidden traumas and decides to make use of them to get rid of an enemy. He could seduce him with money or a new lifestyle, an expression of appreciation and trust that Abel has never known, perhaps also with drugs or even a physical relationship that responds to hidden desires in him. All of this could lead to Abel becoming a slave to Felix. In the end, it would perhaps not take much to entice him to commit a murder that would primarily have symbolic meaning to his inner world, allowing him to avenge a long-past humiliation. This would be the story of a person

         Dignity as Encounter

who, without noticing, moves further and further away from himself. One day, he has a terribly sobering awakening in a prison cell, realizing that he had succumbed to a seduction that gradually undermined his entire authority over himself and his life and eventually destroyed it completely. Lilli, by contrast, had the ability to pause and reflect. During her seduction, these faculties remained untouched. This is different with Abel, as we imagine him here. What Max does to him has precisely this effect: somewhere along his dangerous journey, Abel loses his ability to pause and think. It is this loss that endangers his dignity. 'You bastard! You seduced me and took away all my dignity!', he could say to Felix. The dignity that he speaks of could be understood as the right to be respected in terms of his self-image and its authority. Felix might then start to grin, signifying to Felix that he enjoys his powerlessness, which he spent months working towards. All conditions for humiliation in the fullest sense of the term would be fulfilled.

Overpowering

I can get others excited about many things: a region, a language, a type of music, a sport, but also an idea such as justice, or a feeling like gratitude towards a god or even an entire way of living, for example a monastic one or one dedicated to political activism. I can make someone passionate about something to the extent that he subordinates everything else in his life to this passion. We are able to do such things to one another because we are malleable and formable in our experience: aside from some elemental needs, nothing in our lives is predetermined, but develops and changes through other people's influence – though what we see, hear or read of them.

All of this has nothing to do with manipulation, but is part of being alive: in the absence of such formability through foreign influences, our encounters with others would be lifeless and cold, merely stiff transactions. It has nothing to do with seduction either, in the sense that we discussed earlier: our new desires need not be in conflict with our self-image and internal censorship – they might be entirely new and easily integrate into an existing self-image.

Yet this plasticity of human experiences may also be abused in a manipulative way. This happens when other people's influences are not innocent and spontaneous, but motivated by a plan, aiming to acquire power, or to coerce or subdue others. In this case, someone wants to use me for his goals, and for that purpose not only control my actions, but my entire inner world: what I think, feel and desire shall not be genuinely mine, but of benefit to him. This can only happen if he deprives me of the possibility of resistance and *overpowers* me.

There is a wide spectrum of such instances of overpowering. At the gentlest, most harmless end of the scale are certain advertising strategies: attempts to talk people into having desires that they did not have by themselves and sell them things that fulfil these desires. This is merely about commodities and entertainment. The advertising itself does not rob us of the possibility for resistance: we can meet the ad with a critical distance, ignore it or even mock it – we retain our authority. The situation is a more dangerous one when psychological trickery is deployed, designed to overrule our alertness, or generally betray our conscious perception, with stimuli that are too short to notice. The case that led to the ban of this technique was an innocent cinema ad for lemonade, but it was prohibited as a matter of principle: the intention of the ban was to protect the authority of our desires, that lies in the possibility of conscious choice. It wanted to protect us from being overpowered and becoming the defenceless toys of salespeople.

Yet it is not even necessary to switch off our consciousness and attention in order to undermine our authority. It can also happen when a group applies pressure and threatens us, or when a superior exploits the feelings an inferior has towards him: feelings of affection, for example, trust or admiration. Both are powerful tools for manipulation. They can not only create desires, but also emotions like fear, envy or hatred and prejudices that can become complete worldviews. This is what happens when someone becomes a fanatical follower of a religion, a political movement or sect: the way he sees things and the feelings he has towards those who hold different views – his enemies – are shaped by the pressure of group membership and his admiration for and submission to a leader's influence. Both undermine his ability to pause and examine things from a distance, making him lose the ability to fight back. Indoctrination takes its course without hindrance, seizing its victims' thoughts and feelings. They become entangled in a totalitarian ideology that is hermetically sealed and immune to criticism and refutation. Critics are simply enemies and as such always wrong, both in their judgement and perception, as well as in their different, sick desires. What is especially malicious about it is that this worldview, with its accompanying censorship and enemies, is internalized, and once this internalization is complete it appears to me like my own. I have given up my authority to a group and a leader, who have overpowered me in such a comprehensive way that I experience what is in reality a total powerlessness as an especially strong form of self-determination. The brainwashing is complete.

In this process of ideological brainwashing, language plays an important role. Seductive words, catchy slogans and powerful metaphors clog the mind, freezing it in its hostile fanaticism. The language of brainwashing is like a simplifying staccato that annihilates distinction and nuance. It is marked by a striking use of vague concepts and an intolerance towards other language that might give rise to doubts. The enslaving manipulation through language has been most powerfully described by George Orwell. In the world of Big Brother's *English Socialism*, which people have to call *Ingsoc*, a new language is enforced upon the population: *Newspeak*, which replaces English as it was previously used, *Oldspeak*. Of course the new language incorporates the new worldview. Yet its suffocating tyranny goes much further:

> The purpose of Newspeak was not only to provide a medium of expression for the worldview and mental habits proper to the devotees of Ingsoc, but to make all other modes of thought impossible. It was intended that when Newspeak had been adopted once and for all and Oldspeak forgotten, a heretical thought – that is, a thought diverging from the principles of Ingsoc – should be literally unthinkable. Countless words such as *honour, justice, morality, internationalism, democracy, science*, and *religion* had simply ceased to exist. A few blanket words covered them, and, in covering them, abolished them. All words grouping themselves round the concepts of liberty and equality, for instance, were contained in the single word *crimethink*. In Newspeak it was seldom possible to follow a heretical thought further than the perception that it *was* heretical: beyond that point the necessary words were non-existent.

The annihilation of dignity as autonomy in thought, speech and experience is complete.

Working With a Therapist

When someone, motivated by pure selfishness, plays with the unconscious forces of another person without any concern for her authority and wellbeing he manipulates her. With this manipulation, he takes away her dignity. He helps her suppressed, banned and denied feelings, desires and phantasies resurface and, in the process, as in Abel's story, destroys her authority. Yet this process, in which previously unconscious impulses come to the surface, does not necessarily have to endanger dignity. It may be a *therapeutic* process that respects dignity by increasing a person's authority and inner freedom. What happens during this process?

Therapeutic influence is part of a plan but lacks selfish intention. When I commit to working with a therapist, I know that this work will change me. I know that in the end, I will face others and myself in a different emotional state, that the pattern of my actions will change and that everything might take a turn that I could not imagine in the beginning. Yet there is something that protects me from losing my dignity: the fact that this influence has been *agreed on*. I enter an *agreement* with the therapist, a *pact*, which has the goal of freeing me from emotional suffering and leading me out of a dead end that I cannot escape by myself. A therapy creates a save space in which the only thing that is important is understanding the patient, helping him to reach a better knowledge of himself and changing him in a way that improves his wellbeing. A good and moral therapist is alert towards selfish motives and avoids them in her work. She also does not take advantage of her patients' feelings. Her attitude is the exact opposite of Max's attitude towards Lilli or Felix's attitude towards Abel. Because it lacks self-interest, according to my conceptual story, it is conscious influence but not manipulation. The explicit pact between me and the therapist means that an encounter takes place between us, something that occurs neither between Max and Lilli nor between Max and Abel: unlike them, I am seen and recognized by the therapist as an autonomous person.

Therapeutic influence thus constitutes unselfish seduction towards the good. As with selfish seduction, there are two distinct kinds: the kind of seduction that leaves a person's control and authority intact at all times and the kind that might require temporarily disrupting this authority in order to bring about the crucial internal transformation. In both cases, it will be important to bring light to hidden and censored impulses, explain the content and origin of my self-image and trace the symptoms that arose from conflicts between this self-image and the experiences that I have not been able to make sense of.

In the first case, it is a process of examination, understanding and change that allows me to pause and reflect at any moment. When I envision my life story and work through current conflicts with a therapist, there might be far-reaching discoveries that announce vast internal rearrangements: a radical revision of my self-image, the recognition of powerful desires that can no longer be denied, the discovery that I have misinterpreted important relationships with other people, the uncovering of self-deceit and life-long lies. All of this can be profoundly unsettling, perhaps making me feel as if I am losing the ground below my feet, to the extent that I might even wish to resort to my old, familiar suffering. What matters is that I remain the final authority on whether or not I want to continue on this emerging path. If it becomes clear that something inside me is resisting the necessary changes and I encounter the therapeutic seduction with hostility, I must not fear being overrun by the therapist. I decide which changes are allowed and which are not, and I also determine the speed of this process. This is what my dignity lies in during this risky proceeding, in which so much is at stake.

Yet it might be that things in my inner world are so messy that I have lost the ability to pause and reflect on them from a distance. I might be the victim of a misguided self-image, completely ossified in its erroneousness, which makes me feel either far too small or far too big, without realizing that my hopeless experiences are due to the tyranny of this erroneous image and evaluation. This might be accompanied by inner compulsions or experiences of unfounded fear and suspected guilt that drive me into internal and external isolation. Perhaps all of this goes along with an addiction that also cripples me physically. This is how I can end up in a situation where I can no longer rely on my reason. Then my therapeutic treatment might have to be different: my best chance might lie in committing myself to the effect of drugs and the gentle guidance of a therapist, who will help me break down set images of myself and habitual patterns of experience, in order to find a better understanding of myself and a new flow of experience and action. This makes me temporarily lose my authority, which had already been compromised by my illness anyway. It is like an operation: I put myself in another person's hands in order to allow the procedure to help me win back lost opportunities in life. My dignity is not in danger because nobody is playing with me in a manipulative way, as we imagined it with Max and Abel. The goal of the influence is the restoration of my collapsed authority and self-determination. Although for the duration of my helplessness I cannot be a true partner in the encounter, the therapist still regards me as a person with whom she will one day be able to have such an encounter again. My dignity, one could say, is preserved in this expectation.

When someone hesitates to accept a therapist's help, his hesitation might be founded on an unrealistic idea of mental autonomy – we talked about this in Chapter 1. Yet the hesitation might also be due to another concern, namely that I do not want to expose myself and my emotional need to the therapist's distanced, professional gaze. This does not matter in the case of physical problems, where I am glad about the doctor's sober and distanced looks. But it is different with our emotions. I only want to experience my emotional events as an active participant. Will the therapist's distanced gaze not turn me into a mere theatre for emotions that are dissected and analysed?

This concern rests on a misunderstanding. A meeting with a therapist is an encounter of a special nature because it lacks the symmetry of regular encounters. I do not care for the therapist in the same way that she cares for me. I know far less about her than she knows about me. Nevertheless a therapist's gaze is different from a completely indifferent gaze, threatening to freeze my emotions. The therapist is not involved in my regular life, and thus no real entanglement of feelings can take place between us. Yet the discreet efforts of therapeutic work can produce the kind of closeness and commitment that matches the depth of the emotions that are being discussed.

Do I not have reason to fear the transformations therapy causes to my memories, experiences and actions? Talking to friends is different: we discuss things that I know about and that do not generally escape my perception. I do not have to question the authority of my knowledge. I do not have to consider the possibility that I might be in an entirely different situation compared to what I thought. Generally, much less is up for discussion than with the therapist, who can throw up radical questions. I know how my friends view me and feel safe. Their perspective on me also makes me unfree, as I might establish later on, but it provides a feeling of security. I am secure in their projections.

Yet the concern that therapy might estrange me from myself and, in this sense, even make me lose my dignity is also unfounded. Nothing that a therapist does is designed to overpower me and distance me from myself. A therapist respects my symptoms: they make sense as intelligent answers to my life's challenges. They are not something that must be removed at any cost. There is also respect for my resistance to change: my subconscious has its reasons for wanting to protect me. Emotional resistance must not be broken, and it provides guidance to the therapist: the cure lies where there is resistance, for this is the location of the conflict that needs to be worked through. My autonomy is also protected: the therapist's interpretations are just suggestions, not prescriptions. With time I get to know the limitations of her insights. In the beginning it seemed to me as if she possessed wholly objective knowledge. What she said did not seem to carry the mark of her personality and its limits, which I was glad about. Later, after one of her interpretations completed missed the mark, I learned that because of who she is, she cannot see it differently. This does not mean that these interpretations are useless: I can recognize myself through differentiation from her story about me. Therein lies the autonomy of my insight, which I would not have gained were it not for the conflict with her interpretation. I can also discuss this dissociation with her. But this discussion also has its limits, and the remainder of the work might happen in silent, productive separation, which belongs to my dignity in the sense of autonomy.

No Pity, Thank You!

In Norman Jewison's film *In the Heat of the Night*, the black police detective Virgil Tibbs assists the sheriff of a small town in Mississippi with a murder investigation. At first, the sheriff mistrusts and dislikes him. But this changes after a while, and one night he invites him to his room at the police station. He asks Tibbs what he knows about insomnia and pours himself some whisky. Bourbon can't cure it, Tibbs says.

'I got no wife. I got no kids', the sheriff says, 'Boy, I got a town that...don't want me. And I got an air conditioner that I have to oil myself, and a desk with a busted leg. And on top of that, I got...this, uh...place. Now, don't you think that'd drive a man to takin' a few drinks? I'll tell you a secret. Nobody comes here. Never. You married?'
'No.'
'Ever been?'
'No.'
'Ever been close to it?'
'Close to it.'
'Don't you get just a little lonely?'
'No lonelier than you, man.'
'Oh, now, don't get smart, black boy. I don't need it. No pity, thank you. No, thank you!'

It seems as if the sheriff is fighting for his dignity with this angry outburst; as if Tibbs's pity is a threat to it. How can that be? Does it not help when someone feels for me, sympathizes with my situation? Is it not nice to experience compassion? Is it not nice to feel that the others are not indifferent to me? It makes me less alone in my suffering and I can find solace in the illusion that I do not have to carry the burden all by myself. What is the angry outburst fighting against then?

What the sheriff rejects is not *compassion*. It is *pity* that makes him angry. What is it that bothers him about it? What could be a threat to his dignity? Tibbs lets him see that he understands his suffering, his loneliness. But it cannot be that knowledge alone. The sheriff spoke at length of his lonely life. He *wanted* Tibbs to know about it. It is therefore not the knowledge itself, but what Tibbs *does* with it. Is it the fact that he *pronounces* the sheriff's loneliness? Calls it by its proper name? It need not be words – it could also be a gesture, for example putting an arm around someone who is lonely. This can also lead to an explosion and angry rejection. Is it therefore the fact that someone *mentions* my suffering at all? It is also possible to bring it up in a neutral manner after all, without expressing pity.

Perhaps what happens is that through pity, the other shows me that he regards me as weak and miserable – as someone who needs pity. I can see it in his behaviour: he thinks that I am weak – and he *shows* it. Why is this so difficult to bear? Is it because now that the weakness and misfortune I have felt for a long time has become the subject of another person's actions, it forces me to recognize this suffering in a new way? Because I can no longer doubt whether I am really unhappy or lonely? Is it thus because the other person forces me to be truthful? Is this what the sheriff resents Tibbs for?

The pity of others makes me *small*. This is why it can seem *condescending*: I am strong, you are weak. The symmetry of the encounter is damaged and my dignity is endangered. This is different with sympathy and compassion: it connects people and strength and weakness, being big or small, play no role.

Pity particularly enrages us when we are pitied for our lost autonomy, for example when we have lost the ability to stand on our own feet through illness, poverty or disability. Then what we see in the others' looks and hear in their words of pity is above all the message: you are no longer autonomous. Pity thus becomes a demonstration of powerlessness. It is not mean-spirited and not enjoyed powerlessness, but it is still a demonstration of powerlessness. The other does not consciously induce it, but still represents and stresses it with his pitying gestures. An expression of pity thus comes dangerously close to a humiliation. It is not just the lonely sheriff who does not want pity. A person in a wheelchair does not want it either, because it additionally demonstrates her powerlessness to her, which she already feels constantly. The wheelchair user and the sheriff fight against pity with the same anger with which we fight against humiliation.

Encounters Between Autonomous Individuals

When people who are on their path to autonomy encounter one another, their relationship needs not be confined to the blind control of desires and emotions. We need not experience the relationship as the mere victims of an emotional power play, and then conclude that we either work well together or not. As we are capable of internal distancing, critical reflection and questioning – including that of our self-image – we can also thematize the relationship itself. We have the opportunity to talk about it and ask: What is our individual share in how we both experience the relationship? How do we see the other person, and what do we think about the way she sees us? What are we doing wrong? It is possible to talk these issues to death. But the possibility of such communication belongs to the dignity of an encounter. This is something we realize when we experience the opposite: when we are prisoners of speechlessness and keep locking jaws instead of discussing the situation. We do not just experience this as any kind of misfortune, but as the misfortune of lost dignity – we have lost our sovereignty.

This sovereignty involves experiences that feel like balancing acts. One of them has to do with our self-images. We are not only entangled with each other in our direct experiences, but also because we recognize ourselves in each others' self-images – and sometimes clash in them. I know of the other person's self-image and see that it does not match her words and actions. I recognize self-deceit and fundamental lies. At the same time, I am concerned to respect her in her self-conception. This creates difficult emotions in which I can easily lose my balance. The opposite can also be hard: when I become aware that the other knows more about me than I do myself, thanks to a very deep encounter between us. This may question me as a person. It takes courage to carry on and grow from this experience. Dealing with projections that we have recognized is also a balancing act. There are no intense encounters without projections, that is without the attempt to mould the other according to our wishes. The other will recognize the conflict between the ideal and his own reality and face the task of resisting it, without letting the resistance break the relationship. It belongs to the encounter of autonomous individuals that they do not avoid such challenges.

They will also not run away from another unpleasant experience: conflicts. There are moments when conflicts that we have felt growing for a long time need to be confronted and called by their proper name in order to deal with them. If we keep avoiding them, either by whitewashing them or simply keeping quiet, it not only creates growing tension, it also forfeits dignity.

We remember how Sarah Winter took Bernard to the hospital, where he struggled with a feeling of lost dignity after he begged her to stay. One day, Sarah also has to go to the hospital. It is another Sunday night. It is still early, but she is impatient: 'I want to get it over with', she says with an impassive face that does not want pity.

Nor does she want Bernard to stay in the hospital room. He heads down the corridor towards the exit, but a strange instinct makes him turn around. He quietly opens the door to her room a crack. Sarah lies on the bed. She wears headphones that he has never seen on her before. She does not normally like headphones. Her legs, propped up on the bed, move to the tune. It is a lively, carefree movement. It fits her happy, joyful face. She whistles. Bernard closes the door and drags himself back out. He asks a person who is smoking outside for a cigarette – his first in years. It was a completely different Sarah. She was not only different from the woman with the impassive face who wanted to get the operation over with, but altogether different from the woman he lives with. He debates whether he should confront her straight away: 'Why were you pretending? Are you actually *glad* to spend some time away from me? Are you secretly preparing to *leave* me?' He decided not to do it here, not at the hospital.

Leaving an Open Future to the Other

Inner autonomy is, as we said in Chapter 1, connected to the possibility of having an open future: that is, having the experience that past events, actions and experiences do not predetermine one single possible future for us, that we are not condemned by iron laws to rigidly continue living our history, that we can distance ourselves from this history and try something new – not just at the snap of a finger, but by analysing and understanding the past. This does not yet bring liberation, but it prepares it.

There is also a right to an open future in encounters. It is the right to change in one's actions and experiences and pursue new paths. If I want to leave another person his dignity, I must not constrict him through fixed expectations. I must not have a final image of him, suffocating him with its pressure. This right is a facet of the desire to be regarded as a being who is an end in itself, rather than a being whom others use as a mere instrument of their desires – as water carriers in the race for their own happiness, so to speak. We could not live with someone who was entirely rhapsodic in what she says and does, unpredictable and with no coherence over time. But we also know that dignity can be lost if we are torn apart by a gridlocked relationship in which everything keeps being repeated, like a needle that is stuck in a vinyl record.

Dignity has to do with the willingness to be changed by a relationship and also the willingness to end a relationship. There is a tension between leaving an open future to the other person, as well as claiming it for oneself, and loyalty, without which it would not be possible to have a meaningful relationship. For loyalty, meaning emotional partisanship for the other person, always also involves sacrifice – the sacrifice of other possibilities that could have been lived. Loyalty and openness: we need to be able to talk about them, too.

Dignified Partings

Sometimes our paths part. We might meet again, but our shared life is over. The pain of the break-up contains an awareness of the fragility of all relationships, an awareness of the temporary nature of all experiences, all sharing, all promises and hopes. It is an awareness, a totally unsentimental one, of final loneliness. Dignity is a way of coping with this painful experience. What is it about?

One facet of it is the attempt to *understand*: what the shared life was like, how it began, what kind of logic it followed, where the first cracks appeared; the role played by chance; how emotions and attitudes, the patterns of behaviour, changed over time and why; what the relationship allowed us to understand about the other and about ourselves and what it did not; which elements always remained strange and mysterious.

The dignity of a parting has a lot to do with *recognition*: recognizing who the other person is, what he is capable of, how important he was to us, what he did for the relationship. It involves adjusting the image if we had belittled him, relativizing accusations, separating the important from the irrelevant. It also involves appreciating the other as a whole, as someone with inherent opportunities that we have not seen, did not understand and perhaps even undermined. It is also about generosity. It expresses gratitude for what the other meant to us.

Such generosity is only possible through *self-criticism* – the willingness to do what was not possible before, in the heat of the involvement: recognizing and admitting one's own mistakes, one's failures, cruelties and the unfairness of one's accusations. It is also about recognizing the other's just accusations. Generally, it is important to free oneself from the madness that comes with always wanting to be right. Dignity has to do with *reconciliation*: accepting the other, letting accusations rest, letting guilt rest; bringing to mind the emotions that connected us, without embellishment or sentimentality; realizing that in a sense the other cannot help being who he is; that there were limits to our expectation for him to change; looking at each other with the reconciliatory awareness that two people have only very limited control over how things will develop between them.

Accordingly, an undignified parting is marked by a stubborn, bellicose tug-of-war between two unforgiving individuals, paralysed by hatred and accusations. There is no inner distance. Everything is charged up and avenged – a rule of self-righteousness and pettiness.

What is also part of a break-up is the realization that every union involves unlived life and sacrificing certain things that could have also been lived. This is why the awareness of an open future, that we have discussed already, seems particularly poignant during a parting. It is important to allow the other person the right to an open future, even when the path to this future leads away from me. Perhaps Bernard's interpretation of Sarah's secret whistling in the hospital room is correct: she is about to leave him. She is a woman who, perhaps in the company of another man, could evolve in ways that are completely unfamiliar to him and that he does not actually want to accept. She will thus become estranged from him. To cope with her parting, he will have to tell himself: one must not let closeness and a seemingly complete knowledge of the other person obstruct her future. This thought is an internal step towards freedom. As a result, Bernard might think: I, too, could develop in new directions that might surprise me. Compared to how I have experienced myself so far, in my shared life with Sarah, I might even seem a bit alien to myself – and oddly free. This feeling would help him let Sarah go and live through the separation in dignity.

3

Dignity as Respect for Intimacy

Human dignity has a great deal to do with our need to draw a distinction between what is only our business and what others are permitted to know about, too. We do not want to expose everything. Besides the wide field in which we are visible to others, we need an area where we are alone with ourselves. We have the need for a private space in our lives. When others enter this space against our will, or when we open it to them for the wrong reasons, it can endanger our dignity.

The boundary line between the private and the public is located differently for different people: something that lies on the private, hidden side for one person, another may allow on the opposite, visible side. This can also differ from culture to culture, and the boundary can shift with age. What is crucial for the experience of dignity is that such a line exists *at all*.

The desire to draw this distinction can apply to a range of different things: our actions and skills, possessions, looks and health, our thinking and feeling, wishes, desires and passions, ideas and dreams. With all these things, there are some elements that we permit to be seen or even show to others, and others that we want to remain hidden – we want to keep them to ourselves. When others catch a glimpse of them, or they even fall into the bright light of public attention, this is not merely unpleasant. It causes a serious loss that can endanger our existence. Sometimes we also experience it as a loss of our dignity.

The Dual Need for Intimacy

In order to understand this experience in its full scope and depth, it is important to distinguish between two distinct needs that lie behind the wish for a hidden, secret side in our lives.

On the one hand, we might want to withdraw something from the gaze of others because it represents a *defect* that we therefore wish to *hide*. This is the case when we hide a deformity or serious illness, incompetence or transgression, a vice or abnormal desire, a taboo belief or a daydream that frightens even ourselves. If such things were disclosed against our will, we would experience it as an *exposure*. It would be an experience of *shame*. It could lead to a loss of respect and recognition, to condemnation and exclusion. This threat is one motivation for our desire to build a barrier of intimacy that wards off the looks of others.

On the other hand, the need for a private, intimate area in our lives that others have no access to can also be motivated by a completely different reason that has nothing to do with our consciousness of a defect and the desire to conceal it. It is important for our understanding of preserved and lost dignity to recognize this as an independent motive.

It is the need to *differentiate* ourselves from others. In order to be able to experience ourselves as autonomous individuals, there have to be things that others do not know about. We do not want to be made of glass: transparent in our emotions to all people at all times. We decline to be like that, even when we do not have to fear the discovery of a defect. We simply want to have experiences that we can be alone with. We want to be able to seal off our inner world to the outside. When this seal is broken against our will, it does not just feel like an exposure but like a *loss of boundaries*: we have been robbed of our emotional boundaries and thus of our ability to differentiate ourselves from others. This can also mean a loss of our dignity.

Feeling the Other's Gaze

I am alone on an empty beach or in an empty library. Another person arrives and his gaze focuses on me. This changes everything. The foreign gaze completely transforms my sense of myself in the world. Before, I was completely focused on one thing, absorbed by looking at the water and the sand or concentrating on my book. I was in a state of single-mindedness, not at all preoccupied with myself. The foreign gaze puts an end to this absent-minded dedication to one thing. I now experience myself as an object that a look is focused on. This forces me to confront myself. I used to be merely conscious, taking an interest in the world without being a part of it. Now I arrive in the world and feel myself as a part of it – I feel self-conscious. This first applies to my body: under the foreign gaze, it is present like a body among other bodies, although it still distinguishes itself as the seat of my experiences. My emotions and thoughts are now also different from before. I used to just feel and think them. Now, because I am watched by another person, I perceive myself as someone who feels and thinks them. Before, the feelings were merely felt and the thoughts thought. I was fully *in* them, dissolved in them. Now, under the foreign gaze, they are *present* in a completely different way. I as a whole am present in a different way: I am present for another person's gaze. And I am also present for myself in the foreign gaze, as well as through it. I see myself through the other's eyes.

The gaze of the person who arrives on the beach or in the library may be inattentive, fleeting and casual, lacking any intrusiveness. I am not being watched. I do not have to deal with the gaze. When this changes and a casual glance turns into a gaze that *scrutinizes* me, I experience something new: I feel *awkward*. Awkwardness is caused by the awareness that I am explicitly noticed, watched and assessed by others. This is not about a fear of looking bad. Praise and admiration can also make me feel awkward; it can be embarrassing to be celebrated as a benefactor or a role model. It is not judgement that causes embarrassment, but the undesired, perhaps also unexpected, attention. This attention creates a more explicit and intrusive existence in the world, thwarting the need for and habit of an inconspicuous presence. I believed I could remain unnoticed, and all of a sudden, everyone's eyes are focused on me. All these foreign looks feel like spotlights and make me want to run away, even when there is no reason to fear their judgement.

What is a Defect?

The narrator in Per Petterson's novel *I Curse the River of Time* tells of standing in a bar full of people on a night ferry: 'There was a man there I did not like. I did not like his face when he looked at me. It was as if he knew something about my person that I myself was not aware of, which for him was as clear as day, as if I were standing there naked, with no control over what he saw, nor could I see in his eyes what he saw in mine. But what he saw and what he *knew* made him feel superior to me and, in some strange way, I felt he had a right to. It could not be true, I had never seen him before, I was certain of that, he didn't know anything about my life.'

Awkwardness, as I have described it, is the experience of being the subject of unexpected and unwanted attention. The man on the ferry reports of an experience that is sometimes intermixed with general embarrassment, but that can be understood as a separate phenomenon: he speaks of the frightening thought and feeling that the foreign gaze might see something in him that he does not even know himself. This awareness can turn the foreign look into an intrusive and dangerous one, into an enemy's gaze that he has to protect himself against. Why? Because what this might be about could be a *defect*. But what actually is a defect?

Something is not a defect through its mere *existence* or *presence*. A deformation, stutter, addiction, an abnormal inclination, a life on a dumping ground, being unable to read and write, the scars of a failed suicide attempt, betrayal – it is never the mere fact that they are present, their existence, that makes these things defects. A *defect* is not an objective category, not a fact. It is a category of judgement – of negative, hostile judgement: a defect is an *evil*. The verdict is: it should not exist, it should never have happened. It is censorship that makes something a defect. In a world without censorship, nothing could be perceived as a defect.

Yet a defect is not just something that is *judged* to be a curse. It is not only an *intellectual* rejection. A defect is *experienced* and *felt* as something that should not be: as something whose existence I want to extinguish. I look at myself in the mirror and yearn for the deformations to go away – I want them to be *gone*. Or, when the defect is a past action, for example a betrayal or a cruel deed, I want to *undo* it. The negative verdict stains all my experiences. This is what makes every defect a curse and a burden: I carry something with me – either presently or in my memory – that I want to get rid of, but cannot. And because I cannot do away with it, I have the overwhelming desire at least to *conceal* it. A defect is therefore by nature something that must be hidden.

Not every defect is the same. It makes a difference to my perception of it whether it is my fault, whether I carry responsibility for it or not. There are defects that are purely bad luck, something that just happened to me: a deformation I was born with, a tremor caused by Parkinson's disease, a bald head after chemotherapy, lost control over my secretions, falling into poverty through no fault of my own. Such a defect is often a cause of awkwardness, as I described it, because it makes me stand out and draws others' attention to me. But because it is a defect, there is an additional experience: I feel *ashamed* and *embarrassed* to appear in front of them like that. In Petterson's book, the stranger's gaze particularly bothers the man on the ferry because it is directed at his tumours and scars – that is, at his defect. It could be much worse, of course. Imagine the bailiffs come to your house. Your furniture is carried out piece by piece, making your debt and bankruptcy public, visible to everyone. The neighbours watch and gloat over it. You just stand there. Your face burns. It is not your fault – your employer went bankrupt. It was simply bad luck. Your face burns nonetheless. It is a burning of embarrassment. You feel ashamed.

The burning would feel different and would be even stronger if this were your fault – if there were something for which you had to take the blame. It might have been an *omission*: although you were able to, you did not save any money, which now could have helped you with your debt. If you had been more prudent and careful, there would be no moving van outside your door and nothing for the neighbours to gloat over. This might be similar to the experience of an illiterate person who has to sign a document, but lacks the skill to do so. His face will also burn. He will also feel ashamed. And although his life story explains why he has never learnt to read and write, he will perhaps also perceive it as a failure, as a defect that was not unavoidable.

My face will burn in yet another, even more intense way when I am not just responsible for an omission, but for an *action*. When my hands tremble because of alcohol, it is a different kind of embarrassment from the tremor being caused by Parkinson's disease. The latter is bad luck, the former my responsibility. You would feel similarly if your furniture was carried out of your house because you gambled away your savings at a casino. In this case, your loss is your own fault, making the neighbours' looks cut even more deeply.

The defects in the examples discussed so far have not been *moral* defects: no defects connected to a moral judgement that undermines one's moral integrity. A moral defect – this can be a betrayal, fraud, lie or deception, a cruelty that caused pain, fear and loneliness, a deed that has irrevocably damaged or extinguished someone's life. Such a defect is a *transgression*. When the neighbours stand by the fence because I am led away by the police for a transgression, I again experience their looks in a different way from the case of a bankruptcy, even when I was not entirely blameless. I experience something that is different from the embarrassment felt by those who suddenly find themselves in the spotlight, and it is not just the embarrassment of defeat or weakness either. I feel the full and cruel force of *shame*. I cover my face with my hands. I want to disappear into the ground.

The Logic of Shame

What happened? I have been *exposed*. I could only be exposed – this is a conceptual observation – if I wanted to hide something. What I wanted to hide was the defect. I erected a protecting façade in order to mislead others about the defect. The façade broke down, the defect was revealed. Now I feel *unmasked*, defencelessly exposed to the judgemental looks of others. I suddenly feel as though I am naked. This is the first, rough outline of the experience of shame.

Our linguistic habits around the word 'shame' are rather lax and loose. The way we talk about it is doubly vague. The first ambiguity concerns the scope of the word. I have reserved it for the unmasking of a transgression, that is of a moral defect. But in fact, we also often speak of shame when we talk about defects that are not transgressions, where I have so far only been speaking of awkwardness and embarrassment: we say that someone is ashamed of her addiction, poverty, stutter or illiteracy. And even when a football player, on missing a decisive penalty shot in front of millions of viewers buries his face in his hands we say, 'He must feel so ashamed!' Nevertheless I would like to stick to my limitation regarding the use of this word – because the logic of shame, as we will see, shows itself most clearly with transgressions.

The word 'shame' also carries another ambiguity. It is sometimes the name for the *experience* we have when a defect is exposed, the name for the feeling behind the blush and the burning face. But what is sometimes also meant is not the emotion felt by the person who experiences the exposure, but the experience and conduct of someone who is seeking to *prevent* such an exposure: for example, someone might not mention her drug use to an anaesthesiologist because she is ashamed of it; or a homosexual person who is innocently accused of a crime prefers – out of shame – to be convicted rather than expose his sexual orientation. What we call shame here is actually a *fear of being exposed*, paired with the effort to hide something. Of course, this also happens in the case of transgressions: because I feel ashamed of my lie, I will carry on lying.

Why is it so bad when our defects become visible to others? What exactly are we afraid of when we fear being exposed? What is it that we feel when we feel shame acutely – with its cruel, emotionally destructive force? We feel a *loss*. What we lose is others' respect, recognition and appreciation. Before the defect is exposed, I am respected, my opinion is worth something, and my respect and appreciation of others are valued. Everything changes from the day a serious betrayal or lie is exposed, an act designating me an informer or traitor.

The consequence might be that something *happens* to me: I am led away, charged with a crime or otherwise pilloried. Yet it can also simply mean a new type of *gaze*. I am now the subject of looks of contempt. These are looks that signify condemnation and – biblically speaking – reprobation. 'You're no longer one of us', these looks say. This is what I am afraid of when I do all I can to conceal the defect of my transgression and prevent its exposure: I fear that I will be rejected, excluded and condemned. I know that this means losing my authority as a full member of the community. I can no longer claim respect, and my opinions no longer count. No one values my appreciation and recognition any longer. I am not allowed to use my voice any more. When I try to speak up, I am laughed at. No matter what I say, I am no longer taken seriously. From this moment, I am viewed and exist differently for others. And when I feel ashamed, my existence also feels different to myself – I feel that I should not exist at all. My inner life has a permanent flaw. I feel that I cannot breathe, as if I were suffocating. Now that I no longer have a voice, no claim on respect and authority, life has become something that is no longer lived but merely endured. I no longer have an active life in which I feel confident and evolve as a person.

Shame also changes the way I experience time. The fear of an exposure prevents me from living fully in the present: I might be unmasked at any moment and therefore cannot be free and relaxed in the present. My pre-empted internal shaming overshadows every moment of my life, filling it with anticipatory tension. Every person I meet might expose me. Every person therefore possesses quasi-judicial authority over my transgression, preventing me from being fully in the moment when she is present, as this would require relaxation of my guard. And once the exposure has taken place, the present is forever taken away from me. Shame destroys an actively lived present. It is only if I succeed in doing the impossible that I can win it back: that is, undoing my transgression.

The experience of shame is not a fleeting episode that occurs only when others are present. It is not a passing sensation like the anger or fear that I feel on seeing a certain person, which disappears as soon as I lose sight of him again. The shame of those who feel exposed and embarrassed cannot be *forgotten*. It may be covered up by powerful experiences in the present, for which the shamed person feels grateful because they make him forget his shame for a while. Yet when the force of the present subsides and he is closer to himself again, the shame immediately returns, and the changes in his life that were brought about by the experience of shame are more intrusive and pressing than ever. It is something he wakes up and goes to sleep with. It infiltrates his dreams. To him, it feels as if it would even outlast his death.

Why does shame have such power over us? We experience the exposed defect as something that *surrenders* us to the gaze of others. Whether it is the neighbours' looks, those of the audience in a court room or of television viewers: we feel as if, in our shame, we cannot protect ourselves against these looks in any way, neither through words nor deeds. It is the others who are in control and will remain so forever. It is an experience of *powerlessness*. Because the source of the contemptuous looks is external – they come from others – it may seem like the usual experience of powerlessness: something creeps over me like a landslide, helplessly burying me beneath it. Now it is a landslide of looks against which there is no protective wall. But *why* is there no such wall? Why is there no internal firewall that can protect me against being shamed? I constantly receive critical looks after all, and usually I just let them bounce off and carry on. Or, when the looks are more intrusive and threatening, for example when I am living under a dictatorship, I go into internal exile and seek the protection of my inner citadel. Why is such a move not possible with an exposure that brings to light failure or transgression?

It is because I *contribute* to my powerlessness. The experience of shame acquires its destructive force not simply because others judge me for my defect, my transgression. Shame only becomes truly powerful when I *submit* to the others' looks and judgement. Instead of facing them, as I normally would, with my own view and my independent judgement, which would counter theirs, I *adopt* the foreign judgement and make it my own: I *internalize* it. I view myself through the others' eyes and unconsciously appoint them as my judges. I bow to their judgement, to their annihilating verdict. When the court is located on the inside, it is almost of no relevance whether or not the others are really present. Shame as internalized judgement functions anyway. I adopt the annihilating verdict and from then on live as someone who has no authority towards himself, as someone whose judgement and recognition are no longer of value. The internal campaign of destruction that I lead on the others' behalf is unstoppable. There is no possibility of retreat. My powerlessness is complete.

Shame as Humiliation

We have already encountered Willy Loman, the exhausted and desperate salesman, a number of times. One day, his wife Linda makes an unsettling discovery in the cellar.

> Linda: Last month...Oh boys, it's so hard to say a thing like this! I was looking for a fuse. The lights blew out and I went down the cellar. And behind the fuse-box – it happened to fall out – was a length of rubber pipe – just short.
> Biff: No kidding?
> Linda: There's a little attachment at the end of it. I knew right away. And sure enough, on the bottom of the water heater there's a new little nipple on the gas pipe.
> Happy: That jerk.
> Biff: Did you have it taken off?
> Linda: I'm – I'm ashamed to. How can I mention it to him? Every day I go down and take down that little rubber pipe. But, when he comes home, I put it back where it was. How can I insult him that way?

Loman's despair is so great that he considers taking his own life by gassing himself. For someone who used to believe in the American Dream this is a failure and a defect. That is why he hides the pipe. If he found out that Linda knew about it, he would experience it as *shame*: he would face her as someone who is ashamed of his despair and suicidal intention. This situation would bring an experience of powerlessness with it, and it would be powerlessness in a double sense. One the one hand, it would be the powerlessness of shame, as I described it earlier: he would feel as if he had lost Linda's recognition and appreciation, and because he appropriates her perspective, he would also see himself as someone who no longer has authority and no right to his own voice. On the other hand, he would also feel another kind of powerlessness: he was not able to prevent exposure, the discovery of his defect.

The double feeling of powerlessness is part of the logic of every experience of shame: first, we let the person who is ashamed feel that he did not have enough power to hide the defect. Second, we let him feel the powerlessness of lost recognition and authority, to which he himself contributes by internalizing our perspective. This is already the case when we shame someone for a defect that is not a transgression: poverty, for instance, homelessness, impotence or illiteracy. Someone who must pay but cannot, or should be able to read but cannot, experiences both the annihilating look at the defect and his inability to hide it as powerlessness. And the cheater and traitor will feel this double powerlessness even more strongly when her transgression is discovered: in one go, she loses both her power of concealment and her authority in the eyes of the others. An act of shaming thus fulfils the conditions for a humiliation, as we have defined it in this book: the person who feels ashamed has to witness us demonstrate his powerlessness to him, enjoy it and also feel our enjoyment. This is why shaming someone can be such a cruel form of punishment. What Linda wants to spare her husband is the humiliation he would feel if she showed him what she has discovered in the cellar. She would be the last person to want to demonstrate his powerlessness to him, let alone enjoy it in front of him. But there is also another reason for her hesitation: Loman would experience Linda's discovery as not just an exposure, but also as the overstepping of a boundary. It would thus not only violate the need for privacy that concerns the concealment of a defect, but also the other kind that is concerned with protecting the boundaries of one's inner zone against intrusion. For what the pipe reveals lies at the very centre of his emotional universe: despair at a failed life. Loman hides the pipe not only because he regards this despair as a defect, but also because it belongs to his deepest feelings, which are no one else's business. And now he would discover that Linda knows about it and that through this knowledge she has come closer to him than he can bear. This is also what Linda wants to spare him.

What the example of Loman's pipe makes clear is that the humiliation of exposure can also be a humiliation in another sense: it can tear down emotional boundaries. There are defects that do not involve emotional disclosures: a deformation, bodily decay, unfortunate life circumstances or bankruptcy. But many things that we hide as defects are also concealed because they reveal how we are deep inside: the betrayal, lies, denunciations, and many cruelties reveal what ultimately drives us. Then we are not only naked in front of others in the sense that our defects have been revealed, but also in the sense that a foreign gaze can pass our emotional boundaries unhindered. The power of shame is greatest when both occur at the same time. This can be annihilating. Linda knows that, and this is why she puts the pipe back every night.

Dignity as Conquered Shame

Dignity, we could say, is the right not to be shamed. This is a variant of an idea that we have already encountered several times: that dignity can be understood as the right not to be humiliated. This is the idea that Linda is led by.

Yet perhaps she underestimates her husband. Perhaps he is stronger than she thinks. Perhaps he does not need her consideration. Let us imagine that one day she confronts him after all. The pipe lies on the table. Loman blushes and feels caught out. But he rallies quickly, much faster than Linda expected. 'I'm tired', he says. 'Some days, I simply don't want to go on any more. All the doors I have to knock on. All those people deriding me. Howard who thinks I'm a loser. On those days, the pipe is my solace. And you know what: *I'm not ashamed of it. I admit it.* I hid the pipe because I wanted to be alone in my despair. There are certain things you need to deal with alone. Now that you know about it, I can tell you: I don't care what the neighbours would think, or Howard, or the boys. And ultimately I don't care what you think about it either. You see, I've spent all my life trying to satisfy others' expectations and opinions: that of Howard, the customers, the neighbours who are always watching us, the boys and also yours – your opinions set the standard. A while ago, I was so exhausted I forgot to fill up the car and ran out of gas in the middle of the road. While waiting for help, I thought of the pipe for the first time. I felt scared and ashamed: what would everyone think! When I passed the same place again some time later, after a terrible week filled with failures, something strange happened: I felt much less ashamed when thinking about the pipe than the previous time. Why do I have to follow the opinions of others? I thought. It's *my* life after all, *my* despair and *my* decision. And you know: I felt really good for the rest of the drive. You know how I usually come home hunched, weighted down by the valise. That night, I entered the house with my head held high – internally, at least. A few days later, I installed the new outlet at the boiler and arranged the pipe. Well, now you know what it looks like inside me. I would have preferred to keep this to myself. But now that you know about it: I stand by how I am.'

What Loman describes is no less than this: by conquering the tyranny of the foreign gaze and the imminent shame, he wins back his dignity. This can be generalized: when I have a defect that I want to hide and whose exposure I fear because it would put me to shame, the cause might be either foreign judgement or my own. I hide the defect and fear its discovery because others might judge me or because I judge myself. The fight for one's dignity in the face of the actual or feared shame begins by reflecting on this distinction and asking oneself: is it actually inevitable that I appropriate the others' judgement, which makes what I grapple with appear as a defect, shame and disgrace?

The internal step Loman describes is the step many people take in order to win back the dignity they believed to have lost: homosexuals, for instance, or poor, sick or disabled people. They follow the logic of the famous words with which the black civil rights movement sought to discard shame and humiliation: *Black is beautiful*. It is as if they all shouted: 'You want us to feel ashamed? We're not even thinking about it! This *is no* defect!' This can also be a liberating thought for the heroin addict who picks up his dose; or for the person who needs drugs that reveal her psychiatric illness to the pharmacist. She used to drive to far-out villages to pick up her prescription and would never go to the same pharmacy twice. She found it humiliating that she had to keep driving further out of shame. Now she always goes to the pharmacy in her home village, stands calmly in front of the pharmacist, looking him straight in the eye. 'Yes, I'm ill', her gaze says, 'but I see no reason to be ashamed – no matter what you might think behind your spectacled face.' An illiterate person might turn up with a similarly firm look to sign up for a literacy course: 'Yes, I'm quite old and can't read. I felt ashamed for far too long. That was silly and I'm done with it.' And we can also imagine a beggar who does not look down in shame: 'Yes, I have nothing to eat and depend on handouts. But this is no disgrace, just misfortune. It doesn't make me less worthy than you.'

Those who win back their dignity that way realize that there is no irrevocable compulsion to internalize the foreign judgement – no compelling reason to see themselves only through the eyes of the others. The foreign judges had silently found their way inside me – now I chase them away. This also makes the desire to protect myself through hiding disappear, as there is no longer the self-induced threat of the foreign gaze. I embrace what I used to perceive as a defect and that no longer is one. I stand up to the others, who may now see me as I am. I cannot stop them from continuing to judge me with their dogmatic stubbornness. But they have been thrown out and now no longer have access to and power over me. They can still exclude me, refuse me work and income. But now I can move to another town where I can live in peace with myself. Such an escape would have been futile before, as I would have taken their gaze and their annihilating verdict with me.

What I win back through such internal development are my lost authority and my voice. Perhaps I was a deserter, someone who ran away during the war. I saw no sense in abandoning myself to enemy gunfire. I wanted to live. I escaped. But after the war, I was accused of being a coward and traitor. These humiliations deprived me of the possibility of defending myself. I left the country and hid elsewhere.

I walked with my head low and thought that I had forever lost the chance to enjoy my life. I almost let the shame suffocate me. Then I read about other deserters and spoke to some of them. This allowed my original judgement to take charge again: I regained confidence in my own, divergent voice and straightened up. I was able to revolt against the humiliation and shook off the powerlessness that it had brought. I went home and sought open confrontation. I questioned the justification for the war. I defended myself. I was back in the present.

But what happens when I do not succeed in shaking off shame because I myself also view the uncovered transgression as a defect? What if it so severe and unambiguous that I cannot defend it to myself either? What can it mean to react to such an inner conflict with dignity?

Let us assume that what Willy Loman hides in the cellar is not a pipe but papers that prove that he is a spy and traitor: he betrayed a friend to Joseph McCarthy's witch hunters for money. It ruined the man and his family's lives. He ended up killing himself. His family lives in misery. Linda discovers the evidence. What can Loman do to win back the dignity he has lost because of his transgression? Is there *anything* he can do – something that is not denial, whitewashing or self-deceit? What kind of dignity could this give rise to?

First of all, Loman would have to *understand* how this could happen: he would have to be sincere in his quest for his motives. A political motive seems too superficial and would be a cheap explanation. Money alone cannot be a strong enough motive either, as the sum was not high enough in relation to the severity of the crime. No, this was about him and his feelings towards his former friend. It might have been envy of his success, that stood in unbearable contrast to his own failures. Or it could have been burning jealousy, as he saw how the man flirted with Linda and how she enjoyed it. Or perhaps it was a humiliation that happened a long time ago, but was never forgotten. What is important is that by uncovering his true motive, Loman understands and feels that the betrayal of his friend was no accidental slip, no superficial mistake, but a meaningful episode of his own unhappy life.

Understanding and sincerity alone will, however, not be enough. It will also be important to show what we call *remorse*: the clear and genuine awareness of an inexcusable transgression, paired with regret for the fact that the deed undermined him as a person of moral integrity. Standing up to this loss and recognizing it will be crucial for Loman. It could be the beginning of a slow, silent reconciliation with himself – not in the sense of airbrushing, but rather in that the way he continues to live his life will allow him one day to rediscover himself as a moral person. His newly acquired dignity would lie, one could say, in the constantly precarious equilibrium between the unadorned memory of what has happened and his confidence in his new moral integrity.

Loman will not be able to find this equilibrium on his own. He will also need the perspective of others – those who are ready to stop shaming him and accept him again. They will only be ready for it when Loman's actions express his remorse and regret. Only when they see him trying to make amends will they gradually start to treat him in a manner that will help him win back a sense of dignity. Only then will he have the courage to speak with his own voice again.

The Intimate Space

The French teacher Philippe Claudel spent eleven years visiting a prison in Nancy every day in order to give lessons. He published his observations under the title *The Sound of Keyrings*. One of them was the following: 'Peepholes on the cell doors allow one to see in without being seen. The inmate would hear a hand move a metal lid and notice a prying eye. She might never know to whom it belonged. It was simply an intruding gaze that relegated the concept of intimacy to the pages of a dictionary. – This eye would always look through the hole when Linda B. washed herself or went to the toilet; this constant surveillance led her to develop incontinence and she wet herself during the night. Everything went back to normal when the guard who used to watch her was moved to a different post.' This account inevitably makes one think of George Orwell's world, where everyone is being watched at all times. It also immediately makes one think that human dignity is violated here – it seems crystal clear. But what exactly does it mean? What exactly is destroyed when we deprive a person of the possibility of being able to hide from a stranger's gaze?

We do not want every moment, every action and every expression of our life to be observed. We want to be alone and unwatched when we go to the bathroom or take care of our bodies. We also do not want to be exposed to the looks of strangers when we sleep – this is why I pull my coat over my face when I try to nap on a train. We need living spaces where we are safe from intrusive looks. These are the places where we keep all the things through which we express ourselves as private persons: furniture, books, pictures, bric-a-brac. This is the intimate space that we have created. Only a few are allowed to enter. When we are the victims of a burglary, the material loss sometimes seems less severe than the shock we feel because total strangers entered our intimate space.

We call this space our *private sphere*. It is not something that is predetermined and unchangeable. Every individual, and also every culture, has the power to alter the scope of this sphere freely, to determine its boundaries and also change them in the course of a life. I can develop the desire to open up my intimate sphere by showing more of myself than before. This can happen entirely without coercion and I can experience it as liberating – as something that opens up new experiences for me, new kinds of relationships, new possibilities to develop as a person. Yet it might also be external circumstances and desires that force me to narrow the radius of my private sphere and expose more of myself and my life to others. This might be caused by cramped living conditions or a stay in a total institution like the army, a prison or hospital. There the usual protective walls of intimacy are torn down. This is not merely unpleasant, but can be experienced as a threat. The woman in the prison in Nancy certainly perceived it that way. In the same prison, some especially tough inmates in the high-security wing would decline their right to a walkabout when it involved stripping naked in front of the guard beforehand. It would be a humiliation, demonstrated and sometimes also enjoyed by the guard – it would destroy dignity.

When we cannot stop others from tearing down the protective walls that guard our intimate space, we have to keep moving those walls further inwards. 'Fine then, they'll see *this* and also know *that*', I think, 'but they'll *never* get to see this and that.' It is the retreat into an inner fortress where I remain invisible and untouchable, even when I am flooded by glaring lights and grabbed by intrusive hands. The fortress is narrow and I have to make my experiences small to be able to squeeze inside it and shut the gates.

I am also forced into such an internal retreat when I sell my body for sex or pornographic films and photographs. I need the inner citadel in order to not be shaken up each time someone breaks down my intimate boundaries. I have to place my body outside the gates of my shrunken private sphere, despite the fact that its limits were originally among this sphere's major boundaries. I even have to perform this feat when another person not only touches and feels my body but penetrates it. I have to retreat inside, to a space beyond the body and move the limits that define me to an emotional space that no one can reach through physical penetration – where I am unreachable, untouchable and invulnerable. As the self that matters the most to me and whose dignity is at stake, I withdraw from the body and am no longer present in what happens to me physically

– no one is *there* when I am penetrated. I am not selling *myself*, but just my *shell*. This makes it less bad. I pull out of my body while it happens. I am essentially inanimate during the process. Even the physical sensations, one could say, are lifeless. And when the others come and think they can take away my dignity, I say to them: You are out of luck! I have already left. You're attacking a bastion that I abandoned a long time ago. You are ridiculous – like an army that is excited to invade a ghost town.

The Innermost Zone

The reason why Willy Loman hides the pipe in the cellar is not necessarily that he considers his despair a defect and is therefore ashamed of it. It might also be that, although he admits and is not ashamed of this deep and universal emotion, he feels that it is simply no one else's business. He wants to be *alone* with it. If this is the case, he is led by the second need for intimacy that I spoke of at the beginning of this chapter: the need to use secrecy in order to distinguish oneself from others. If he found out that Linda knew about his secret, it would mean the loss of a protective barrier for him. He would have the disturbing experience of an emotional loss of boundaries and an external seepage. In this case, there would not be the threat of shame, but that of an *externalization* of the inner world: something that was meant to stay inside would be turned to the outside. There would be the danger, one could say, that he would *lose* himself and become *alien* to himself.

How can we better understand this need for the delineation and protection of intimacy, so that we can be sure that when talking about it, we do not just conjure up empty words but describe a real experience? What is precious about this form of intimacy? And how is it embedded in the way of living that we are tracing here in order to make sense of the idea of dignity?

Every person possesses an emotional boundary that nobody can cross because it constitutes a conceptual boundary: nobody else can have *my* experiences and live *my* life. Experiences always belong to a certain person and are part of her identity. In that sense, they cannot be shared: two people can never share an experience in the same way that they can share a space, a job or an object. Without needing particular protection, this intimacy is irrevocable, its conceptual seal unbreakable. The protection we desire for the inner zone of our experiences therefore cannot concern the *possession* of these experiences, but only their *knowledge*. What I have to guard is the extent to which others know about my experiences. But *why* is it important to protect it?

There is a practical reason that we might also call prudence: what others know of my inner world determines their picture of me, which in turn determines how they encounter me. That is why it is prudent only to let favourable things be visible to others. The things that I keep quiet about do not need to be defects. The thoughts, feelings and desires that I leave in the dark may be innocent. I simply do not want to give others the potential to calculate my behaviour and wishes. In that sense, it might be prudent to remain impenetrable and mysterious to others.

But this prudence is neither the whole story about intimacy and secrecy, nor is it even the most important part of this story. Let us assume that I keep a diary. It does not contain any dark secrets or confessions. Nobody who might read it would have reason to point a finger at me. On the contrary: the diary might tell of overcoming fear, hatred or disappointment. It might testify to an inner struggle that deserves the highest respect. It might reveal sacrifice, renunciation or true moral greatness. It might show magnanimity, compassion for an enemy, empathy for someone who did wrong and is now suffering. If others read this, their image of me would change for the better. It would make me appear a highly generous person, a role-model for others, a beacon of good character. Why am I nevertheless drawn to keep it a secret?

The diary entries might also be about things that do not require moral judgement: a shocking experience, hope, love, admiration and respect. They might describe the inner parting from an author whose works I followed for many years or an artist or a type of music that used to be important to me. The entries might also talk about religious or political views, about grief and suffering, about a longing for fog on autumn days. I might have noted down my fondness for a perfume or a colour. And perhaps I also captured daydreams and memories that I did not want to lose. Why do I want to be alone with all this? Why do diaries have locks?

We do not want another person to know *completely* who and how we are. A part of us must remain uncertain, in the dark, vague – even for those with whom we share our lives, day by day. Why? Let us assume that someone finds my diary, breaks it open and the next day everyone can read in the newspapers what has preoccupied me in my quiet moments. I would experience it as a disaster. But what is actually so terrible about it – when, as we assumed, it does not reveal the slightest flaw or transgression? What are the right words to describe the harm that is done here?

I might perhaps want to say that I feel *vulnerable* and *exposed*: everyone is now able to see what I am like. I could say that I feel like the woman in the prison in Nancy, but even worse: her privacy was destroyed, but her inner world remained safe, closed to the guard's intrusive look. I, by contrast, have also been hurt in my innermost zone by the newspaper stories discussing my private experiences. This is admittedly different from the aftermath of a shaming: there are no contemptuous, spiteful looks directed at me. But the others' looks still pierce me in the same way and I cannot stop them. Even when I receive understanding, admiring or compassionate looks: I did not want these knowledgeable looks. I wanted to walk the streets unnoticed.

We could also use other terms: we could say that the publication of the diary abolished an important *space* between me and others, a space defined by secrets – by the fact that there are things that remain hidden from them. Those who respect the need for this space are *discreet*; those who disregard it are *indiscreet*. Discretion is the sense for distance, the respect for others' secrets. We could continue this line of thought and say: only such a distance from others allows us to be *ourselves*. Consequently, the person who robs us of this distance not only does something that is merely offensive and unpleasant, but commits a serious and highly destructive act: he causes us to *lose* ourselves. Holding the newspaper that makes the entirety of my emotions public, I feel that I am losing myself under the gaze of others because there is no longer an inner zone to which I can retreat, no final secret that I can draw a line around.

And even this is not yet the full story. Something else happens to our experiences when they are ripped out of our innermost zone and exposed to the spotlight of public attention: they *change*. We can describe this change in the following way: we are *robbed* of the original experience. Once it has been discussed in public, it cannot be experienced as before. It is *lost* to us. 'If only I hadn't spoken about it!', we say to ourselves after thoughtlessly blabbing out a valuable, fragile feeling. 'I wish I hadn't mentioned it!' Now we have to fear that we will not be able to relive this feeling in its original, unuttered form. And when we lose one feeling after another that way, we end up being completely *estranged* from ourselves.

In one of the numerous monologues Christa Wolf conducts in her book *City of Angels*, she says to herself: 'And so you kept your silence when people started pestering you with questions and accusations. At some point, the sentence formed: We loved this country. An impossible sentence that would have earned you nothing but mocking jeers if you had spoken it out loud. But you didn't. You kept it to yourself, the way you were keeping so much to yourself.' Christa Wolf is not a person who was ashamed of her feelings for the GDR, and neither would she have been unable to bear the contemptuous reactions to this politically incorrect sentiment. The reason she withheld the sentence that was so important to her is that she did not want the emotions that went into it to be destroyed by sardonic and mocking discussion. Others' derisive sentences would have created new emotions in her, and even if they had not changed anything about her attitude, the original emotion would have been irreversibly altered by the storm of indignation and the anger of her resistance. She wanted to protect the love for her country through distance – a distance of discretion and silence.

And in the end, is silence not just important externally, but also internally? We might hesitate with certain words not just towards others, but also towards ourselves – hesitate to say something to ourselves or write it down, even though we are certain that no one will find out about it. The reason might be that we want to deny something to ourselves: fear, envy or spiteful joy, for example. It is better not even to think about it. But it does not have to be like that. It might also be that I want to protect the emotion in its verbal virginity because I sense that it would change in its substance if I put it into words: that it might even seem banal or kitschy to me if I named it. It does not have to be a negative judgement or an unpleasant discovery, as if I had to say to myself: this is what I'm feeling then. Could we say then that by naming it, the experience loses its *magic* – the magic that lies in its unpronounceability, its mystery and secret? Does the survival of our innermost zone in that sense also depend on our silence?

Dignified Disclosures

As we have seen, human dignity has a lot to do with looking after the boundaries of our intimate space and refusing to mindlessly open the innermost zone of our thoughts and feelings to others. Yet we might end up revealing our most secret emotions in public in a way that makes precisely that the expression of our dignity. We can, for example, imagine this happening in court: I show myself in my vulnerability, my pain and my hatred that had driven me to commit the crime. Or at someone's grave: I let everybody see my shock, my tears of grief and loneliness. It might also happen during a political speech, where my anger and indignation at humiliation, oppression and injustice break through: triggered by the situation, I pour out all my emotions. The dividing wall between the private and the public is torn down, and everyone can now see inside me. These used to be carefully guarded and secret feelings, desires and thoughts – now they are revealed in what we call an emotional outburst. The emotional eruption, the emotional lava that breaks forth, sweeps away the protective barrier. Unplanned, I *show* myself in a way others did not use to know me. And in the process, I feel: it was high time for me to admit my feelings in public, too. In that moment, my dignity lies in that I no longer hide myself.

This can evoke deep respect. I see it in the looks of those present and also the next day while walking down the street, I feel how they respect me for publicly standing up for myself. What matters is that my emotional outburst was spontaneous and genuine. When we decide to show ourselves that way, it cannot be a staged performance or show – nothing calculated and exhibitionist, no plan or tactic. The overpowering must be genuine.

When I break down at the grave and only shortly after, when leaving the cemetery, crack jokes, people will say: 'How undignified – deep emotions shouldn't be a show.' And it is similar with an emotional speech that seems to come from the bottom of someone's heart: when we get hold of the manuscript and discover that the outbursts were meticulously scripted stage directions, we will feel nothing but disgust. It will be the kind of disgust we feel in the face of forfeited dignity. Political candidates who show anger and indignation ten times a day, strictly according to plan, risk seeming ridiculous: it is the ridiculousness of lost dignity.

Being in court, standing at someone's grave or at a lectern: all of these are important situations that are framed by symbolism. Their symbolic weight is decisive for our willingness to show to the outside what normally remains inside. We could say that this willingness in part defines these situations – the public outcry is symbolically embedded. But what happens when we hear this outcry outside of any symbolic framework? When someone cries out her grief, hatred or desire on the village road or in the marketplace, when a drunkard staggers through the streets at night and lets his misery break out in a raw, loud and helpless manner? Is this just funny, embarrassing or sad? Or is dignity also involved, perhaps in the genuine, undisguised and honest manner of the outcry?

Symbolically motivated disclosures from the innermost zone also occur in another form: as literary journals. 'I've said before that I'm an alcoholic. Now I'm no longer saying it just to make myself interesting. I am an alcoholic', Max Frisch writes in his *Drafts for a Third Sketchbook*. 'I have never made a serious attempt to put an end to my life. No unserious one either. I have just – at all ages – thought of it', we read in *Montauk*. And: 'Lying on the summery balcony with its view across Rome, I slept with my face in my own vomit.' If a stranger attacked us with such confessions, we would find it repellent and perhaps turn away: this is not something we wanted to know. We would perceive it as lacking in distance, as indiscreet – as undignified. Why is it different when these are sentences in a carefully composed book? Why is dignity less in danger when it is an artistic disclosure instead of cheap, indiscreet chatter? Why does a skilful description, an expert choice of words and a successful textual flow make the issue appear less indiscreet and objectionable? Why does it seem less like forfeited dignity than in the case of an artless, uncontrolled exposure? Is it because the artistic work betrays a process of reflection and the author's intellectual distance to his confessions, which revoke the lack of distance that we would normally find objectionable? Or is it because, when the sentences are embedded in a work of art they acquire the dignity of universal insight although they are still about this single person? Is that the reason why we do not regard autobiographies, which typically lead us into an author's innermost zone, as undignified impositions but as sources of understanding?

Disclosures of intimate information that do not involve a violation of dignity also happen in another context: during therapy. Those who hesitate to see a therapist often do so because they dread the idea of disclosing their most intimate desires, feelings and fantasies to a stranger. What helps one get over this fear is the thought that these will be *healing* disclosures. They are necessary in order to reach a better understanding of one's own experiences and actions. This is about self-discovery and sincerity towards oneself; and also about the growth of one's inner freedom: about overcoming dependence, compulsions, pretence, unnecessary taboos and false shame. To accomplish such change, we sometimes require the outside, expert viewpoint of a person with whom we are not entangled in our regular lives and who, for that reason, is able to show the selfless solidarity that we need. Exposing my secrets to her can be liberating. I can now call them by their proper name, which is the first step to taking away their threat and eventually integrating them into my identity. When I disclose myself to the therapist, it happens within the framework of a pact against the inner forces that cause my suffering, against incomprehension and unfreedom. My contribution to the pact is openness. Her contribution is her experience with emotional issues. The pact creates intimacy between us, yet it is intimacy of an unusual kind: it is asymmetrical because the disclosures are one-sided, and this intimacy is not, as in other relationships, an end in itself and also limited in time: one day, there will no longer be the need for it.

Part of the logic of therapeutic situations is that we trust the person to whom we open ourselves to be discreet. It is discretion that makes me feel that I can safely talk about things that I have never been able to put into words before, even for myself. While doing so, I might momentarily stumble and wonder whether this is the right thing to do, or whether it will cause me to lose myself. With luck, it will become obvious in retrospect that it was the right decision, for the difficult, perhaps agonizing and shameful disclosures helped me to win back my dignity – in the sense of inner autonomy, which we discussed in Chapter 1.

But what happens, also in terms of our experience of dignity, when the therapeutic process brings up such dark, powerful and destructive disclosures that I end up wishing I had never walked down this corridor of memory? In his book *The Lost Art of Healing*, Bernard Lown writes about a patient who compulsively bought groceries. After a long time, she finally got over her fear and told of a horrible experience she had had at the concentration camp. 'Then she suddenly composed herself, looked at me angrily because I had brought this long-buried nightmare back to light and fell silent again.' How can we interpret this silence? How can we interpret it if we want to understand it in terms of the experience of dignity?

Undignified Disclosures

A person can gamble away her dignity by revealing intimate information to the public without the need to do so and in a crude and unreflective manner, thus making it accessible to people who normally have nothing to do with her life. In this case, there is no encounter that provides a context and reason for her to break down the barrier of intimacy and open herself up to the gaze of others. This is an exposure in front of total strangers. She is responsible for blasting away the protective wall around her experiences and switching on the glaring lights. This might happen, for example, when someone accidentally finds himself at a party where such revelations are considered desirable. Someone might also disclose his most intimate thoughts, feelings and obsessions in front of TV cameras or to voyeuristic tabloid journalists and photographers; or he might use social media. Sexual preferences, even perversions, are revealed, together with terms of endearment and affection, hidden fears and hopes, religious convictions, bizarre habits and tastes. And even the symptoms of illness and decay, up to the announcement of an imminent death, are offered up to the curious, sensation-seeking gaze of the anonymous audience. Those behind the cameras believe that the more the innermost zone comes to light, the better.

When I have heedlessly ended up in such a situation, I might wake up as though from a bad dream, thinking: how did I get myself into this! What have I done? This can upset me for a long time. I experience it as a loss, and if I had to name it, I would say: it is a loss of my dignity. No other word captures it. This example shows that we cannot do without the concept of dignity. If we did not have it, we could not make sense of an important facet of our lives.

Yet the experience of such a loss is not homogeneous, not all of a piece. What matters for our intuitive judgment about lost dignity are the *reasons* why we exposed ourselves to the intruding looks of the public. It might happen out of *carelessness*, out of inexperience and rashness: it just seemed novel and exciting to go public. This sometimes happens to teenagers who are not yet sure of their limits and want to experiment. In that case, there is no plan, no calculated advantage: it was just 'cool' to do it. Then we are less offended by the indiscreet behaviour. We might not even consider it a loss of their dignity, but a part of a learning process in which they are still developing their sense of dignity.

We might also be forced by *social compulsion* to reveal more of ourselves than we actually want, betraying our need for distance and discretion. I do not actually wish to go to the sauna: others should not see my naked body. I do not like telling strangers about my sexual habits; nor do I like sharing my partner's words of affection. I do not want to disclose my daydreams, which reveal my hopes and fears. When I reluctantly do these things nonetheless, it is to avoid being excluded. Intimate information can thus be extorted through the threat of exclusion. Defending the dignity of discretion here equals defending the dignity of autonomy and not allowing anyone else to dictate the boundaries of my privacy. Failing to defend these boundaries is a sign of weakness. I might of course choose to violate discretion because it is the lesser evil – this is an understandable endangering of dignity, taken for fear of isolation, and cannot yet be considered an active forfeiture of dignity that is motivated by self-interest.

Something that we might find repulsive and that might lead us to make a harsher judgement is when someone *sells* the intimate side of her life – for money or for attention. I might agree to go on a talk show and expose my inner life to the eyes and ears of millions of viewers – because I was promised a generous fee or because I finally want to receive lots of public attention. Or I might call the voyeurs from the tabloids. My home is invaded by cameras, microphones and make-up artists. I allow spotlights to pour into my private rooms. My intimate life is appropriated and rearranged by strangers. It is a violent act, and this is also how I experience it. When the gang leaves or I return home from the talk show, I ask myself if I have perhaps just destroyed something valuable.

The destruction of a person's dignity through the destruction of his intimacy can also be accomplished from the outside. We are all familiar with the ambivalent emotions we feel on seeing a television camera move very close to faces showing grief, agony or despair. Why do these tears have to be made public in such a way? They are not a piece of *news* or *information* after all, which some audience has a claim to. Why show them? Their emotions are visible to those who are part of the situation, those standing at the grave or by the wreckage after the disaster. This kind of visibility does not endanger dignity, as it is natural and unavoidable. The camera, by contrast, makes these emotions public in a special and artificial way: visible to millions, for whom they are just one image among thousands of others that they see in their living rooms – foreign, fleeting and of no consequence to their own actions. They can simply switch to another channel. You cannot say that it is a show. A show is planned and arranged. This is not the case here. There is no director of action, just a director of images. What shall we call what the camera is showing, then? A public scene? A public emotional drama? The emotional life of others as entertainment? Those who film and broadcast it might not intend it that way. There might be no cynicism or shabby voyeurism involved. But is it not still a problem? Is it not a problem of dignity?

Sometimes the issue is even more complicated. The point might be to show viewers across the world something that they would otherwise struggle to believe. Then the respect for intimacy gives way to the desire to educate – educate in the sense of truthfulness and knowledge of the world. This is the case when we are shown pictures of emaciated naked people behind barbed wire fences, or other pictures of cruelty and suffering, photographs of dead people, mutilations or maltreatment. The victims sometimes approve of being filmed: they want their misery to be known. Filmed executions are not part of this. Here we feel disgust and anger at the lack of dignity. In such cases, the rhetoric of information and education is too flimsy – this is pure sensationalism.

Finally, there is the voyeur's lost dignity: the person who gloats over others' intimate details and sells them as a commodity. We have already been able to observe several times: when someone steals another person's dignity, he also gambles away his own. This is also the case when someone snoops around another person's private life without permission. Paparazzi are the reckless and undignified pirates of the private sphere who, with their cameras, not only violate good manners and provoke disgust; their private snapshots that end up on the front pages of the tabloids are also repellent in a deeper sense: they violate human dignity in the sense of respect for intimacy. It is a miserable way to earn one's living.

Shared Intimacy

Sometimes we wish to open the intimate space that we inhabit to others. We let them enter our rooms and even live in them. They are allowed to see our books and pictures, use our bathroom and cook in our kitchen. In turn, we are invited to enter their intimate space. This creates relationships that we call intimate relationships. There are different stages to such shared intimacy. The question is how far we open ourselves and how much of us we allow to become visible. Intimacy grows to the degree to which, beyond the intimate space, we also allow insight into our inner life, the innermost zone of our thoughts, feelings and desires. In a very intimate relationship, we show ourselves to another person in a way that only few and perhaps no one else knows us. We show ourselves in our desire, our fear and longing, our hate and contempt, our envy and jealousy, our hopes and dreams. We let the other see our tears and disappointment, our euphoria and despair, our irrationality and obsessions. We allow the border to the innermost zone to become permeable. And of course, physical relationships, passionate encounters, create a special form of intimacy. There are moments when the force of desire disables all control and makes us completely vulnerable.

Intimate relationships are encounters, as I described them in Chapter 2: people in their thoughts, desires and emotions relate to those of others, that they can in turn relate to their own. Those involved are thus intellectually entangled with one another in a complex way. This structural entanglement already creates a type of closeness uniquely known to humans. This closeness acquires an additional dimension when we share intimate knowledge and experiences. We now also mutually respect our intimate secrets and have a reciprocal trust in this respect, that is also a trust in each other's discretion. It is this respect and trust that make this intimate relationship so valuable. An essential part of this is the expectation that the relationship will be symmetrical, as far as the scope and depth of intimate knowledge is concerned. It is horrible to realize that I was mistaken in this expectation and opened myself in a way that is not reciprocated: I took this step, the other person did not. Even when the other's refusal to open up is not a demonstration of my powerlessness, so that we cannot speak of a humiliation, it might be experienced as a grave offence, in the sense of an affront. Everyone knows this and we are all familiar with the strange and awkward situation that we find ourselves in when we are confronted with unexpected and premature disclosures of intimate information: to avoid insulting the other person through an imbalance of openness, we sometimes reveal things beyond what we actually wanted. One could speak of an unintentional extortion through unwanted openness.

Intimate relationships possess a certain form of *exclusivity*: each such relationship is different from all others and none is replaceable by another. When the inner worlds of two people become entangled, an emotional connection develops that is unique and distinctive in its intensity, tone and atmosphere. This brings along emotions that have to do with dignity. We avoid carrying over gestures, words and rituals that have developed in one intimate relationship, and have helped define it, unchanged into a new relationship. It might be impossible to live a new relationship in the old apartment. We do not simply take a new partner on the same holidays, and we avoid certain restaurants. We might feel unsettled if old emotions occur in unaltered shape in the new relationship. It disturbs us because it endangers the uniqueness of a relationship. Intimacy as routine: we sense that this would be a problem. We would not just fear staleness. Even more would be destroyed: the dignity of an intimate relationship as the respect for its unrepeatability.

Intimate relationships can break apart. What happens with shared secrets? With what only I and no one else knows about this person – her dreams, yearnings and disappointments? Her demands on herself and her self-image? This can also be considered a question of dignity: whether we keep the secrets despite the break-up, or whether we betray them and with them our past intimacy by telling them to others. This question also poses itself when the other person has now become an opponent or even an enemy.

Betrayed Intimacy as Lost Dignity

The step into an intimate relationship is a dangerous one. Intimacy means that a foreigner possesses knowledge of me. And because it includes knowledge of my weaknesses, it is dangerous knowledge, as it gives the other person power over me and makes me vulnerable. The other has seen what I am like behind the façade I show to the world in order to protect myself. She has got to know the impulses and desires that exist inside me, beyond the internal censors, and whose public knowledge would make me vulnerable. She knows of my uncontrollable prejudices, my ugly envy and my excessive hatred. She knows how much blind compulsion, utter unreason and intolerance there are behind my façade of sobriety and control. She knows my weaknesses and incapacities and has learned how petty, unforgiving and unfair I can be. She knows my dark sides. By allowing her to get to know them, I have in a certain sense surrendered myself to her. Intimacy can thus become a weapon. A person might be blackmailed with the threat to betray his intimate secrets, and feel humiliated when this exposure of private information in front of others actually occurs. All of this can mean a loss of a person's dignity.

The logic and dynamic of such a loss of dignity can be observed in Edward Albee's piece *Who's Afraid of Virginia Woolf?* George and Martha, who have been married for a long time, know everything about each other. No weakness has remained hidden. One person's weakness is the other's strength. Their relationship largely subsists of their mutual knowledge of failures, misleading self-images and life-long delusions. It is a *folie à deux*. It has worked and got them so far because it has always been their private matter – an entanglement that only concerned the two of them. This changes when a young couple, Nick and Honey, arrive for a late-night visit and break down the protective wall of intimacy that George and Martha had erected around themselves.

Martha, the daughter of a college president, as we learn from George, despises her husband because he did not make it to head of department. 'Martha tells me often, that I am *in* the History Department...as opposed to *being* the History Department...in the sense of *running* the History Department. I *did* run the History Department, for four years, during the war, but that was because everybody was away. Then...everybody came back...because nobody got killed.'

> Martha: George is not preoccupied with *history*...George is preoc-
> cupied with the *History Department*. George is preoccupied
> with the History Department because...
> George: ...because he is *not* the History Department, but is only *in*
> the History Department. We know, Martha...
> Martha: George is bogged down in the History Department. He's an
> old bog in the History Department, that's what George is.
> Ha, ha, ha, HA! A SWAMP! Hey, swamp! Hey SWAMPY! God

knows, *some*body's going to take over the History
Department, *some* day, and it ain't going to be Georgie-boy,
there...that's for sure. Are ya, swampy...are ya? I had it
all planned out...He was the groom...he was going to be
groomed. He'd take over some day...first he'd take over
the History Department, and then, when Daddy retired,
he'd take over the college...you know? That's the way it
was supposed to be. That's the way it was *supposed* to be.
Very simple. And Daddy seemed to think it was a pretty
good idea, too. For a while. Until he watched for a couple
of years and started thinking maybe it wasn't such a good
idea after all...that maybe Georgie-boy didn't have the
stuff...that he didn't have it in him! You see, George didn't
have much...push...he wasn't particularly aggressive. In
fact he was sort of a...FLOP! A great...big...fat...FLOP!

Martha exposes something in front of the visitors that is only her and
George's business: her contempt for him. There are mutual opinions
between people that are no one's matter but theirs. This exclusivity
of certain views, like the exclusivity of certain emotions, accounts for
the intimacy of their relationship. Martha breaks apart this intimacy
and betrays it. What belongs to intimacy is the trust that the other
person will never do such a thing – when it happens, it therefore
also constitutes a breach of trust. The witnesses thus learn of two
things: Martha's contempt for George and furthermore the fact that
she is prepared to betray her intimacy with George and break the
trust between them.

George must experience this as a humiliation that violates his
dignity. Nick and Honey's presence is critical. Let us assume George
and Martha were alone when she says to him: 'You are a big fat
flop.' That would be insulting and offensive. Would we also call it a
humiliation? Not according to the definition of the concept that we
have developed so far. What is missing is the experience of powerlessness. If they were alone, George would have the ability to *protect*
himself: he could respond to it with a similarly grave insult, so that
they would be even; or he could laugh at Martha, thus showing that
she could not hit him; or he could leave the room in silence. But now
the guests hear it. What is so terrible about this? What is it that turns
the insult into a humiliation?

If it belongs to the nature of a humiliation that it includes a demonstration of powerlessness, the guests' looks would have to cause
this powerlessness. How far is that the case? First, George does not
have the power to *erase* the guests' knowledge of Martha's contempt.
They now know how Martha sees him – he can no longer change

anything about it. They see him with Martha's eyes: as a flop. George must moreover feel powerless because he does not have any suitable reaction at his disposal. Whatever he might try – it would do nothing against the annihilating remark. 'I'm not a failure!' – This reaction would be ridiculous, because Martha's comment was not a statement that could be rebutted but an attack. George would appear an idiot who failed to comprehend this. He could give her a taste of her own medicine: it would seem weak and mechanical, like every tit-for-tat response. Laughter: it would be a tense laughter of helplessness. Leaving the room in silence: George would appear a weakling. Do nothing: he would look as powerless as he feels. None of these reactions can break the spell of this crushing remark. With anything he might try he would run the risk of looking like a ludicrous, pitiful character who is leading a hopeless battle. It is like every humiliation: it undervalues any defence in advance – this is what is vicious about it. And finally, George also has another experience of powerlessness: he knows that he cannot halt the destruction of intimacy that has been launched by Martha's tirade. Such an attack is irreversible.

This is confirmed to him some time later when Martha divulges a dark episode from George's past that also affected their relationship. We first hear it as a story about one of George's school mates: he accidentally shot his mother dead and then drove into a tree. His father who was in the car with him died. When the boy learned that he had also killed his father, he could not stop laughing hysterically. What Martha now goes on to reveal in front of the guests is a humiliation for George that could not possibly be greater.

Martha: Georgie-boy had lots of big ambitions – in spite of something funny in his past...
George: Martha...
Martha: Which Georgie-boy here turned into a novel...His first attempt and also his last...
George: I warn you, Martha.
Martha: But Daddy took a look at Georgie's novel and he was very shocked by what he read. A novel about a naughty boy child...
George: I will not tolerate this!
Martha: ...ha, ha! A naughty boy-child who...uh...who killed his mother and his father dead.
George: STOP IT, MARTHA!
Martha: And Daddy said...Look, here, kid, you don't think for a second I'm going to let you publish this crap, do you? You publish that goddamn book and you're out...on your ass!
George: I will not be made mock of!

Martha: And you want to know the clincher? You want to know what big brave Georgie said to Daddy?
George: You will not say this!
Martha: The hell I won't...He caved in is what he did. He came home and he threw the book in the fireplace and burned it!
George: I'LL KILL YOU!
Martha: Coward!

George grabs Martha by the throat – that is how unbearable the humiliation of her betrayal is for him. This betrayal is complicated: first, a family secret is revealed in front of total strangers, forfeiting shared intimacy. In addition, the secret represents a defect in George's life: he was, though only accidentally, involved in both of his parents' deaths. Martha's revelation thus constitutes a shaming. George had previously made the attempt to conquer his shame and win back his lost dignity by writing about his misfortune. Martha's mighty father thwarted this project – another experience of demonstrated and even enjoyed powerlessness. And when Martha accuses George of being a coward in front of others, we are dealing with a humiliation of a second order: George is humiliated because a previous humiliation is set out in front of strangers.

George now fights back against the humiliation by calling it by its proper name. This allows him to be more than just a silent victim.

George: We've played *Humiliate the Host*...we've gone through that one. What shall we do now? There are other games. How about *Hump the Hostess*? Not yet...so I know what we'll play...We'll play a round of *Get the Guests*.

'Game'. Everyone knows that it was not a game. Calling it a game is George's sarcastic way of announcing that, following the boundless humiliation he has had to experience that stole all of his dignity, he will no longer show consideration for anything or anyone: *Anything* is now possible. And the names of the games announce that he is now marching over scorched earth – such games are only possible after a total betrayal of intimacy and a complete loss of dignity. It is as if he was saying: 'Ok, let us pretend that we have never heard of intimacy and dignity...' His revenge campaign is merciless.

It begins with him convincing Nick to reveal the intimacies of his own marriage: marriage for money, a father-in-law who embezzled church money, Honey's hysterical pregnancy. And then we reach the bitter, cruel finale in which George destroys Martha. He invents a telegraph:

George: Martha...our son is...dead. He drove into a large tree.
Martha: NO! NO! YOU CANNOT DO THAT! YOU CAN'T DECIDE THAT FOR YOURSELF! I WILL NOT LET YOU DO THAT!
George: Now listen, Martha; listen carefully. We got a telegram; there was a car accident, and he's dead. POUF! Just like that! Now how do you like it?
Martha: He is our child!
George: And I have killed him!
Martha: You have no right...you have no right at all...
George: I have the right, Martha. We never spoke of it; that's all. I could kill him any time I wanted to.
Martha: But why? Why?
George: You broke our rule, baby. You mentioned him...you mentioned him to someone else.

Their imaginary son – it was the greatest, holiest lie between them, after they had remained childless. Talking about him and inventing a life for him – this was their anchor, a resting point in their crazy, destructive relationship. It was what held them together despite all the disappointment and hostility – a remainder of substance in a rotten, cracked relationship. And what is crucial for our topic: this substance could only keep its binding power as long as it remained their secret and was invisible to others. There had not been much dignity between George and Martha for a long time. But this was still there: the dignity that lay in their shared secrecy surrounding their imaginary son, their soothing lie that underlay their whole shared life. Martha broke the rule of this secrecy and thus destroyed the remainder of dignity in their relationship. Now George sees only this one possibility: destroying this lie in public, in front of their guests. The annihilation of all dignity and the destruction of their relationship are complete.

Nick and Honey witness their hosts' mutual annihilation campaign. This results in an exchange between Nick and George whose powerful emotionality reveals just how great our anger and disgust can be when we become the witnesses of betrayed intimacy and the accompanying loss of dignity.

George: Do you think I like having that...whatever-it-is...ridiculing me, tearing me down, in front of...YOU? Do you think I *care* for it?
Nick: Well, no...I don't imagine you care for it at all.
George: Your sympathy disarms me...your...your compassion makes me weep!
Nick: I just don't see why you feel you have to subject *other* people to it. If you and your wife want to get at each other, like a

> couple of animals, I don't see it why you don't do it when there aren't any...
>
> George: Why, you smug, self-righteous little...
>
> Nick: CAN...IT...MISTER! I've never hit an older man.

Unless we are undignified voyeurs, we do not actually *want* to know what other people's sphere of shared intimacy looks like. We feel embarrassed when we become the witnesses of betrayed intimacy – so much that we have the strong urge to get up and leave. How would we describe it if we had to explain this desire? 'It's none of my business' is not a justification but just an expression of how we feel. It means: I want to keep a distance. Why? One answer might be: because I feel that the betrayal of intimacy and the resulting removal of distance between us concerns not just one *aspect* of our lives, a single facet among several others, but an *entire way of living*. We can imagine Nick and Honey getting up to leave already at the first signs of the catastrophe. 'We won't listen to this', they would say. 'And you know why? Because we simply *don't want to live like this*.'

When George and Nick meet on campus the next day, things will be different: the knowledge of betrayed intimacy will stand between them. It is impossible to pretend that this unwanted insight did not occur. Perhaps George will try to take the bull by its horns:

> George: Now you know what my wife thinks I am: a flop. And generally, you know what it looks like inside us and between us.
>
> Nick: Must have been hard for you to hear this, especially in front of us, in front of strangers. But you also know a few things about us now – things it would have been better to keep to ourselves.

Where could it go from here? Is there a way for both couples to win back their dignity, between each other and in front of each other? What would be the character of this new dignity? The catchphrase could be: *Dignity as truthfulness*. The next chapter is dedicated to this idea.

But before we get to that, let us hear a fictional voice that radically questions everything we have said about the respect for intimacy. Addressing this scepticism is an opportunity to further deepen our understanding of this kind of respect. Our task is to make the sceptical challenge as strong as possible. Only when it is entirely clear and uncompromising will it help us understand what exactly it is we are defending when we defend the dignity of intimacy.

A Challenge: Intimacy as a Lack of Courage

'We are THE OTHERS. You will call us the *indiscreet* ones, those *without distance*, perhaps also the *shameless* ones. But we don't care! Because the truth is: we are the brave, the enlightened and the truthful ones. We don't hide. We stand by our ideas, desires and emotions and aren't shy about showing them. Of course we know that sometimes prudence demands not to bear it all – so others cannot easily calculate, cheat or control us. But prudence is also the only reason why we accept secrecy and silence. Apart from that, we are exactly the people who go to the parties and talk shows where highly personal things are discussed. These are the important things after all – the things that many people are interested in. And for the same reason, we also display our personal lives online. This is not youthful carelessness: we are mature and experienced adults. And there is no social pressure either: we don't feel vulnerable to extortion. And when you accuse us of being greedy for money and attention, that's defamation. No, no, we are neither thoughtless nor sensation-seeking or voyeuristic: we are just *open* and *engaged*. You simply *learn* a lot when you open up and share personal experiences with people – especially the *very* personal ones, the ones you would like to hide. How else can we broaden our horizons, educate ourselves and deepen our understanding of what it means to be human? Surely you cannot do it by isolating yourself. Privacy, secrecy, distance, closeness: aren't these obsolete concepts from a more repressed era? Are they even *concepts*? Or are they just *words*? Is it perhaps all just talk, mere chatter? In the end, do you perhaps just lack the *courage* to be yourselves in front of others and boldly show yourselves as who you are? Is THAT not the real question of dignity? We know you and we wouldn't be surprised if you called this attitude *the new shamelessness*. But we would be more amused than bothered by it.'

The opening is clever: they talk of openness, engagement, learning and education – as opposed to privacy and secrecy as isolation. *The personal*: this choice of word is also ingenious. It avoids and undermines the *private–public* distinction. We have to be on our guard.

'This isn't about living in isolation and knowing as little as possible of one another. *Of course* we are interested in how other people live and experience their lives. And we're also interested in what it looks like inside their innermost emotional zone – as we do in fact want to understand what it's like to live a human life, in as much depth and as comprehensively as possible. That's why we keep reading, travelling and watching films. And we also have intimate conversations with a select group of people. What matters is that every individual can determine himself how much he reveals and to whom. Dignity lies in this freedom. Respect for intimacy means respect for this freedom.'

'That's indisputable – and misses the point. What we advocate is not a totalitarian compulsion to be public. We're not grabbing diaries out of people's hands. And of course we don't want to terrorize people with secret surveillance either. But there is a tremendous difference in our views: when someone goes public with her most personal experiences and doesn't distinguish between people who are close to and know a lot about her and those who only know her superficially and to whom she wants to keep a distance, you view it as a loss of dignity. That is precisely what we see differently. We don't believe in the importance of what you conjure up by the word of *intimacy*, neither in its applicability to individuals nor in its extension to relationships. We think that it is a *fetish* and perhaps even just a *rhetorical* fetish, a magical linguistic tool. It certainly isn't an irrefutable, meaningful and particularly precious experience. And above all, it isn't something that should or in fact could define the idea of dignity.'

How do you argue about something when the question up for debate is what constitutes an experience? Many other arguments can be decided by measuring the conflicting claims against real experiences. But what do you do when the argument is about what counts as an experience?

'We certainly want to know what others experience. But we don't want to know it about *anyone*. And we want to determine ourselves *if* we want to know it. We also simply want to keep certain things to ourselves: our desires, fears, longings, disappointments. We need this secrecy to be able to feel ourselves. Don't you know what I'm talking about?'

'No. And we don't actually understand this expression: *be ourselves*; nor the other words you have used to describe the topic: *lose oneself, become alienated from oneself*.'

'And how about the situation where George and Martha gamble away something precious the night the guests come over? And that Nick and Honey would have preferred not to witness it – because it means a dramatic loss, a loss of dignity?'

'You see: of course there's always *change* when we learn more about others and they learn more about us. Sometimes this change is pleasant, sometimes it is not. And such change can also mean that the relationship becomes more *complicated*. This is what happens when George and Nick meet the next morning: it's harder than before, when they could simply say: *Hi!* All of this is true but also trivial.

You unnecessarily mystify it, calling up this great word for it: *dignity*. The desires, fears, longings and disappointments that we, the new shameless, discuss in public: you also have them after all, you just deny them. We're simply more *honest*, and we feel repulsed by your insincerity. It's *undignified* because it's dishonest. How hypocritical!'

'If this was about denial, you would be right. But it's not. This is about something else: the difference between what we keep to ourselves and what we make public. This indeed has something to do with secrecy but not with denial. Protecting the private is not the same as lying. The accompanying emotion is a very straightforward one: this is nobody else's business. It is, for example, also nobody's business when I *don't* have certain greed – *this* does not concern other people either, those on the bus, in the street or at work. It must remain a blind spot on the map others have drawn of me. And the wish to keep certain things out of public discussion is not a wish for dishonesty and thus not an undignified wish. On the contrary: it *constitutes* dignity.'

'Fine: if it's not dishonesty, it's still *cowardice*. You won't publicly admit who you really are and what you want. That's undignified. Dignity – this is the willingness to stand by who we are and what we want with our heads held high: being homosexual, for example; or not wanting to have children; or wanting to become rich or powerful; or dismissing bourgeois culture with its churches, museums and concerts as boring, vain and dull – just sickening. Doesn't it show a lack of dignity when one isn't willing to admit these things? The anxious, forced defence of a blind spot: in the end, that's just a lack of courage, a lack of willingness to deal with the others' looks, their judgement, their possible rejection and contempt. But that's exactly what dignity consists in: facing these looks openly and without fear; speaking with one's own voice, loudly and clearly, instead of damping it and making it unrecognizable. And the blind spot: this is the domain of taboo. Don't you also find that taboos are a threat to dignity?'

Whether this is a clever move or a twisted train of thought: the attempt is made here to turn one reading of dignity against another – enlightened, courageous self-confidence that speaks with its own voice against a desire for intimacy and secrecy. This twist is an example of something that I described in the introduction: dignity is a multi-layered experience, with the layers sometimes overlapping in such a way that they become indistinguishable – it is the task of a conceptual representation such as this to show them as different themes and experiences. This is the only way to detect sophisms – of which our topic contains many. This is why I will now drop some catchwords that will only be properly used and developed in the following chapters.

'This isn't about taboos. A taboo is something that we are *banned* from speaking about under punishment. The private sphere, which dignity commands us to guard, is something that we *choose* to protect. And everyone determines for himself how large the radius of his intimate circle is: what lies within and what lies outside and how he might want to alter the boundaries in the course of his life. Taboos violate dignity: because they obscure things, stifle one's voice and suppress questions. Depriving taboos of their power belongs to dignity in the sense of enlightenment. And as far as one's own voice is concerned: the fact that it is one's *own* and expresses individuality does not mean the same as using it to talk *about everything*. It's the voice of our own thought, feelings and desires, and what matters is that they are truly ours, genuine and not prompted or touted. The contrast therefore is not open or secret, but genuine or dissimulated. The authenticity of our voice does not suffer when it remains silent on certain things. Dignity is not damaged by silence, but by a lack of authenticity. And on the subject of cowardice: it's true that silence about private things also has to do with protection, protection against being hurt, as it for example happens when tabloids drag someone's private life through the dirt. But first, not every desire for protection is the same as cowardice. Cowardice is a specific avoidance of confrontation, in cases where there are reasons not to avoid it. And second, dignity is not the same as the desire for protection, even though one might perhaps say that it also offers protection.'

'What is it *then*?'

'It lies in the distance that secrecy about private things creates between me and others. We need this distance in order to then create intimacy by loosening secrecy. If we were made out of glass – there wouldn't be any closeness, because there would be no distance that needed to be transcended in the first place. Everyone would know everything; we would like some people but not others – and that would be the whole story: a rather banal story, a story without the magic of intimacy – and without the happiness brought by this magic.'

'And what if I show my innermost to the public, not for money, but just like that? Because I feel like it and enjoy it? And what if more and more people did the same, until *everyone* was doing it, and there was no one left to mourn your loss? What would happen *then*?'

Would this be the end of *experience*? Or would it just be the end of *words*? If someone looked down on us from far above – what would she say: 'They have lost part of their dignity', or 'They have lost part of their vocabulary about dignity'?

4

Dignity as Truthfulness

༺༻

In his book *L'Adversaire*, Emmanuel Carrère tells the true story
of such an enormous life lie that it takes one's breath away and
is impossible to forget. Having grown up in the Jura, Jean-Claude
Romand enrols for a medical degree at Lyons. After two years, he
does not show up for his first exam. He stays in bed, watching the
hand move over the clock face. His motives remain obscure, even
to himself. Years later, he claims that two days before the exam, he
had fallen down the stairs and broken his wrist – a lie. He tells his
parents on the day of the exam that it went well. Three weeks later
he declares that he has passed and will be admitted to the next year.
He uses a fake doctor's certificate to keep signing up for the second
year of study for the following twelve years. It is a purely bureaucratic
process. No one asks any questions. The other students do not ask
questions either, since he carries around the same scripts as them. He
pretends, also to himself, that he has cancer. This makes it easier to
cope with the fake enrolment: everything will soon be over anyway.

But then he marries and has two children. His wife doesn't suspect
that anything is amiss. He claims he is doing research in Lyons. Later,
he invents a job with the World Health Organization and the family
moves close to Geneva. He goes on fictitious trips: conferences, all
over the world. He studies travel guides. His wife packs his suitcase.
He spends days living in a hotel near the airport, looking at the planes
taking off and landing. He watches TV, calls home every day, reports
on the weather abroad. He misses her and the children, he tells his
wife. After a few days, he returns with presents from the airport gift
shop. He says he is tired because of the time change.

Because of his position, he surely must know many important people. But the family never receives any invitations. Nor can he be reached in his office. The only way to contact him is via a special service – in reality his mobile phone. He uses a visitor's card to access the library, post office, travel agency and bank at the World Health Organization. He avoids the top floors with the security personnel. He sends his parents a postcard of the building and marks where the window of his alleged office is. The children want to see daddy's office. He drives them to the parking lot and points up – that is all.

This is the life he leads for fifteen years. He brings the children to school in the morning. Then he buys piles of newspapers and reads them at a café or in a parking lot. He drives around neighbouring towns. He spends days hiking in the Jura forests. The newspaper *Libération* would later write: 'He lost himself, alone, in the forests of the Jura.'

He finances this life through large-scale confidence scams. As he is popular and trustworthy, friends and relatives hand over large savings to him so he can make profitable investments at Genevan banks on their behalf. When his father-in-law demands his money back, he happens to fall off a ladder and die, coincidentally after his son-in-law comes to visit.

How was it possible for this web of lies to stay intact for so long? Carrère writes: 'It's impossible to think about this story without feeling that there is a mystery here with a hidden explanation. But the mystery is that there is no explanation and that, as unlikely as it may seem, that's how it happened.'

The story finds its horrible ending when the financial scam can no longer be concealed. Romand's mother receives an alarming letter from the bank. By that point, he also has a mistress whom he takes out for dinner in Paris every week. She has also given him lots of money and now wants it back. After fifteen years, his fake life is about to fall apart. Romand drives to his parents' house and shoots his father and mother. Then he also kills his wife and children. He also tries to kill his mistress, but fails. He takes sleeping pills and sets his house on fire. The firemen save his life.

During the trial, he suddenly declares that he remembers the reason why he missed the exam: that morning, he had received a letter from a woman who was in love with him and who took her own life because her feelings were not reciprocated. Someone commented: 'He lies. That's his mode of being, he can't do otherwise, and I think he does it more to fool himself than to fool others.' Romand himself confessed to the forensic psychiatrist: 'I am a murderer, I'm seen as

the lowest possible thing in society, but that's easier to bear than the
twenty years of lies that came before.'

Lying to Others

The life Romand leads surpasses most people's imaginations.
Nevertheless, we can try to envision what his misfortune consisted
in and what it had to do with lost dignity. It is obvious that at some
point in the course of this life he gambled away all of his dignity.
But why exactly was that? And what part did his dishonesty play in
the process?

Romand takes his children to school, and then he has to kill time:
in parking lots, cafés and forests. He does not work, does not receive
any recognition, gains no sense of his own worth, does not develop
as a person: he does not, in short, know the dignity created by work.
Nor does he know the dignity of autonomy: he is dependent on the
money he has embezzled. His lies, moreover, undermine true encounters. The social façade was fake, but his feelings were genuine, he says
in court. This is hard to believe. He pretends to be an important man,
looking forward to calling home from abroad and bringing the children presents. His wife, children and friends show feelings towards
him that lack any foundation. It is impossible for him to respond to
this with genuine emotion – the awareness of his lie prevents it. He
can only simulate his feelings as well as his entire relationships. It is
all a mere façade, a bluff. While napping in parking lots and marching
through the forests of his youth he becomes alienated from himself.

We could say that Romand's lies annihilate his dignity because
they annihilate his autonomy, undermining his ability to have true
encounters. Put this way, the lack of truthfulness would be something
that only affects dignity indirectly, via its consequences. But we could
also say: he already loses his dignity through his complete dishonesty, simply because he moves so far away from the truth – not by
mistake, but because he lies. When described this way, the experience
of dignity becomes connected with his commitment to truthfulness
– with the willingness to stick to the facts in what we say, feel and
do. This, we could add, is the basis for a person's *authenticity*. An
essential element of this authenticity is the courage to face up to the
facts. Romand gambles away his dignity because he entirely lacks
this courage.

There are lies that do not present a threat to dignity – white lies or
lies told in an emergency, for example. But even more elaborate lies
need not necessarily destroy dignity, as in Romand's case. A spy or

undercover agent, for instance, needs a cover story: a false account of his identity. It requires simulating feelings and faking encounters. These characters may occasionally spin out of control, stumble and feel that they are doing something undignified. When they decide to quit their jobs, it sometimes has to do with their desire to regain lost dignity. But there is a difference with Romand: their lies serve a cause which they believe in and consider worthwhile, for example, uncovering crimes or the defence of their own country. And there are some people – their employers – with whom they do not have to pretend. The encounters they have with them – when they can speak the truth – are like an anchor that makes them feel a core of truth. There was no one Jean-Claude Romand could have this experience with, once the harmless lie about an exam had become a veritable life lie that swallowed everything else.

Romand kills his relatives because he cannot bear being exposed by them as the fraudster that he is. What they could accuse him of is related to what Lilli from the scrap yard could also say to Max, the police inspector, who led her to believe in the fake world of Felix, his bank and the big deposits made by the wholesale meat dealers. She is not only upset because of his lies. She also feels wounded in her dignity: he faked their encounter and let her develop false assumptions and illusory feelings that lacked any foundation. Romand's wife similarly could accuse her husband of having never taken her *seriously*. This would be the accusation that through his fakery, he led her to lead a life devoted to a delusion. 'I can't believe', she might say, 'that I genuinely cared when I packed your suitcase, that I was happy to hear your voice when you were – supposedly – far away, when the kids were excited about their fake gifts! I lived for a façade, behind which there was nothing! *Nothing*!'

Lying to Oneself

A life lie does not need to consist of lying to others. One can also deceive oneself. What is forged is not one's social identity, but one's self-image: I view and evaluate myself in a way that I am not. It can be simple, harmless errors: it turns out that I have less influence over an issue than I assumed; that an achievement was not as significant or a transgression not as severe as I thought; or that I am less affected by someone's death than I expected. Harmless errors in one's self-image are those that, once they have been uncovered, do not shake my emotional identity – overall, I can continue living with myself as before. Life lies are different. They create an identity that encompasses large parts of my life: that of a successful businessman, artist or scientist; a selfless, loving mother; an honest and generous friend; an enlightened, responsible citizen. If these self-images turned out to be false, my whole life would be in turmoil. Many of the stories about the motives governing my actions would need to be rewritten, my emotional world reordered. My entire life's worth and meaning would be in question. All of this would bring fear and unhappiness. This is why we tenaciously hold on to familiar self-images, even against the force of obvious facts. We do not *want* to know the truth.

Willy Loman, the ageing salesman, is ignored by former clients and laughed at by colleagues. We heard earlier how he admitted this to Linda. It is a moment of truthfulness. But the truth is hard to bear, and Loman therefore immediately seeks refuge in the lie of success and popularity again: 'I'm vital in New England. One thing, boys: I have friends. I can park my car in any street in New England, and the cops protect it like their own. Be liked and you will never want. You take me, for instance. I never have to wait in line to see a buyer. "Willy Loman is here!" That's all they have to know, and I go right through!...Someday I'll have my own business, and I'll never have to leave home any more.'

Sometimes life lies that we see in other people seem merely amusing. We smile. Yet sometimes we are also repulsed by them. And when we uncover them in ourselves, it can be horrifying. Why? Because it might be that the lack of truthfulness has morally problematic consequences: for example, when a surgeon does not admit that he can no longer control his hands, or when an alcoholic continues working as a construction supervisor. Yet we might also feel repulsed when there are no such consequences to fear, and we are in no way affected by the lies. Then it is the lack of truthfulness itself that we are disturbed by. Why?

In the case of Romand's lack of the courage to admit the facts, we said: he gambles away his *authenticity* and thus his dignity. Perhaps this is also the right answer here: lies undermine our dignity in relation to ourselves by preventing us from being genuine in our actions and experiences: from acting and living as we really are. This has consequences. One is that we take leave of our own lives and become alien to ourselves. Because I wanted to see myself as social, popular and successful, I forfeited my identity as a difficult loner. Because I carry the self-image of an angry revolutionary from my youth, I ignore my need for a quiet, private life. I am not the person who I really am, and therefore I do not live a large part of what could be my life. Life lies thus undermine our possibility of living a full life. Is this not what makes the discovery of self-deceit so oppressive? Even when others are not affected by it?

But sometimes others do suffer because of my lies. Lies can poison encounters and thus endanger the dignity of everyone involved. We heard about the shared lie of a son that connects George and Martha in Albee's play. George kills the son through an invented telegraph. 'Did you...did you...have to?', Martha in the end asks into the silence. 'It was...time', says George. And after a long pause: 'It will be better.' 'Just...us?' Martha asks anxiously. 'Yes.' 'I don't suppose, maybe, we could...' 'No, Martha.' The play is a veritable purgatory of humiliations. Yet it produces a reformed relationship: its dignity lies in overcoming a life-long lie and thus reconquering a piece of genuineness.

Honesty and Its Limits

In Christa Wolf's novel *City of Angels*, which is throughout motivated by an unrelenting will for truthfulness, there is one particularly dignified moment. She enquires about her true feelings concerning the opening of the Berlin wall and writes: 'Were my feelings ambivalent when we were stuck for ages in our car on the drive home, at the intersection of Schönhauser and Bornholmer Streets, because the stream of Trabis and Wartburgs pouring toward the Bornholm border crossing did not let up? What did I feel, actually? Happiness? Triumph? Relief? No. Something like fear. Something like shame. Something like depression. And resignation. It was over. I had understood.'

In the midst of ecstatic happiness, honking and hugs, Christa Wolf admits to herself that she feels very differently about this situation. She will neither let herself be talked into having certain emotions, nor pretend to herself, just because others expect it and might look at her disapprovingly when she does not feel what is considered politically correct. She is honest, genuine and true to herself.

Similarly, we can imagine a soldier returning from a war who says: 'I loyally did my service. But now I'll tell you the truth: I felt nothing but fear, disgust and total senselessness out there.' Another soldier might say to an audience of pacifists: 'I know that you reject this war, but I can tell you: every minute out there, I felt proud and grateful to do this service.' Both soldiers emanate dignity, owing to their honesty and the courage to be themselves, even in front of others.

There are also experiences of dignity through truthfulness in our private lives. After fiercely resisting it for a long time, I might finally summon the courage to admit difficult things: relief upon someone's death or a separation, the desire for revenge after a humiliation, the humiliation itself, anger, jealousy. And I might also need to admit that I do *not* have certain feelings – affection or pity, for example. I wait for it – but it does not arise. By getting rid of self-deception and recognizing my experiences as they really are, I feel a new closeness to myself that might bring relief. Above all, it brings a feeling of dignity, in the sense of authenticity. Even when others know nothing of this inner development, I now encounter them differently – with more autonomy and confidence.

Dignity as honesty and authenticity plays a crucial role in every committed encounter. It involves admitting emotions that are painful and bring disappointment – because they force me to admit that something has always been missing and the relationship was never as I imagined it. Here dignity also has to do with courage. We need this courage to mourn, to remember and recognize certain things. We also need this courage to raise difficult issues with the other person: to name painful emotions and to seriously ask whether they require a separation or at least a change in the way we live together. Do we even want to continue this shared life? Is it good for us? Or has it become mere habit, paired with fear of the pain of separation?

A serious discussion of these questions will inevitably involve a conversation about both partners' self-images – about how they see themselves and their partner. We established in Chapter 2 that as autonomous partners, we are not only entangled in our immediate experiences, but also through the fact that we recognize each other in our self-images and sometimes also clash in our perception of them. Another person's self-image does not always match the reality of her experiences and action. We are aware that it often involves self-deception and life lies. It is possible to detect this even with someone to whom we are not particularly close: a doctor might detect evidence of suffering that the patient is in denial about. A teacher might see a student's lack of ability. A manager might realize that an employee is overwhelmed with work. In those cases, one can keep one's distance. If there is a question of dignity here, it is: how long can one watch this in silence? But when I am close to someone, I will eventually be forced to share my observation. In return, I will have to listen when others tell me of their impression that I am lying to myself. Being challenged in one's self-image like this can be deeply wounding, less so when we have no sense of a life lie at all, but even more so when we feel that a nerve has been hit. Then it is perhaps the deepest kind of insult we can experience. Nevertheless, such openness is part of the dignity of a long and deep relationship. It is the dignity of shared truthfulness.

This kind of dignity does not lie in the fulfilment of a demand made by someone else. What the need for openness instead reveals is our desire for a kind of intimacy that is only possible through mutual understanding: we want to know and understand how the other experiences herself, her life and our relationship. Our intimacy grows with this knowledge and understanding. This need for understanding orients itself in the first instance by what the other *says* about her thoughts, feelings and desires – we take her at her word. Yet from the beginning we also read the other in the *silent* messages of her behaviour: in the wordless expressions of fear, shame or anger, for instance. The longer we have been together, the clearer we see the dissonances between saying and doing, between self-image and reality. Intimacy and the detection of self-deceit thus go hand in hand.

A relationship defined by closeness also involves talking about what we do and do not understand about the other and always working on reducing the areas that are not understood. This is the only way to maintain development and vitality, instead of living in stagnation and monotony. That is the reason behind our impulse to confront the other when we believe we have detected a life lie. 'Are you only campaigning against hunger to gain recognition? Is your vanity perhaps the motive after all?' 'Do you write for poetry's sake or in order to get applause? Are those poems really genuine?' 'Isn't your legendary tolerance just a fear of confrontation?' 'Did you perhaps just join this party to get back at your parents and not because you agree with its manifesto?' Or one might say: 'You buy all these encyclopaedias, all those complete editions – I never see you read them.' When we decide to voice such doubts and risk deeply offending someone, we do it because we do not want to lose each other. Hushed-up life lies erect barriers and create distance. They estrange us from one another. One day Bernard Winter will have to confront his wife, whom he saw secretly humming to herself in the hospital room.

Yet even if honesty is a standard for dignity, arising from a need for intimacy and understanding: is it an *absolute* standard? Is it valid at every moment and for any life story? Our judgement on this matter is vague and unstable, and it is important to give this vagueness sharper definition. It is related to the notion that life lies are not accidental, rhapsodic and unpredictable, but that they have strong motives, of which we often cannot be conscious: motives such as the fear of admitting something, especially weakness, ineptitude, transgression, loneliness; or strong desires, such as a craving for recognition or the need for love; or ideological convictions about what is allowed, prohibited, sinful and evil. Such motives may be the reason

behind our violent and bitter resistance to the attempt to address and
question the lies. What do I do when I recognize and understand this
defensive urge? What does dignity demand? Do I still need to follow
the maxim: humans must always face up to the truth?

It may be that Bernard Winter's subconscious loyalty to his reli-
giously oppressed parents precluded him from doing many things in
his life, such as radically differentiating himself from others, fully
developing his sexual desires and insisting on his needs in general.
This affected his choice of profession and partner, as well as the
nature of his education. It defines the temperature and nature of his
relationship to Sarah. She has recently been growing more and more
aware of it. Her attempt to discuss it was met with fierce resistance.
In the process, she found out about many life lies: concerning the
parents' character and integrity, their feelings towards their son and
their alleged sacrifice. Bernard's self-deceit also became apparent:
wrong assessments of achievement, denial of aggression and self-
righteousness, a wrong understanding of relationships, including his
relationship to Sarah. She went on a trip in search of distance, trying
to gain clarity about her feelings and a possible attitude for the future.
She senses that this also raises questions of dignity.

The first thing she will tell herself might be: I have to respect the
hidden motives behind his many deceptions. They are part of his
emotional identity. He wants to leave them in the dark because he
does not feel strong enough to face them. It would be destructive to
force them to light. It would be an attack on him. It would be cruel.
Even a therapist might hesitate to deflate Bernard's parents, on seeing
the potential threat of this to his emotional equilibrium.

What will follow from this? Sarah can tell herself: I will avoid
these reefs and shallows in the future. No life is free from lies after
all. And this is a question of my dignity, in the sense that I respect
Bernard's emotional identity. Everyone has the right to defend his
identity – together with its incongruities, lies and self-deceptions. I
will try the following: I will take a distanced attitude to these topics,
suspending a commitment that would require confrontation. Our
relationship will be redefined on those occasions: I step out of it –
not completely, just every now and then. This is to prevent Bernard's
powerlessness towards his own emotions from being exposed – so
that he does not have to feel humiliated. I will do it out of respect for
his dignity.

Yet Sarah will also ask herself: What about my emotions, when I
find myself confronted yet again by his blatant life lies? My spontaneous reaction is that they feel undignified – there is so little honesty.
What shall I do? Sarah can go down one of two conceptual paths.

The first: she recalls that the idea of dignity is sometimes relativized by someone's emotional strength. When lies are the structural supports of the emotional architecture, without which it would collapse, we are gentler in our judgement: the accusation of a lack of dignity becomes quieter. Dignity seems to be less in danger when the lie is excusable given the magnitude of the potential inner damage, such as when a terminal illness is denied or an ineptitude confessed that would crush a person's self-image. In those cases we think that we cannot expect this of anyone. Sarah might tell herself that life lies should only be deemed undignified when the liar would have the strength to withstand their demolition. This is not the case with Bernard. If I grasp that, my spontaneous perception of a lack of dignity might pale.

The second idea Sarah can try out is this: perhaps we should not say, in cases where someone is clearly overwhelmed, that dignity is in danger. We could instead *factor out* the entire aspect of dignity. We hold our breath with the dignity-judgement, so to speak. And perhaps we could add that this is a question of our own dignity, the observer's dignity. This fits with a basic idea from the Introduction: dignity as a way of living is a response to the threat to human life. What belongs to this idea is that we gauge appropriately when the notion of dignity can be applied to someone and when it cannot.

The question about the limits of honesty is not just confined to others. I can also ask myself whether my lie inevitably undermines my dignity. As long as I do not recognize the lie as such, this question does not arise – there is silence. But in certain moments of clarity, truth might flare up and make the lie visible: about a marriage, a friendship or a profession, a party membership or a commitment I entered for deluded reasons. We saw how this happens to Willy Loman, who suddenly admits to himself that in the eyes of his colleagues he has become a mere figure of fun, who is miles away from his imagined success. Is it then possible to do something like this: slip back into the lie on purpose, without damaging one's dignity? Can we not, in those moments of clarity, be like doctors and prescribe ourselves the continuation of the lie, because we are not yet strong enough to face the truth? Would that not be an act of self-awareness and self-determination that has its own dignity?

There is also another phenomenon: the methodically, artfully developed life lie. As the situation I am in is so hard to tolerate, lying is not just an uncontrollable reaction, but a purposeful, tactical retreat from reality, an escape into a web of self-delusions: in order to endure the doctor's dreadful diagnosis, for example, or the time spent in prison or in a camp, or loneliness, a misdemeanour or a failure. It is an act of self-defence, perhaps even against oneself. Can it also be understood as an act that serves the preservation and protection of dignity – because it represents a form of autonomy?

We can develop this idea even further: dignity as a defiant, perhaps even grotesque, attachment to a life lie that also always appears as such. Is this how we could speak of Loman's dignity? In this case, is it the lie's anchoring in despair that ennobles it? If there is something to admire about it: is it the defiance of his will to live, the fact that he does not surrender, although he has lost everything and everything speaks against him? Is it the case that he can only carry on by holding onto this lie, as if it were a flagpole – despite the fact that it is he who erects and carries this flagpole? It is like soldiers shouting to each other in a desperate situation: 'We will hold the bridge!' Or when someone makes plans on his deathbed – booking holidays, signing contracts – with a poker face and the ghost of a smile. Is this not also a form of dignity?

Calling Things by Their Proper Name

Willy Loman hides a piece of pipe in the cellar: he wants to retain the option of ending his life by gassing himself. Linda finds the pipe, but does not say anything. Let us imagine that Loman notices Linda's discovery because the pipe lies in a different position. But he does not say anything either. Now the pipe is a *taboo*: something that cannot be spoken about. The taboo will destroy their relationship. His knowledge of her knowledge will throw a shadow over everything that Linda does and says to him. He will feel that she treats him like a fragile patient whose illness is so advanced that one cannot expect anything of him. Loman feels that her behaviour and emotions are no longer direct and spontaneous, no longer *genuine*. He has lost his authenticity as well: he can no longer believe in what she does and says and yet has to pretend otherwise. He has to deceive Linda. His behaviour and his emotions inevitably become determined by tactics, by dishonesty. Things will get even more complicated when Linda watches him discover her discovery: she sees his shock on discovering that the pipe has been moved. Perhaps he turns around and catches a glimpse of Linda disappearing through the door. Now he also knows that she knows that he has discovered her knowledge of the pipe. They both now know that the secret is no longer really a secret. If they continue to pretend that the other did not have this knowledge, their lies will become fixed. This is because neither their conduct nor their emotions match their state of knowledge. It is

an important criterion of authenticity that there should be no consciously maintained gulf between knowledge, conduct and feelings.
Loman and Linda cannot look at each other without their gaze
betraying that each knows about the other's knowledge. This would
not be bearable. But above all, it would be a situation in which they
would forfeit their dignity. In order to save it, they would have to
take a decisive step: defy the taboo and talk about the pipe. 'Okay',
Loman might say eventually, 'you know about the pipe and I know
that you know about it. Let's talk about it.' This truthfulness would
create a new dignity.

It is, however, not always liberating to set aside a taboo and call
things by their proper name. It can be an act of cruelty to utter the
dreaded words and this will create a new threat to dignity. Mary
Tyrone in Eugene O'Neill's play *Long Day's Journey into the Night*
is addicted to opium. Back from a sanatorium, she seems to have
beaten her addiction, but then relapses. This relapse is at the centre
of the play and leads to the exposure of her family's delusion.

Mary: Come to think of it, I do have to drive uptown. There's
           something I must get at the drugstore.
Tyrone: Leave it to you to have some of the stuff hidden, and pre-
           scription for more! I hope you'll lay in a good stock ahead
           so we'll never have another night like the one when you
           screamed for it, and ran out of the house in your nightdress
           half crazy, to try and throw yourself off the dock!
Mary: James! You mustn't *remember*! You mustn't *humiliate*
           me so!

Unlike in Loman's case, there is no secret to discover here. Mary's
addiction has been well known to everyone in her family for years,
overshadowing all their lives. The humiliation Mary speaks of thus
cannot consist in being robbed of a closely guarded secret – in that
someone enters her innermost zone which no one should have access
to. What she experiences as a humiliation is something else: that
her addiction is called by its proper name and that a memory is
recalled of a traumatic scene caused by this addiction. What this is
therefore about is her misfortune being *brought up* again. It is about
the act of *putting it into words*. It is this act that Mary experiences
as a cruelty.

By putting something into words we publicly articulate that we
mean *that* specific thing and not something else, for example: war,
betrayal, a lie. Naming something forces us to recognize the facts
and all the things that follow from them. In the case of addiction, it
forces us to recognize that someone is a slave to a compulsion and

no longer the master in his own house. When is this the beginning of liberation and when an annihilating humiliation?

Tyrone could also speak differently to his wife: 'The drugstore: not again! Don't you realize this is how you succumb to that damn drug again? Do you want to be its slave forever? Addiction – it's not *fate*! Pull yourself together, fight it! This is about *your life* after all!'

What is the difference? It might seem like a mere difference in *tone* and perhaps also in Tyrone's emotions. But it is much more: it makes a difference to Mary's dignity. In this imaginary conversation, Tyrone's words ascribe an open future to Mary: the possibility of dropping her old habits and changing. We saw in the second chapter that when we want to leave someone his dignity, we must not suffocate him with fixed expectations. Even when certain habits seem all-powerful, we must still acknowledge the possibility for change. Tyrone's former words lacked this openness. In his sarcasm, he presented Mary as a hopeless case. Evoking the ghostly night scene did not serve as an inspiring plea, which it could have had he chosen different words, but as a reminder that said: you have been a slave to your addiction forever and will always remain one. He is denying an open future to her. He is demonstrating her powerlessness to her. This is why she feels humiliated.

Although this is not what he actually does, we could imagine Tyrone saying to Mary: 'You're a *junkie*.' This is like saying: 'You're an *alcoholic*.' Aside from the fact that this definition puts an end to all euphemisms and denial, might the humiliation simply consist in *saying the word*? Uttering the word changes the situation. It changes the relationship between the person concerned and the person who says it. Such a change even takes place when both had already thought about the word and also when both knew about this silent thought with the other. Why is this the case? What makes such words dangerous?

Once the word has been uttered, there is no more scope for denial and euphemism – no possibility of pretending that this suffering is not real. Besides, such words carry a certain tone and a range of associations with them, that might make the phenomenon appear worse than it is. *Junkie, alcoholic* – these words carry overtones of transgression and open up whole corridors of disgrace in our imagination. This is what someone might mean when he says that saying such words is brutal. There is something else that can also be terrorizing: *junkie, alcoholic* – these sound like generic names and therefore like something that gives a person an indelible identity. It takes away the possibility of an open future. A person who merely drinks too much can stop. An alcoholic no longer has a chance to be anything else.

Saving One's Face

We spend a large part of our lives living under the gaze of others. We have to present ourselves in a certain way. We have to show a certain face. This face is our visible identity, the social façade and also the mask that we can hide behind. One part of this is the 'face' in the narrow sense: the facial features and expressions we put onto it. But a lot more also belongs to it that has nothing to do with facial features: our social role, the skills, influence and power we ascribe to ourselves, the pattern of habits and attitudes that we call our character, the ideas and emotions we express. We spend our whole lives working on this social face. Losing it would be dangerous. It would make us vulnerable and powerless. Losing one's face would be connected to an experience of humiliation.

We will do almost anything to save face. Sometimes we also help others save theirs. This is not possible without lies. These are sophisticated and subtle lies: their purpose is not to make false claims, but rather to avoid the truth. The language of such lies is the language of diplomacy, euphemisms and embellishments. It is the language of meaningless compromises, purported respect for political enemies, supposed progress in protracted negotiations, the alleged achievements of those who have failed. 'I made a *mistake*', people who have been apprehended for a transgression tend to say. 'Don't we all make mistakes?' And already it looks as if the great loss of face has been averted. The language of expert reports and job references also often contains such lies: obvious things are highlighted as special achievements, while deficiencies are silently ignored. The whole thing is false, though nothing incorrect is said. A person might be forced by virtue of his function to deliver a eulogy on a deeply loathed opponent. This is an occasion where we hear a masterpiece in the art of falseness through silence. This falseness is only surpassed by the thank-you speech of the person honoured.

Lies that help a person save face are therefore astounding, as they are completely transparent: both those who lie and those who are lied to know that the truth is not being said. And still – it works. Everyone acts as if the lie was truth because it might be dangerous to cause embarrassment to someone. George W. Bush instigated a war in Iraq that was based on lies and violated international law. '*We're running out of time*', his people preached on all channels. Many people knew that those were lies. Yet no one said, 'They're *lying*.' This was taboo. Even the country's critical newspapers were afraid to call things by their proper name. They spoke of the 'L-word'. They would not even say the word at a point when *everyone* knew that they were lies. People waited in vain for governments that were opposed to the war to *declare* that it violated international law. This was also taboo.

Bush's lies and the dishonesty of all those who did not call them by their proper name violated dignity in the sense of the will to truthfulness. But things can also be more complicated. We might stubbornly, and against our better judgement, refer to a suicide attempt as an 'accident'. And perhaps James Tyrone used to tell his children, 'Mummy is tired and needs her medicine.' This is the *regulation of language*: we choose certain words although we know that they obscure the truth. We do this to allow someone to save face. There is a silent agreement to cover up the truth. Yet this manoeuvre may be regarded as something that nevertheless protects dignity, instead of annihilating it. Why?

It must have to do with the *motive*. The motive is the protection from cruelty. It would be cruel to appear and be talked about as someone who wanted to kill himself, or as a mother who is addicted to morphine. The blurring, euphemistic words prevent that. 'But how can they do that, when everyone involved actually knows the truth?', Tyrone's sons might ask their father one day. 'What kind of dignity is it, when people are using open lies? Isn't it a strange kind of dignity if it rests on playing back a well-rehearsed lie?' 'I'm not sure about this myself, boys', the father might reply, 'This dignity thing – perhaps it's a misunderstanding. A misunderstanding marked by despair. Perhaps – if we are completely honest – this is simply about being afraid. Being afraid of words that hit hard. Somehow you can cling to the gentler words, and one wants to cling to something...'

Bullshit

To the extent that our dignity is determined by our will to truthfulness, it is also concerned with an attitude that we might call *intellectual honesty*. Formulated as a maxim, it demands that one should not pretend to know things that one does not and cannot know. We may mention and discuss many different assumptions and ideas – including uncertain ones. This is not prohibited by intellectual honesty. What it prohibits is passing them off as knowledge – as something that others can build on. This is particularly common and obvious in statements made by politicians. Their subjects are often so complex and confusing that no one really knows how matters stand and what should be done. But heads of governments, ministers and party spokespeople stand up and claim to be the only ones who know the

answer. Everybody else is wrong. What they say about the situation
and what they plan to do lacks an alternative. Parties and ministries
devise formulas and conjure up metaphors that are laughable in their
simplicity. They try to compensate for this with energetic arm movements. When we turn off the volume and watch their body language,
we see people who are trying to mask their lack of knowledge with
gestures of self-persuasion. A person with solid knowledge would
not need such gesticulation. Turning the volume back on does not
improve matters. It is a strange spectacle.

It could be done differently. 'You know the facts', the speaker
could say, 'And it's beyond question that we have to take action.
But what needs to be done is far from obvious. There are many
factors that we can't predict – that nobody can predict. You heard
very different proposals presented in this house. There are many
serious arguments that contradict one another. It would be dishonest to pretend that we, the government, simply know better than the
opposition. The truth is: everybody in this room has to decide under
conditions of uncertainty. Those who have listened to the others and
are honest, will cast their vote under doubt. They know the others
might be right. I present our policy, promote it and hope for a majority because out of all the arguments that I have heard, I am most
convinced by those made by our party. But I refrain from making
presumptions, being self-righteous and polemical – this is for fools. I
can't rule out that our plan will turn out to have been a mistake. We
act to our best knowledge and according to our conscience – but not
without doubts and with respect for the others' objections. Things
that concern a human community are so complex and confused that
there can be no certainty. This is what we have to admit to ourselves,
and this insight is what should guide us in our dealings with one
another. This institution's dignity demands this.' How different the
atmosphere would be! No one would want to turn off the volume.

Besides the acceptance of uncertainty, intellectual honesty also
demands the acceptance of facts, especially of morally significant
facts. This is the reason why we even take legal action against a lack
of truthfulness: the denial of genocide, for instance, is punishable in
many countries. Even when no one directly suffers as a result *it is
not okay*, it is *unbearable*. We do not want to live like that. We are
disgusted by it. The disgust is caused by a lack of dignity.

Superstition can also be in conflict with our dignity. Many hotels
do not have a thirteenth floor because the number is considered
unlucky. We smile in the elevator and forget about it. Yet for a
moment it can also make us feel uncomfortable. Why? Because there
is no evidence at all for this fairy tale. So what? What troubles us is a

more general aspect of this ludicrous little example: the fact that the idea of *reasons* is not taken seriously, the idea of a reason as something that may, and in fact should, change one's beliefs. *It's not okay to believe anything you like!* we might want to shout out. And this principle has something to do with the will to truthfulness – because the idea of a reason is an idea of something that makes the things that we believe in more likely to be true.

There are people who spend days and weeks sitting at roulette tables in casinos, writing down the numbers. Future numbers will have nothing at all to do with where the ball has fallen before. At a regular roulette table, that is not rigged, there is no system to uncover. Each run is like the first. It is hard to watch these fanatics write down numbers: their superstition is a threat to their dignity.

We can also damage someone's dignity by seducing him into superstition. Lourdes is an example. Lourdes is a nightmare. The place is not just suffocated by swathes of kitsch and commercialism. What is worst are the many paralysed and disabled people who go there because they have been promised a miraculous cure – it is the final straw they desperately cling to. There are indeed what we call spontaneous recoveries, rare healing processes with as-yet unknown causes. Emotional factors might perhaps play a role. But holy water cannot cure damaged nerves. We know that. There is not the slightest reason to believe the contrary. Leading someone to believe this therefore violates his dignity.

Besides a lack of intellectual honesty, lies and superstition, there is also another way to damage dignity in the sense of the will for truthfulness: through blather that lacks any connection to facts, truth and even falseness. I do not mean absurdities like 'yesterday's Sunday was better than today's' or confused statements like 'Lisbon to New York – it's a pleasant stroll'. This is not about saying things that make no *sense*. It is about the case where the speaker does not care about the seeming content of his words, although these word have a sense. He not only does not care about *this* content, but about *all* content, like Howard, Willy Loman's boss. He tells him that he cannot continue working for the company.

Loman: Howard, are you firing me?
Howard: I think you need a good long rest, Willy.
Loman: Howard –
Howard: And when you feel better, come back, and we'll see if we
          can work something out.

We can imagine Loman yelling at him: '*Bullshit!*' What that would mean is: 'None of this blather!' Loman could continue by saying:

'*You know exactly* that what I need isn't rest, but another job. *You know exactly* that there can be no question of rest when someone is fired. And more than anything: *You know exactly* that you will *never* give me work again. So stop blathering on about finding a later solution!'

Howard has humiliated Loman by letting him feel his dependence and powerlessness. Now he additionally humiliates him through blather. He has retreated from a genuine conversation, which was about facts, and tries to get by with bullshit. He does not believe in what he says, and he does not even lie: he simply *babbles*. What he says is humbug, verbal bluffing. This is another way to gamble away the dignity of an encounter.

Blather that pretends to speak of facts but is actually nothing but hot air occurs everywhere, happens to everyone and is often completely harmless. We sometimes meet up with others just to let off some steam. This is not about truth or falseness or about reasons. This is about venting oppressive feelings – about regaining one's inner balance by speaking freely. There is also a quieter variant of this: chatting. We chat about this and that, and chatting is primarily what this is about. It does not matter so much what is right or wrong, as not much will follow from this conversation, but all will soon be forgotten. One's dignity is not in danger.

It is only in danger when the situation becomes too serious for chatter. This is the case with Howard and Loman. This is also the case in public contexts where something important is at stake. The economy is booming, unemployment is falling. 'Who did it? *We* did it!', the government official keeps chanting. 'Doesn't he realize that he is being ridiculous?', asks the man at the table next to me. 'What a bullshitter!' 'If Spain wins the European Championship, it could end the country's crisis', I hear on the radio. 'Have a carefree future with low-cost loans!', the poster from the bank says, showing a couple in debt – beaming. 'Just be sure to be polemical!', the talk show host who wants to invite me to a panel discussion says. It does not count, not even a bit, what is right and what is wrong. What counts are *sound bites*, sensationalism and folly. What counts is *bullshit*.

5

Dignity as Self-Respect

As subjects we are beings who can explain our actions to ourselves and to others by telling stories about the motives that govern these actions. These stories express our identity: we are the ones who these motive stories are about. They are stories about where we have come from, how we have become who we are and what we are planning for the future. As I said at the beginning of the book, these stories create our self-image: an image of how we see ourselves. This is not only an image of how we *are*, but also an idea of how we *want* to and *should* be. As subjects, we can evaluate ourselves and ask whether we are content with our actions and experiences: whether we approve or disapprove of them. This evaluation determines whether we can *respect* ourselves for what we do and experience or must *despise* ourselves for it. Beings who live with a self-image are therefore familiar with the experience of maintaining and losing self-respect. This is of great significance for how they experience their dignity.

Dignity Through Limits

Human dignity in the sense of self-respect means that we wouldn't do *anything* in order to achieve a goal. There are *limits* to our actions – things that we would not do under any circumstances, no matter what advantage it would bring us. In order to maintain self-respect, we must remain within these limits. We lose our self-respect when we cross them. These limits belong to our self-image and define it: I refuse to do something, because it contradicts my sense of myself and would imperil my identity. Looking after one's self-respect means maintaining this kind of coherence in our lives. When someone stops caring for his self-respect in that sense, he loses his dignity.

The limits that define a personal identity and determine a person's self-respect may be moral limits. In this case, they involve showing consideration for others and are motivated by the desire to combat cruelty. But often crossing those limits would not necessarily lead to a moral transgression or bring harm to anyone. And yet, we could no longer respect ourselves if we violated them.

Perhaps Bernard Winter, whom we already encountered earlier in this book, is a scientist, committed to enlightenment and rationality, impatient and also contemptuous of superstition. Now he is ill – incurably, as scientific medicine assures him. Someone tells him about a miracle healer. Her method *cannot* work according to rational principles – it is not an open question. Sarah and his friends urge him to try it anyway. 'It won't do any *harm*, and your life's at stake after all, so *everything*'s at stake!', they say to him. 'All my life, I've believed in proof, science and rationality: why would I all of a sudden follow pure superstition', Winter says. 'It's out of the question!' 'But wouldn't it be *sensible* to try everything in this case?' 'No, because there isn't the slightest *reason* to believe in its success. I might as well eat grass. And you're wrong to say that it won't cause any harm: it would harm my self-respect.'

Winter's symptoms become more severe, the pain worsens. Winter secretly goes to the healer's address. He walks up and down outside her house. He is about to ring the bell. He does not do it. If someone asked him what had stopped him, he would perhaps say: 'It would feel like a *betrayal*. A betrayal of myself. I'd feel as if I am *losing* myself – and thus also my *dignity*.' Perhaps he goes to see her in the end. He endures the holy water, the Bach flower essence, the touches and spells. Afterwards, he would give a lot to undo it. 'But nothing actually *happened* to you!', Sarah says when he tells her about his disturbing experience. 'Oh yes,' says Winter, '*a great deal* happened. Inside me. If only I had stayed *true* to myself! I feel so *alienated*!'

We can also imagine the opposite scenario: Sarah is ill. '*Of course* I'll go!', she says. 'Why not? I won't accept any dogma, not even that of science! I have an open mind. I'll try anything! Worst case scenario: it was a waste of an afternoon. And who knows...' She returns from the healer. 'God, what a strange person! And those dark rooms! But somehow it was also funny...' He looks at her. She knows this look. 'A loss of self-respect? Not at all. Perhaps if I had betrayed the ideals of a revolution. But certainly not because of this trifle!'

152 *Dignity as Self-Respect*

The example shows: every person sets individual limits for his or her self-respect. The judgement about self-respect and dignity thus has nothing to do with limits imposed by a foreign authority. The only thing that counts are the limits that we set ourselves. Something that is irreconcilable with self-respect for me does not have to be so for others. According to this reading of dignity, no action is undignified *in itself*. The question of dignity only ever arises in relation to a self-image and the limits that it imparts to one's actions.

It might seem to be different. Jean-Claude Romand, who spent years on parking lots, in cafés and the Jura forests, forfeits his dignity in the sense of truthfulness through an enormous life lie. Does he not also forfeit it in the sense of his self-respect? We cannot imagine what it must be like to be him. This is also because we feel he must be so full of contempt for himself that it is unbearable. We are completely *certain* that, because of his lies and his wasted life, he has lost his self-respect. Do we seriously want to say here: it all still depends on how he sees himself? Is there not something like an objective standard for self-respect after all?

We might feel similarly when we encounter extreme cases of opportunism: someone makes a fortune from tacky films about the Holocaust. A person who always used to curse the tabloid press, all of a sudden starts promoting it. Someone who used to fight racism becomes a speech writer for a racist politician; the legacy hunter who tells his insufferable, but rich, aunt exactly what she wants to hear; the actress who sleeps her way to the top; a man who submits to the rituals of a cult to get the woman he wants. Or a comedian who would use anyone for a punchline. Or prostitution. Or American electoral campaigns where candidates will say *anything* to win. Are all of these not repulsive, undignified acts? Is it not *clear* that self-respect is forfeited here? *Objectively* clear?

But there is ultimately no objective position, independent of a self-image, from which this could be determined. It would be impossible to develop a coherent idea of such a position. Our deceptive impression of objectivity arises from two sources: from projections and from the cultural commonality of our self-images. Imagining what it would be like to waste my life on parking lots like Romand, I conclude: such a loss of self-respect would be unbearable. The fact that this judgement, which in the first instance reflects my individual self-image, appears to be valid beyond myself rests on the fact that I share this self-image with many other people: there is hardly anyone who would not shudder at this thought. This is also the case with contemptible cases of opportunism: we apply our own standard, and because we can be certain to share it with many others, we consider the loss of dignity that we see to be universal.

This impression may be further reinforced when the self-image in question belongs to a certain social role, carrying its obligations with it. In Chapter 1, we encountered a doctor who overrode another person's judgement when it came to a blood transfusion and a Caesarean. 'I *couldn't* act any other way, I *had* to do it', he says afterwards. He sensed that unless he followed his conviction, he would lose himself. His decision had to do with his self-respect as a doctor: as someone who, in his self-image, is bound by the Hippocratic oath. This is a self-image that he shares with his colleagues and one that would also be recognized by a court. Nevertheless it is not *more* than that: a self-image – a culturally contingent internal arrangement that has a history and also the capacity to change. If it changed, dignity in the sense of self-respect would change with it. By bearing in mind the cultural contingency of such arrangements, we can avoid oppressing others with our ideas of self-respect and dignity.

Fluid Self-Images

Self-images that influence our self-respect do not develop in a vacuum. They are the result of long and slow processes of upbringing, education and cultural formation in which others play an important role. Their approval and respect determine the firmness of our self-conception. Their criticism and contempt can undermine and overthrow our self-image. In that sense, self-respect is also a social phenomenon. This does not mean, however, that there is no such thing as the dignity of the outsider: it might be an essential part of my self-image to live according to principles with which, in this place and society, I am alone. But even such principles are never really invented by one person single-handedly.

The fact that self-images develop through exchange with others who participate in the same culture also means that self-images can change. An earlier understanding of myself may be replaced by another, contrary self-image. Questions of self-respect then take a different shape, too: something that would have previously brought inner conflict and alienness can later be experienced as harmonious – as something that I can respect myself for. What is crucial for the question of dignity is how this change came about and what motivated it. Perhaps a political party that I used to have nothing to do with offers me a well-paid position. I even become its spokesman. 'Why shouldn't one change one's political views?', I ask those who look at me with suspicion. Perhaps – in a feat of self-persuasion – I bring myself to believe that my U-turn was a process of intellectual evolution. But in quieter hours, I know that my new self-image and self-respect have been bought – and I feel my dignity crumble. I would feel similarly if I changed my views because I wanted to marry into a family. This is the wrong kind of motive. This is opportunism.

What is it like when the emotional force of a relationship shifts the internal limits of the possible? When love, admiration or gratitude lead to a change of mind that makes new things compatible with one's self-respect? Perhaps Bernard Winter allows a new love to seduce him into moral, political and aesthetic positions that would have earlier been completely anathema to him. He now opposes abortion, advocates lowering taxes and admires Andy Warhol. He once abruptly left the table on hearing that his neighbour was from the tabloid press. Now he is willing to go to this man's party because he is a friend of his new girlfriend. He visits a public sauna for the first time. He uses words that earlier would have never crossed his lips. He used to run riot when Sarah tidied the living room before receiving guests – now he will do it himself. These changes in conduct are no vile calculation – the feelings behind them are genuine. But they are still problematic, because the change in attitude is motivated by an emotional development that has nothing to do with the new themes and interests in his life themselves. He has not formed new judgements, but has merely experienced an internal shift that was caused by outside influence. This is how a gulf can develop between things we allow because of what a relationship and its emotions demand and the limits we draw outside this relationship. When the relationship is over and Bernard Winter returns to his old standards of self-respect, he might say that – in retrospect – he feels as if he has been seduced into forfeiting his dignity. 'I wasn't fully present', he could say, 'it was as if I was standing besides myself. It makes me feel rather silly.' It would be different if his attitude towards these things changed as a result of reflection, new experiences and a maturing process: for example, if his left-wing attitudes slowly gave way to more conservative sentiments; if he became more open towards different types of art and more socially tolerant. 'Oh yes,' he would laugh, 'that used to be! I would have never done this! But today – I feel completely comfortable doing it.'

Then he falls in love again – with a woman from a strict religious family. They leave nothing out: grace, Mass, confession, religious dying rituals, Lourdes. What does Winter, the atheist, do? Does he sit there stiffly, silently when they say their prayers? Or does he murmur them as well – as a lip-service, words without conviction? How can he make a distinction between concessions that leave his self-respect intact and those that are out of the question? *Is* there such a distinction? Can he kneel during Mass, as a kind of lip-service, too? Is paying lip-service harmless to our self-respect? These are not *just* lip movements after all: one *says* something. At least this is what it looks like from the outside. 'Confessing – that's so undignified', he used to say. 'The motive of truthfulness may make confession look noble. But it's ultimately a disclosure of most intimate things to a stranger. It involves submission, since it is ordered. It is done for the despicable purpose of ransoming oneself from guilt. And it does not contribute the slightest towards internal development.' Can we imagine him one day entering the confessional box despite this attitude?

For this to happen, a religious conversion must take place. It is hard to say how something like this comes about and what it actually *is*. Many inner standards can change and with them the experience of self-respect. When we learn that someone adopted a new belief to prepare himself for the Last Judgement, do we find it opportunistic and therefore undignified? *Does* it exist: a distinction between dignified and undignified conversions? What would be the criterion to distinguish between them?

Destroying Self-Respect

People are capable of destroying other people's self-respect. It is among the cruellest things they can do. Friedrich Dürrenmatt tells of such a cruelty in his play *The Visit*. It is a story of revenge. When Klara Wäscher was a young girl, she became pregnant by Alfred Ill. He denied being the father. He bought two witnesses who swore in court that they had slept with Klara Wäscher. The charge was rejected. 'I became a prostitute. The judgement of that court made me one', the woman says. She learns that everything is a question of money, and she goes on to buy everything: brothels, companies, people. As an old, sick woman of incredible wealth, who now calls herself Claire Zachanassian, she returns to Güllen, the place of her former disgrace. She wants justice, and one could also say: she wants revenge for Ill's betrayal and the injustice she has suffered. She says to the citizens of Güllen: 'I'm giving you a billion, and I'm buying myself justice.' 'Justice can't be bought', says the mayor. 'Everything can be bought', says Claire. 'A billion for Güllen if someone kills Alfred Ill.' 'In the name of all citizens of Güllen, I reject your offer', the mayor replies. 'I reject it in the name of humanity. We would rather have poverty than blood on our hands.'

This is the reaction of self-respect, as we have discussed it: there are limits to what we are prepared to do. We cannot be bought. 'I'll wait', the old lady says dryly. The wait yields its fruits. The citizens of Güllen start buying more expensive food, clothes and furniture, all on credit – for they expect the billion to come. Ill senses his impending doom: every new sign of wealth means his death is closer. After a long inner struggle, he says to the mayor: 'You must judge me, now. I shall accept your judgement, whatever it may be. For me, it will be justice; what it will be for you, I do not know. God grant you find your judgement justified. You may kill me, I will not complain and I will not protest, nor will I defend myself. But I cannot spare you the task of the trial.' Dürrenmatt lets Ill die. The old woman keeps her word. Money flows.

As Dürrenmatt tells the story, it is above all a story about revenge on Ill, revenge through murder. Beyond that, the old woman also seeks revenge on the citizens of Güllen: she seduces them into gambling away their self-respect and also their dignity. We could also imagine a version of the play that is exclusively about revenge as the destruction of self-respect. After the vote, where the citizens unanimously decide on Ill's death, Claire could say: 'That's all I wanted: that all of you prove to be corruptible and forfeit your entire self-respect. Alfred Ill – why would I want him killed! Sure, he betrayed me, but he wasn't even twenty at the time – still half a child, who panicked when faced with the responsibility. This was tough for me, but not the worst part. What was worst was how Güllen, this miserable dump, treated me after the trial: like a whore, like filth. It's this humiliation that I sought revenge for. And God, have I succeeded: all of you, who wanted to kill Alfred out of pure greed for money – you have lost something that is more important than life: your dignity. You'll have to go on living with him, day after day. You will have to withstand Alfred's gaze. Every time he sees you, it will say: you have no self-respect. You would do anything for money, simply anything. You are a corruptible, undignified nothing. Besides, you also have to pay back your debts, as I won't give you a penny. I don't feel any obligation to keep a promise towards boundless opportunists like you. I have shown you what a miserable pack you are. My contempt is without end. May you all suffocate on Ill's scorn, a little bit more every day!'

The old lady destroys the people of Güllen's self-respect by seducing them into boundless opportunism: she seduces them into transgressing their inner limits. It is a destruction through seduction. Self-respect can also be destroyed in a different way: though fear and pain. Nobody has described this in a crueller manner than

George Orwell. O'Brien, the chief torturer of Big Brother's regime, has alienated Winston from himself to the extent that he is ready to declare that two and two is five. Winston reacts to the humiliation as we described it in the first chapter: through a retreat into an inner fortress. 'He obeyed the Party, but he still hated the Party', Orwell writes. 'In the old days he had hidden a heretical mind beneath an appearance of conformity. Now he had retreated a step further: in the mind he had surrendered, but he had hoped to keep the inner heart inviolate... For the first time he perceived that if you want to keep a secret you must also hide it from yourself... he must keep his hatred locked up inside him like a ball of matter which was part of himself and yet unconnected with the rest of him, a kind of cyst...' Even if they shot him dead: 'The heretical thought would be unpunished, unrepented, out of their reach for ever. To die hating them, that was freedom.' This is the thought that allows Winston to experience a remainder of self-respect. And something else belongs to this respect: the sacred resolution that under no circumstances will he betray his former lover Julia. This is the final, ultimate line he would never cross. Then he is brought to room 101, the innermost circle of hell. This is where O'Brien unleashes starved rats onto his victims' faces. There is only one thing that can save Winston from his ordeal: he has to offer Julia in his place. 'He had suddenly understood that in the whole world there was just one person to whom he could transfer his punishment – one body that he could thrust between himself and the rats. And he was shouting frantically, over and over. "Do it to Julia! Do it to Julia! Not me! Julia! I don't care what you do to her. Tear her face off, strip her to the bones. Not me! Julia! Not me!"' There are some things, Winston thinks later on, from which you could never recover: your own acts. 'Something was killed in your breast: burnt out, cauterized out.' Winston and Julia later meet again. They admit to one another: 'I betrayed you.' And they say: 'After that, you don't feel the same towards the other person any longer.' As Orwell writes: 'There did not seem to be anything more to say.'

Sacrificing Self-Respect

In William Styron's novel *Sophie's Choice*, Auschwitz inmate Sophie licks the boots of camp commander Rudolf Höss. Reading about this is unbearable, and one is so outraged and disgusted that one feels the impulse to toss the book in the corner. This *should not* have been allowed to happen. From his office, Höss sees the crematoria of Birkenau, continuously emitting the smoke of thousands of gassed and burnt Jews. Höss is in charge of this factory of death. It is impossible to imagine licking *anyone*'s boots – the thought of having to do it makes us stiffen with disgust. But what is outright unthinkable is licking *this* man's boots. One wants to cry out that there are *no circumstances, absolutely none*, under which this would be reconcilable with human dignity. When Sophie does it nonetheless, she forfeits her dignity in a manner that cannot be exceeded in any way. It is the ultimate loss of self-respect. It is the ultimate loss of dignity.

But things look simpler than they really are. One has to envision the situation in all its complexity in order to examine the first, intuitive judgement that seems so unambiguous and dominant. Sophie is not a Jew. She is in Auschwitz because she is Polish. Höss has selected her because she speaks German, can write shorthand and type. She takes dictation, and in return she can sleep in his cellar. She gets more sleep than usual, she can be alone and eat leftovers – an unheard-of luxury in Auschwitz. She can also get away from a lesbian guard who raped her. The opportunity to escape violence, hunger and all the other subhuman conditions makes Sophie eager for the job. These are reasons that everyone comprehends and respects. No one would therefore struggle to understand why Sophie agrees to sit at the desk in Höss's office and type. We must remember though that it is Höss, Eichmann's henchman, the commander over a death camp with millions of dead; that over by the crematoria, which are in sight of the office, the smoke is so thick that one can taste it on one's lips – like sand, as Sophie later says; that what Sophie has to write are sentences like these: 'The mechanism for Special Action at Birkenau having become severely taxed beyond all expectation, it is respectfully suggested that, in the specific matter of the Greek Jews, alternative destinations in the occupied territories of the East be considered.' If there is a human dignity that consists in having firm and unmoveable limits for what one is prepared to do: how do we feel about Sophie's willingness to write such sentences, with the Birkenau smoke in sight? And what is the meaning of the fact that the suffering that Sophie can temporarily escape from by writing those sentences is greater than anything we can imagine?

We then read of Sophie's attempt to seduce Höss – in order to make him release her from the camp. An intimacy is developed with this man that the reader finds insufferable. He asks her how she got there. 'Fate brought me to you, because I knew only *you* would understand.' He gives her a piece of chocolate, removes a crumb from her lip and puts it in his mouth. He would like to have *intercourse* with her, he later says in his bureaucratic speak. They do not get around to it. All of a sudden, Höss acts like the distant commander of Auschwitz towards her again. She shows him an anti-Semitic pamphlet that she, the daughter of a fanatical Polish Jew hater, carries with her. She tells him everything he wants to hear. She has now crossed all limits, both physical and emotional. Her inner fortress is destroyed. How can she continue living after this, one asks. How can she live *with herself*?

We then discover that she does not cross the limits of her self-respect for her own but for her child's sake. She begs Höss: '*Herr Kommandant*, I know I can't ask much for myself. But I beg of you to do one thing for me before you send me back. I have a young son in Camp D, where all the other boys are prisoners. He was with me when I arrived but I have not seen him since six months. I yearn to see him. I am afraid for his health, with winter coming. I beg of you to consider some way in which he might be released. His health is frail and he is so very young...' She later reports: 'I couldn't help myself and I threw myself against him, threw my arms around his waist and begged him again. I said, "Then at least let me *see* my little boy, just once." And when I said this, I couldn't help myself and I fell on my knees in front of him. I surrounded Höss's boots with my arms. I pressed my cheek up against those cold leather boots as if they was made of fur or something warm and comforting. I think maybe I even licked them with my tongue, licked those Nazi boots.'

In Orwell's book, Winston betrays Julia and thus himself to escape the ultimate cruelty – it is about him. This is a different case: Sophie is not concerned with herself, but with her child. This is, one could say, a case where someone *sacrifices* one's self-respect to protect another person. Dignity is the sacrifice and when the good to be protected is great enough, this greatness and idealism annul the loss: *Sacrificed* dignity is not *forfeited* dignity. Could we say that we lose our dignity, but through the sacrifice, win a new one? Or was dignity not lost at all? Dignity is lost when we cross the limits that should delineate what is beyond consideration for our own advantage. Perhaps it is also lost when we cross these limits in self-defence, like in Winston's case, though then the loss is forgivable. When it happens out of self-lessness, however, like with Sophie, we could say that we rise to a new kind of purpose: It is no longer about my good but that of others. Can we say the question of dignity has moved to a higher level? And thanks to my new, selfless will I can be certain of my dignity and no longer need to take care of it in the usual manner? Or even: The old criteria simply no longer apply? They have been suspended by this new purpose. So that, because they are no longer valid, no dignity has been lost at all?

Or is it perhaps different in yet another way? Towards the end of her account, Sophie says something that might silence any reflection on lost dignity: 'Such a terrible place was this Auschwitz that you really could not say that this person *should* have done a certain thing in a fine or noble fashion, as in the other world.' This is, one could add, simply the wrong *standard*. The dignified way of living, I said in the Introduction, is a way of responding to the threats and challenges of human life. This response requires a certain degree of freedom and sovereignty. When people are so beset by misery that they no longer have this room for manoeuvre, every ideal of dignity is extinguished. The question simply no longer poses itself, one could say, and any judgement about it becomes ridiculous.

Breaking Self-Respect

When we want to say that Sophie sacrifices her self-respect for her child's sake, we mean: From a certain point, self-respect is no longer an issue for her. The tension between the need for self-respect and the desire to help others is radically dissolved. In many other cases, however, this tension remains unresolved: The person concerned does not want to transgress her own limit of self-respect, but feels clearly that she thereby violates another precept of self-respect – that relating to the welfare of others. This is what happens to Jones, the greying chief mate in Joseph Conrad's novel *Lord Jim*. Captain Brierly has jumped overboard without explanation. Jones disliked his arrogant manner and yet secretly admired him. 'I am ready to answer for him, that once over he did not try to swim a stroke, the same as he would have had pluck enough to keep up all day long on the bare chance had he fallen overboard accidentally. He was second to none – if he said so himself, as I heard him once.' Brierly also had in a letter to the company recommended Jones as his successor. But someone else is appointed, 'a little popinjay, in a grey check suit, with his hair parted in the middle.' He speaks ill of the dead Brierly in front of the crew. Jones cannot tolerate this – it would be incompatible with his self-respect. ' "I may be a hard case," answers I, "but I ain't so far gone as to put up with the sight of you sitting in Captain Brierly's chair." I left the saloon, got my rags together, and was on the quay with all my dunnage about my feet before the stevedores had turned to again.' He has preserved the limits of self-respect that he had drawn for himself. But he is also responsible for others, and they belong to his self-respect, too. ' "Yes. Adrift – on shore – after ten years' service – and with a poor woman and four children six thousand miles off depending on my half-pay for every mouthful they ate. Yes, sir! I chucked it rather than hear Captain

Brierly abused.' One could say that a fissure goes right through this man, a fissure of self-respect: In order to respect himself in one way, he has to do something for which he will not respect himself in another way.

We can also see such a crack in another character: Inspector Matthäi in Friedrich Dürrenmatt's novella *The Pledge*. He promises to the parents of a girl who was raped and murdered that he will find the murderer, no matter what it takes – promises it 'on his eternal salvation', as the text says. The alleged suspect confesses after an endless interrogation, but kills himself in his cell shortly after. Matthäi has doubts about his confession. But his service for the Zürich police comes to an end that day, and he has to catch a plane to Jordan to start his new job. He makes a momentous decision on the runway. 'The stewardess who had led the travellers to the plane held out her hand to receive Matthäi's ticket, but the inspector turned around once more. He looked at the crowd of children, who were waving, happily and enviously, at the plane which was about to start. "Miss", he said, "I'm not flying," and returned to the airport building, and walked under the terrace with its vast crowds of children, through the building and toward the exit.' Seeing the children made it clear to Matthäi that he had to find the real murderer – as he had promised the mother. It is a question of self-respect for him. Not so much as an inspector – he is no longer in service – but must rather because he has made a solemn promise. 'I simply owe it to myself', he might say. Yet Matthäi is told that it is too late: He cannot return to the service. This is the beginning of a story in the course of which he becomes an alcoholic and loses everything, including his moral integrity. He concludes, based on a child's drawing, that the murderer is from Graubünden. So he leases a petrol station on the road from Chur to Zürich and waits for him to stop by. The former star of the Zürich police now sits in front of a petrol station, drinks, smokes and stares into nothing, for days and weeks on end – because of the promise, because he thinks that he owes it to himself. For that, he is ready to do something that would have never crossed his mind in his previous life: He joins forces with a prostitute and uses her child as a decoy – he uses them both as mere means to an end. He thus does something strikingly immoral – something that lies beyond the limits of his moral self-respect as he used to know it. 'You are a swine', the child's mother says to him afterwards. What Matthäi does is crueller than what Jones, the sailor, does to his family; or at least cruel in a different way. But here too we could speak of a fissure that goes right through the inspector: He tries to stay true to himself in one way and thus betrays himself in another.

Responsibility for Oneself

It is not only possible to lose one's self-respect by transgressing one's inner limits, but also by refusing to take responsibility for oneself and one's life. In Jean-Paul Melville's film *The Red Circle* two gangsters plan to burgle a jewellery shop. Their main challenge is the motion sensor of the alarm system. It needs to be deactivated by a single, precise shot from a great distance. Then they remember the former policeman Jansen, a sniper. He has completely let himself go: he lives in a dump, drinks and has visions of beasts that appear to be living in a closet. The gangsters offer him a third of the booty if he takes part. He pulls himself together, quits drinking, practises shooting, moulds special ammunition and gets in shape. The central lock for the sensor is far away, the first shot must hit. That is why on the night of the burglary Jansen brings along a tripod to stabilize the rifle. But to everyone's astonishment, at the crucial moment he removes it from the tripod, shoots freehand and hits. He proves to himself and the others that he is as good as he used to be. He pulls out a flask, smells it and puts it back without drinking from it. He will give up his share, he tells one of the partners. When he objects, Jansen reassures him: 'It was thanks to you I locked the beasts away.' It is as if he was saying: What you gave back to me is much more important than money – my self-respect.

Jansen had lost control over himself and his life. He had thereby lost his dignity in the sense of autonomy, which we discussed in the first chapter. In the process of losing it, he must have felt that he was not just a helpless victim of uncontrollable events, the victim of an internal landslide. He must have felt that he had *omitted* to do something that was indeed within his power: taking *care* of himself; and that in this omission, he not only gambled away his autonomy, but also his self-respect.

Taking responsibility for oneself has multiple dimensions. One of them is about taking care of one's health, cultivating one's skills, fighting against inner compulsions and for greater autonomy, developing a growing understanding of the logic of one's life and giving this life a meaning and sense of direction. Failure is not a problem. Self-respect is only in danger when we stop *respecting* these things and in that sense *give up* on ourselves. This is not about fixed standards either. Although a certain lifestyle is unhealthy and even life-threatening, someone might decide: this is exactly how I want to live my life. His self-respect then lies in the consciousness of his decision. This is the awareness that Jansen had lost and that returned when he redis-covered his talent.

Taking care as opposed to giving up on oneself: This question may also preoccupy us when we see a beggar. When this happens in a country where being born in the wrong neighbourhood means bad luck in life, we feel differently about this case than we would about a case in a country with a social welfare system. In the former, we will not hesitate to be compassionate and supportive, for we know one can easily end up in such a situation, no matter how hard one has tried. Here, there is the dignity of the beggar: openly admitting that one did not make it and cannot stand on one's own feet. Those who pass by know how much this has to do with luck – that's why they will not hesitate to give money. They would rather hesitate in a country with employment agencies and social welfare. They know that one can still go to ruin there. But they will ask themselves whether the beggar really took responsibility for himself to the fullest extent, whether he perhaps gave up on himself too soon – and what that means for his self-respect. Another question can also arise: Is it undignified when the beggar uses her ragged child to evoke pity? Or can this be part of a dignified admission of neediness? What is the difference between showing oneself in one's weakness in a dignified manner and an undignified display of weakness?

An essential part of having responsibility for oneself is being *true to oneself*: to one's convictions, feelings, desires and one's entire way of living. This means having the ability and courage to *differenti-ate* oneself from others. This also means having the strength not to avoid conflict. Self-respect has to do with fearlessness here. We have encountered Bernard Winter as a man who trusts his reason. He has no problem differentiating himself and being true to himself in this respect. Things might be different for him with feelings, with close-ness and distance in personal relationships. There, he easily feels under pressure. Perhaps when he was young, he lived in a student house-share where drug use was fashionable. It was hard to say no and to bear the mockery. It felt good to be able to do it nonethe-less. This small victory of self-respect was something that he often remembered when he had to confront difficult issues in his marriage or friendships. He felt his self-respect suffer whenever he kept avoid-ing, glossing over and denying conflict, just to preserve peace and harmony. We encountered him when he discovered Sarah humming to herself in the hospital room – a person very different from the woman he thought he knew. As he smoked his first cigarette in years outside the hospital building, he felt he would have to find out the meaning of his discovery – and that this would become a question of his self-respect.

When someone decides to stay true to himself in the face of resistance, it can mean a great and serious conflict. For example, a dissident who only narrowly escaped the secret police might decide to return from exile for the sake of his self-respect and his life's coherence. But self-respect, according to this understanding, can also be at stake with issues that at first glance seem ridiculously small. Right from the beginning of his career as a conductor, Leonard Bernstein was extremely ambitious. But when someone suggested that he should take a more Anglo-Saxon-sounding name, he reacted with sarcasm. And it can be about things that are even smaller: I refuse to share a table with a certain person or choose to leave the cinema because I find the film that I am watching with my friends repulsive. The courage to publicly declare an unpopular opinion also belongs here. It belongs to the dignity of the outsider. It is always about the same thing: not to betray oneself for the sake of others' approval; not to endanger dignity through a craving for admiration.

In his humiliating talk with Howard, Willy Loman first asks for sixty-five dollars per week, then for fifty and finally for forty. Going even lower, I said in the first chapter, would destroy the rest of his self-respect. We can now specify what I had in mind: Self-respect can also consist in claiming what one has earned. This is also a way of being true to oneself. There are many reasons why workers or trade unions can demand a higher wage. One of them can be self-respect: We finally want a wage that matches our performance. A minimum wage is a wage one can live on. It is also a wage that is compatible with the workers' self-respect. Self-respect here is the awareness that one deserves a certain kind of recognition.

Finally, there is a dimension of responsibility for oneself that has to do with our changing emotional identities. We can imagine an author, a friend of Bernard Winter, who has written something that he later distances himself from. He hastily buys up all the remaining copies of his book. When someone gets in his way, he nearly turns violent. Winter watches his anxious friend. He finds his conduct ridiculous. He feels sorry for him. His dignity is imperilled. 'But Martin', he says, 'this was *also* you. Sure, you see it differently now, and you're embarrassed about those words *because* they were yours. But it can't be the solution to cut them off and deny them. You must find a way of standing up for them despite everything. You have to stand up for yourself – as someone who has changed in the course of his life; as someone who has – like all of us – lived many different lives. It's no *accident* that you used to think and feel in a certain way, and it's no *accident* that you have turned into a person who now thinks and feels differently. There is something to *understand* here: how an old life tune has become a new one. These internal events have a logic. They are unlike mysterious tectonic movements. You can make sense of these inner events and thus recognize something that's a part of your life. Taking responsibility for one's life means these two things: understanding and recognizing. It allows you to face the world with a gaze that says: Yes, I was all these things! – or even better: I *am* all these things!'

6

Dignity as Moral Integrity

ᏃᏉ

I can find myself in a situation where I have to sacrifice something in my life for another person's benefit, perhaps because he is ill and requires my help: for example, I might give up a trip, a job or a relationship. Then it is not, as is usually the case, my needs that determine my actions but the needs of another. I embrace his needs and placed them above my own. This characterizes moral action and lies at the core of moral respect and consideration: allowing the interests of others to be the reason for me to do or abstain from doing something. This attitude and pattern of action also determine a part of human dignity. Yet their logic is not always easy to comprehend, and in drawing out the conceptual implications we become disoriented very easily. How can we best make sense of the experience of morality? What idea of dignity does it reveal, and how is it connected with the other ideas that we have discussed already?

Moral Autonomy

Sacrificing the fulfilment of one's own wishes for the benefit of others: only beings with an inner distance to themselves, who can evaluate and control their actions are capable of it. These skills are the defining features of subjects. They make us into beings who are not just powerlessly drifting about, simply following the dictates of their desire. They make us into beings who have mastery over themselves and are not slaves to their passions; beings, therefore, who can determine by themselves which desires they allow to translate into action. This means that the experience of moral decision-making and renunciation involves an experience of self-determined distance and control. This is not the only experience of this kind. Yet in each instance, it is also a confirmation of this ability and thus an experience of inner freedom.

But is this not an illusory, perhaps even deceptive, description of the experience of moral action? When I allow myself to be defined by the needs of others does it not invariably entail a loss of self-determination? Does it not inevitably lead away from me? Is it not necessarily an experience of self-alienation? This is what we feel when our moral actions are motived by fear of an external authority and its punishment: fear of God's wrath, for example, or of a religious institution's sanctions, or of social exclusion. Then our moral decisions are like those of slaves. It is not very different when we fear an internalized authority: the voice of conscience, which might sound like the voice of important people in our lives. It makes us enslave ourselves. In both cases, we do not make moral decisions of our own volition, but out of compulsion. Self-determination then only exists in this one shape: in our decision to succumb to this inner extortion or not, to risk feeling pangs of conscience or not. But it remains an experience of inner enslavement either way. Our moral action does not arise from spontaneous moral perception and is therefore not *genuine*. And because it does not develop from spontaneous moral sensibility, responding to the nuances of a particular situation, this action – for lack of any other guide – uses rules, duties, imperatives and maxims for orientation. It is as if we were working through a bureaucracy of rules and edicts that pertain to moral decision; as if we had to sit hunched over dusty files of moral commands and prohibitions, joylessly going through them with old gloves and tight lips, feeling full of sorrow.

But we do not *have* to understand the experience of morality in that way, and most of the time this is not how we *experience* it either. Those who make moral judgements and decisions use a sensibility that has grown over the course of a lifetime and, like any sensibility, develops and becomes refined through trial and error. Unlike the purely bureaucratic inspection of a catalogue of moral prescriptions, this approach is based on a detailed perception of a given situation. It acknowledges the fact that morally significant situations are usually very *complex* and bear no resemblance to one another. This moral sensibility is governed by an experience that is among the most valuable experiences that we know: the experience of *moral intimacy*. It rests on the particular way in which subjects encounter one another – we discussed this in Chapter 2. As I said then, in the course of such encounters, subjects become internally entangled in manifold ways. Their thoughts and feelings address the thoughts and feelings of others; the needs and desires of others are present in their own needs and desires. And there is also another way in which we can become entwined: by imagining what it would be like to be in the other person's position. We do not just have to listen to a story about an experience from a neutral remove. We can also make the attempt to *re-enact* it internally and ask ourselves how we would feel in this situation. Then we are using our sensitivity, our social imagination. And re-enacting it is not all. We will respond to what we have envisioned in our own life and actions, and this response will in turn have an effect on the other. We are now involved in the other's life. The relationship has become what I called a *committed encounter*, a relationship that contains the heat of mutuality. As we tend to say: we take *part* in the other person's life.

This participation in the other's life can take different forms. One is that of moral intimacy: the particular closeness that develops when I embrace the other's needs and put aside my own desires. We then become *important* to one another in a way that is impossible without moral intimacy. For the other person, it is an importance that goes beyond a feeling of gratitude. For me, it does not represent selflessness in the sense of making a sacrifice that leaves nothing of me. Generally speaking, the language of gratitude and sacrifice is not adequate in the case of this experience. What is perhaps more suitable is the language of bond, shared life and solidarity, all of which enrich our life and give it depth. And we can only grasp this experience in its true meaning when we put aside the idea of moral authority and the need to consult commands and prohibitions. When I forego something for the benefit of a sick person just in order to obey a moral principle, it does not produce the moral intimacy that I want. It does not come about, because instead of being my own wish, the act of renunciation was ordered; it was something that was imposed on me. What pushes itself between me and the experience of moral intimacy is resentment at the fact that this was a sacrifice I did not want to make. Moral intimacy is destroyed before it could even develop.

Two things merge in our moral consciousness, as I have described it: the experience of self-determination and the experience of moral intimacy. These two experiences together give moral action its worthiness. They not only occur together, but are also entwined in each other: Moral intimacy is experienced as something valuable because it is an expression of freedom. And when we look for acts of renunciation that are self-determined, it is because such experiences give rise to the special closeness of moral intimacy. This connection is not just an abstract intellectual insight: It is *felt*. If there is anything that we want to consider as the foundation of morality, it would be this felt connection. But perhaps we should not even speak in those terms, but simply say we *want* to live according to this principle, because it is a good, precious and joyful way to live one's life; because we want to be members of a community that lives that way.

Moral Dignity

When we violate other people's dignity we can thereby also damage our own. This is what the citizens of Güllen experience when the old woman pays them a visit. Having sacrificed Alfred Ill to Mammon, having humiliated and eventually killed him, they are themselves left with no dignity at all. They have not only lost it in the sense of their self-respect, but also in the sense of their moral integrity: they have lost the natural willingness to show consideration for another person's life and needs.

We have already discussed the connection between our own dignity and the dignity of others in the Introduction. It exists because dignity, when understood as a way of living, is not something that we can experience in isolation. We experience it as social beings who become who they are through the way in which they treat others. Moral intimacy is in that sense a source of dignity: By respecting the needs of others and aligning our actions according to them, we acquire a form of dignity that we could call *moral dignity*. It is a kind of dignity that a completely amoral person, if he existed, would not know; the entire dimension of thought and feeling that belongs to it would be alien to him. Jean-Claude Romand, who lost himself in the silent forests of the Jura, had, despite all his lies, not lost his moral dignity entirely; a great deal of what he did for his family expressed his aptitude for moral intimacy, or at least seemed to express it. What makes his deeds so hard to comprehend is the suddenness and coldness with which every remnant of moral dignity was extinguished. 'It is true', he says in his last words during the trial, 'that silence must be my lot.'

But moral dignity can mean even more than the capability and willingness for moral intimacy. It is a particular form of moral integrity, concerned not just with *any* interest others might have, but with needs that are connected with the very core of their dignity: their need for autonomy, for genuine encounters, for safe intimacy and understanding, for truthfulness and self-respect. There are many modes of inconsiderateness that can disgust us, but which we could not accuse of hurting their victim's dignity. One can be beaten, robbed, deceived, lied to and betrayed without having to experience a humiliation that would endanger one's dignity. Although the perpetrator loses a part of his moral integrity in the process, he retains his moral dignity in the sense of the words that I am using here. The latter is only lost when he steals his victim's dignity: like Inspector Matthäi who uses a woman's child as a decoy, a mere instrument for his investigation; or like the torturer O'Brien who forces Winston to betray Julia; or like Romand who robs the people in his life of truthfulness and genuine encounters. In those cases, moral integrity is not merely damaged, but actively forfeited as moral dignity.

There are laws with which the state tries to protect its citizens' dignity by precluding others from damaging it and thus forfeiting their moral dignity. The categorical prohibition of torture is one example, the prohibition on dwarf-tossing and peep shows another. The protection of this dignity is also what drove the German supreme court to prohibit the pre-emptive downing of passenger aircraft that could be used as weapons and steered into high-rise buildings. The court argued that by killing passengers as a means to save the lives of others, the state would be treating them as mere objects. 'Such treatment would disregard the individuals as subjects with dignity and inalienable rights.' In line with the idea that we are introducing here, we could also add that the moral dignity of those who would have to shoot down the plane also requires protection – the protection that the pilots of the Hiroshima and Nagasaki bombers would have deserved.

A perpetrator's moral dignity is destroyed when his deed is *cruel*. There are many things that are cruel. But true cruelty consists in damaging someone's dignity: for example, by plunging her into poverty and dependency or driving her towards a humiliating addiction; or by dragging someone's guilt and shame through the tabloids; or by lying to someone for his entire life; or by destroying someone's self-respect through torture. All of these things already entail a loss of moral dignity. But this loss can be even deeper and more comprehensive when someone commits a cruelty *for its own sake* rather than as a means to an end. Both drug lords and the tabloid press want money, which is why they act cruelly. Romand commits murder because he does not want his lies to be exposed. And even O'Brien has a goal with his torture: he wants Winston to identify with Big Brother's state and come to love its ever-present eyes. All of this is not yet the final step in the loss of moral dignity. This stage is only reached when someone treats another person with cruelty simply *because he likes to see her suffer*. Then his will is a will that desires cruelty and suffering as such. Were it not for the word's metaphysically dubious connotations, one could even call it an *evil* will.

In Chapter 1, I described humiliation as a powerlessness that the perpetrator enjoys visibly in front of the victim; when a grinning drug dealer lets the addict beg for the drugs; or when an audience laughs at someone because of a physical deformity or embarrassing weakness and delights in its amusement. Through this enjoyment, the perpetrators lose their moral dignity as I understand it here. Yeltsin humiliated the formerly powerful Gorbachev by forcing him to read out a text in public that he had never seen before. Gorbachev was distressed, but kept reading. The camera showed a member of the audience consuming this spectacle of humiliation with pleasure. His grin showed enjoyed powerlessness, enjoyed humiliation. It was repulsive: the man was forfeiting his moral dignity.

One can also feel repulsed by another betrayal of the experience of morality: *vanity*. I act morally in order to appear noble to myself: to appear virtuous, selfless, full of integrity. This conceit might be motivated primarily by the desire to secure the good opinion of others: for example, when I ensure that they see me give money to a beggar or when I publicize my larger acts of charitableness and renunciation. Yet there is also silent moral conceit: enjoying the awareness that one has surpassed others in selflessness. It allows me mentally to raise myself above them as the better person.

What is wrong with this? Moral acts thus become primarily a means to increase the sense of one's own worth: outward selflessness turns into boundless self-centredness – morality as an ego trip. This is a paradox and might seem perverse: an action that purports to be entirely about others and precisely not about me is in fact only about me. Those for whom this moral action is intended are just the playing field for my narcissism. This narcissistic shift undermines the moral experience. One might object: 'But there simply must be something about moral action that *I* benefit from as well – otherwise I wouldn't be able to bring myself to do it!' And yes, it does exist: an experience of self-determined moral intimacy without narcissism – just the experience itself as something good that does not count towards anything and is not mentioned on any inner balance sheet. This is part of moral dignity.

What is also a part of moral dignity is the capacity for *loyalty*. According to my understanding of the word, it is the title for a long-term commitment. It is not only longer than momentary moral action, but is in a way also more abstract: further removed from the turbulences of powerful moral feelings. One could say that there is something unconditional, absolute about it, and it is not so much an experience as an attitude – one could speak of emotional partisanship. Doing something motivated by this kind of loyalty means not repeatedly questioning and measuring one's acts against the current moral perception. Loyalty is an attitude that eludes any moral calculation. It is still valid when the usual balance of moral action is not in my favour. It is rooted in a long shared history. The lives of the people involved intersect and overlap, such that it is impossible to imagine one's life without the other. This loyalty develops through the kind of bond that is common in long marriages, friendships and perhaps also among neighbours, in a professional community, or that has emerged in consequence of a joint commitment to a political cause. The attitude is: given our long history together, I stand by this person – no matter what else has happened. Nevertheless, loyalty can also break. But this requires more than a conflict of interest and also more than a momentary moral difference of opinion. It must be something very severe: a serious betrayal, ideological delusion or involvement in crime. Then loyalty dies because an entire part of our life dies. Yet the depth of a former loyalty is still palpable in the strangeness and coldness that stay behind once it is gone.

Dignity in Guilt and Forgiveness

We can harm other people and become burdened by guilt. What does guilt do to our dignity? What does our dignity do with guilt? What might a victim's dignity consist in?

When we are guilty of harming someone, the consciousness of our guilt is the consciousness of having destroyed moral intimacy. When the harm we have done destroys the dignity of another, it is consciousness of the loss of our moral dignity. We feel distressed after behaving in such a fashion – distressed by ourselves. This feeling of distress is the feeling of guilt. Different emotions flow into it. We have disappointed others by failing to be considerate, and we recognize their disappointment as justified. We feel isolated by the deed, as it has lost us the recognition that others used to have for us. We know that their good will is going to turn into rejection and that there will be anger and a desire for revenge. We not only expect this reaction, but find it appropriate. All of this makes us wish that we had never done it. It makes us search for the possibility of making amends.

The culprit's dignity lies in her attitude towards her guilt and the action she takes to restore the lost moral order. This depends on what the guilt consists in exactly, for guilt can be varied and challenge dignity in manifold ways. A child might dart in front of my car. I caused his death, but I am not guilty: I could not have prevented it. Yet I dream of how my wheels crushed the little body. There is nothing for which I, from a moral perspective, need to atone. Nevertheless, I might visit the parents, and perhaps it will feel like the visit has something to do with dignity. This would not be the dignity of an apology, but that of visible regret and grief for their misfortune. It would be a dignity that shows that I am not unaffected by their suffering, even though I am not to blame for it.

Perhaps I run over the child while driving drunk and leave him paralysed. It was not my intention, but I am guilty. Aside from my legal responsibility, what can I do in terms of dignity? The minimum: acknowledge my guilt, without denial, without white-washing, without sophistry – dignity as truthfulness. I can ask for forgiveness. Not for my intention, but for my negligence, my lack of responsibility. I will do what I can to alleviate suffering. I will show myself to the child and his parents as a person who does not steal himself away. I will also not hide from the parents' justified anger and the child's understandable, perhaps life-long, resentment. What would be undignified is if I considered the issue settled by setting up a monthly payment for them.

What about myself? What do I do with myself? Remembering is not enough. But dignity also cannot mean being paralysed by guilt, suffocating because of this one thought. Perhaps it is about growing through this experience by taking more responsibility for my life as a whole and examining my priorities. Then my dignity would relate to the kind of dignity we discussed in the last chapter: dignity as responsibility for oneself.

I can fail in an even more serious way: I leave the injured child lying in the street at night and drive off. The guilt is now founded on my will: not in that I wanted his death, but in that I did not find the will to help – out of fear, perhaps, or because something else was more important to me. The exact motive is important. But in both cases, I am guilty because of neglect, because of a lack of will. This has more to do with me and my identity than the drinking. This is why I will experience a deeper feeling of guilt: I have lost moral inti-macy because of who I am. I have isolated myself not because of a loss of control, but because of a character flaw. In court, others will look at me differently than if I had been driving drunk. Although I did not actively hurt the child's dignity, as in the case of abuse for example, I did not protect it either. It was not important enough to me. I cannot make it up to the child any more. I can face the parents and try to withstand their hatred of me, without attempting to white-wash my actions. What else can I do?

In his novel *Reservation Road*, John Burnham Schwartz tells the story of a man who, while driving home with his young son late one night, runs over a boy and flees. It was a dog, he tells his son. The accident happened by a gas station and the dead boy's father saw his son being hit by the car. The book is about the deep disruption this causes to the dead boy's family and about the father's search for the offender. In the end, he finds him in a cabin where he is spending time with his own son. He hears him talk to the boy. Then he confronts him and forces him to go outside in the snow, a gun to his back. He trips over and gives the man who killed his son a chance to strike him down. The man takes the gun and leaves. But then he returns. 'I had taken from him everything there was to take, and had wanted none of it, had hoped and tried to avoid it, had regretted it deeply. But I had taken his boy just the same. And so now I went back to him.' He drops the gun in the snow in front of him. 'I've got a son', he says, 'Ten years old like your boy was. That doesn't seem fair to you, and it's not.' The father says: 'You took his life like it was nothing and then you went on with your own as if you had a right.' 'I was afraid', says the man. 'That's not good enough', says the father. He aims the gun at him. The man nods. 'Yes', he says. The father recounts: 'I tried to avoid looking him in the face, but I could no longer help it; though neither of us moved an inch, the silence and the passing seconds seemed somehow to be pushing us together. His eyes, set wide in a broad, weather-beaten face, were brown and surprisingly soft, and I saw the pronounced dark circles beneath them.' The father asks the man if he will surrender himself to the police. 'Yes', he says. ' "No," I said. I saw him with the police, and it meant nothing, changed nothing. "No." I was shaking my head, seeing his son awake now and standing in the cold, empty house. "Go back to your son", I told him.'

This story is not a model or a guideline for anything. But there is still something that we can learn from it: If dignity has to do with conquering guilt, it can only succeed when there is an encounter between victim and perpetrator, an encounter in which they see and experience one another as humans *beyond* the offence. I am not sure whether this is possible, but we could try carefully to develop the story further. After some time, the two men meet again. Their guilt and pain are unchanged, and animosity threatens to flare up at any moment. But they ask questions about each other's lives, about their lives as fathers and in general. Both at times feel the impulse just to get up and leave. It is pointless. But then they continue their conversation after all. This would be a story about the changeability of our feelings towards guilt. The guilt does not fade and cannot be talked away. However, when both men keep learning more about and understanding one another better, their feelings can become more nuanced, more delicate. Guilt is then no longer like a silent, icy rock between them. The man who was at the steering wheel can now better understand what a tragedy it has been for the father, what it has done to his life. He can find a richer, more precise language with which to ask for forgiveness, a language no longer at risk of trying to shrug off the issue with empty words of apology. And once he knows more about the father's life, he will perhaps also find gestures and actions beyond the words that will express his regret in a credible manner. The father, once he knows the driver better, will not be able to forgive him in the sense of a complete recovery of moral equilibrium. But he will no longer just be the enemy, the reckless offender who took his son from him. He will grant him an open future, a future that is not obstructed by this one offence. This is where the story could go. It would be a story about dignity as processed guilt.

The changeability of our feelings towards guilt, encounter, development and having an open future are all also issues when guilt is not founded on a lack of will or an omission, but on clear and conscious intention to cause suffering. Such guilt can be varied and challenge dignity in a variety of ways. How the story continues beyond the episode of the offence depends on the details of the incident and its significance. One might become culpable while acting in self-defence: through a deed that allows one to escape unbearable suffering, but which annihilates another person. This happens in an episode that Roman Frister recounts in his autobiographical book *The Cap or The Price of a Life*. He was raped in a concentration camp, and the offender stole his cap. 'A prisoner without his standard-issue cap was as good as dead. At morning roll-call the kapo and SS officer regularly killed anyone not having one.' Frister creeps through the barracks at night, looking to snatch someone else's cap. 'He was lying in a top bunk, his face covered by his blanket. The tip of his cap stuck out from the crook of his arm. I tugged at it gently. He didn't awake. The cap was in my hand. I stuck it under my shirt, its rough cloth scratching my chest. I was overjoyed.' The morning roll-call arrives. 'Somewhere behind me was a man waiting to die. I had no idea what the man without the cap felt. I had no qualms. I refused to think about it from his point of view. His existence didn't matter. Mine did. The officer and the kapo walked down the lines. I counted the seconds as they counted the prisoners. I wanted it to be over. The capless man didn't beg for his life. The shot rang out without warning. I didn't want to know who the man was. I was delighted to be alive.' Frister writes down the story in a single night. The journalist who reads it wants to publish it. Frister refuses. 'Why did you write it then?' 'I don't know. Because I had to.'

It is the story of guilt incurred in self-defence. The will to live is stronger than anything else. In the camp, Frister even suppresses the feeling of guilt. It cannot unfold. But it is there. Many years later it all of a sudden breaks through, and he writes it down. And many more years later, Frister can finally go public with it. It is a way of admitting his guilt and integrating it into his life. Two things belong to this process: first, the awareness that he is no longer the person who he was at the time. This does not diminish his guilt, but gives it another emotional location and role in his life. And second, Frister can now also have a different perspective on his guilt than before, both at the time of the deed and the time when he abruptly wrote the story: 'Can the acts of a time of blackness be judged by the values of a time of light?' He does not deny any guilt. But he makes the attempt to find the right perspective on it, instead of locking it up inside him and not making sense of it. This is also what dignity can look like.

Guilt through self-defence: this may also happen when a dictatorship's security forces blackmail me into betraying my father, a friend or lover to save my own life. I do not just betray the person, but also the precious good of loyalty. How could the betrayer and the betrayed later encounter one another? What might the dignity of such an encounter consist in? It will be important for the victim to understand the betrayal: the particulars of the threat that the betrayer felt and – especially – that of his inner conflict. Only when the betrayed can re-enact the inner struggle, will he perhaps come to the conclusion: this could have also happened to me. Then the following development can commence: two people, who have lost one another through betrayal, try to find each other again. And of the traitor we could say: he tries to *win back* the person whom he has betrayed, through reconciliation and rectification. They can try to find a new commonality in their lives. The condition for their reconciliation is understanding, and its limits are the limits of social imagination.

In Chapter 3 we imagined a Willy Loman who betrayed a friend to McCarthy's witch-hunters. The betrayal destroyed the man and his family. Let us assume that he did not take his life, but that he and Willy Loman meet again. What kind of dignity might there be? What kind of reconciliation? Loman did not do it in order to protect himself. Is there also another motive that his former friend could accept and use as the starting point for a reconciliation? If it was envy or jealousy, he will not even try it in the first place. Yet perhaps it is different when both discover that Loman sought revenge for a humiliation or another cruelty, the extent of which was unknown to the friend. What he wanted to establish through the betrayal was a balance of suffering – as is the case with every revenge, every retaliation. It is doubtful whether this can give rise to reconciliation. This is better, however, than if the motive was pure self-interest or even plain malice. In any case, the friend would need to see remorse: Loman's admission of an inexcusable transgression, paired with the grief for having lost himself as a person of moral integrity as a result of his deed. The friend would also have to be ready to do something that I have already mentioned a few times, but the nature of which is hard to understand – harder than the word's familiarity suggests: to *forgive*.

Nelson Mandela spent 27 years in jail as a political prisoner. When he was released, he reached out his hand in forgiveness to the people who had stolen half his life. He rejected the need to create equilibrium of suffering, not only in action but also in feeling. The dignity that lay in this will to reconciliation rested on the capacity for forgiveness. It was the willingness and strength to let past injustice rest. It seems that this was only possible because Mandela was concerned with something greater than personal conflict and suffering: the peaceful future of his country. This was so significant that even half a life spent in prison could appear small and unimportant. Perhaps this also applies to the act of forgiveness on a smaller scale: we leap over the shadow of a past injustice to create a future. We stop reckoning up in order to let the next stage of life be a success. It is a form of generosity that arises from something that we will discuss in the next chapter: dignity as a sense of proportion. To get over a betrayal, we need this step: to turn back to the other for the sake of a meaningful future. When we see this happen, we experience it as an expression of dignity.

Punishment: Development Instead of Destruction

Many forms of guilt are punished. Punishment means purposely inflicting harm on someone in response to harm that he has inflicted on someone else. In the case of private matters, we carry this out ourselves. When laws have been violated, punishment is enacted by representatives of the state. What is the motive behind it? And how does it affect the dignity of the punished and the punisher?

Someone who is guilty has broken a norm: she did something that she was not allowed to do. The breach of a norm cannot stay without a punishing response. It cannot simply be ignored – otherwise the norm would lose its force; it would be as if it did not exist. When the state punishes a breach of law, it defends the law for the sake of other citizens. This is one motive behind the punishment. It is, one could say, a *conceptual* motive, ensuing from the logic of normativity.

When someone consciously inflicts suffering on us, we feel outrage, anger and even hate. Such emotions require action: an equalization of suffering that helps to calm the anger. We call this revenge or retaliation. This is what victims expect from the law: putting the perpetrator behind bars and thus requiting suffering with suffering. When they call a mild verdict unjust, what they mean is: this is not enough suffering to offset our suffering. And also those who take private vengeance outside the law sometimes speak of justice: 'We choked Wilczek's son to death on the train to Auschwitz', Frister writes in his book. 'I say "we" even though I took no part in it. I watched the fingers wrap themselves around his throat. I was for them. It was natural justice. Not every criminal could be tried by an impartial court. Wilczek's son paid the price of his vileness.' This kind of emotion is a second motive for punishment.

Another motive is less concerned with the victim's perspective and has to do with the perpetrator's future. In this case, we consider punishment a form of forced education: we see it as the perpetrator's obligatory change towards greater control and responsibility, towards greater respect for the law and consideration for others. The main purpose of such coercion is not to make the perpetrator suffer, but to effectively exert influence over him. The only reason why we want him to feel hardship is to force him to develop the will to change.

This last motive does not endanger the perpetrator's dignity. It grants the punished the right to an open future. The rehabilitative process means hardship and compulsion, but it is guided by the intention to help him break free from his reckless past and open the possibility for him to see himself and behave in new ways. It also regards him as an end in itself. What counts is not how likely this approach is to succeed or fail. Cynicism is of no interest. What counts is that this motive of punishment preserves the possibility for encounter and thus the dignity of the punished.

Things are different when retaliation is the guiding motivation. Then the desire for compensation through suffering threatens to destroy the punished person's dignity. This is obvious with the death penalty. The terrified prisoners, deprived of a future, wait for their state-prescribed death. Any dignity, that would also include the dignity of an open future, has been taken away from them. In California, a murderer was executed after twenty years. He had renounced all violence, had written children's books on this subject and advocated the ability for profound human change. The governor knew this, and yet did not reprieve him. Such a loss of moral dignity makes one's blood boil.

The conflict between the motive of retaliation and the motive of education can be observed in any prison. Hundreds of little details challenge the prisoners' dignity every single day. Prisons are total institutions and as such a threat to dignity. Before their incarceration, the prisoner had a self-image, a repertoire of defence mechanisms, rights, a place in society. All of this disappears when the cell door closes behind him. It brings social death and sometimes also emotional death. He is now cut off from the outside world. Even visitors are frightened by the gates. Once they close behind the inmate, he enters a world of humiliation. During the admissions process, he becomes an object that is fed into the institution's administrative machine. In many prisons, he has to be naked during this procedure. There are no personal possessions. There is the loss of one's full name, disfiguration through a uniform haircut and prison uniforms with numbers, hostile stereotypes promoted by the staff. What hurts the most is that one no longer has autonomy, no more determination over one's own life. The time schedule is prescribed. Communication is controlled. The inmate learns nothing of decisions that affect his fortune. The work he is forced to do is worthless. The point of this is to break his will.

Philippe Claudel, the teacher who taught in the prison of Nancy for many years and whom we encountered in Chapter 3, writes: 'The prison is like a factory. A big factory that produced nothing but trimmed time, muted lives and restricted movement.' And he makes us recall what a hell prisons can be: 'Washing in front of others, defecating in front of others, living in front of others, sharing less than ten square metres with – often three or four – others. Sometimes living in a cell of fourteen, sharing only one sink with just cold water. Hearing the others' dreams, their nightmares, their farts, their cries, their hateful rants, enduring the others, letting them rape you.'

I have a meeting with the prison director. He shows me around, gives me time to see the cells and talk to the inmates. When I later sit down in his office to talk, two scenes haunt me. The first: I am in a cell with four men. One of the men sits at a table; the others lie on their beds. I sit with the man at the table – a dark-skinned giant. He draws with crayons. He does not look at me. He cannot find words. But I have the feeling that he is glad about my visit. All of a sudden he says: *On a trop de temps ici.* You have too much time here. *Ça ne va pas.* It is not okay. I try out two different readings of his phrase: 'It is unbearable' and 'You can't do this to a person'. *Ça ne va pas. Vous comprenez?* Do you understand? Yes, I say, I understand. Then he looks at me. I had never had to endure such a look. I would have liked to stay longer. At the same time, I had the urge to flee.

The other scene: I am in a single cell with a slender man. The cell is about five by three metres. There is a small passage between the bed and the desk. You have to move sideways to get through. We sit on the bed. I ask him how long he has been there and how much he has left. *Réclusion à perpétuité*. Life imprisonment. This is a horrible phrase. But *perpétuité* terrifies me even more: it sounds like eternity – eternity in hell. I ask him what he finds the worst about it. He silently leads me to the door. He takes my hand and puts it where the handle should be. I had never felt so distinctly that something was *not there*. When we sit on the bed again, I stare at the door and the missing handle – I cannot keep my eyes off it. I feel a pain as if I was having a heart attack. *Ça ne va pas*, I hear the other man say. I want to say goodbye. I do not find the words. All common words and phrases stay stuck in my throat. I touch his arm and leave. The door is open a crack. The guard is waiting impatiently outside. He locks up. The sound of the key haunts me.

I sit across from the director in his office. He is a man who does not lack openness and sensitivity, but who also easily becomes stiff and defensive when someone questions this place and the work he does. Rehabilitation and retribution: he knows of both purposes and glides back and forth between them.

'This is not okay', I say. This is, of course, the wrong opening. But I have to repeat the drawing giant's words, so as not to suffocate on them, to carry them out into the open.

'I don't understand', says the director.

'Locking them up, all this wasted time. It doesn't improve people, it destroys them.'

'This isn't a hotel. It's a prison.'

'I know. A penal colony.'

There is a twitch in the director's face. It is not a nervous twitch. He would like to get rid of me.

'They are already prisoners in here, who cannot lead a normal, independent life. Why the need to lock the doors as well? Why make them endure the shock of being locked up several times a day? The lack of door handles – what's the idea behind this? It doesn't contribute toward any change for the better, but rather the opposite: It fuels anger, hatred and frustration. What is it for? Simply to keep imposing the evil of being locked up on them, this experience of powerlessness, this humiliation? Just for this evil's sake? Simply to hurt them? Despite knowing that each sound of the keys adds to these people's annihilation? Pure revenge in other words and not on behalf of the victims, but on behalf of the state, administered by civil servants who will receive a good pension and sometimes still kill themselves?' 'This sounds as if we were inflicting evil for evil's sake. As if what we did was inherently *bad*. But this is not the case. We *punish* – this is different. And the people in here have caused great suffering, really great suffering – you shouldn't forget that!'

'I don't forget that. I understand the victims' need for retribution, and I understand that you and your people are exacting vengeance on their behalf. But punishment is *one* thing, annihilation *another*. There is a limit. The daily lock-up lies beyond this limit. It's an unnecessary captivity within the captivity, as they are already imprisoned in here anyway. This is pure torture. "It destroys you", one inmate told me.'

'What if this inmate had done something to your children, your wife or your parents? Would you still feel so repulsed by his daily humiliations? Or would it feel just to you – like a balance of suffering that is restored that way, since the victim's suffering can no longer be undone?'

'The daily humiliation of being locked up is not just *any* kind of suffering, no mere inconvenience, harassment or nuisance. This hundredfold, thousandfold humiliation destroys the soul. One suffocates when one does not see a single day in years without one's cell door being locked. Can you really want this? Isn't the only reason you do this your lack of imagination – because you can't see the true extent of this humiliation?'

'And what if your children...'

'No. I think that I'm in favour of punishment, also in the sense of restoring a balance. A life dominated by compulsion is all right – compulsion towards change or towards compensation for the victim. Lifelong, painful sacrifice for the victim's sake, a sacrifice that benefits the victim – that, I accept. But what I don't accept is humiliation that turns into emotional annihilation.'

'Let's assume that you meet the person who raped your daughter. The girl no longer talks, is stuck in her trauma, emotionally broken. Wouldn't you want to annihilate the person who did this to her?'

'Yes, I can imagine that – that could be *my* emotion. But that's not what this is about. This is not about the impulsive emotions of the victims and those who see their suffering. This is about reasoned, balanced punishment on behalf of the state. And the standard of this punishment should be moral dignity. This means making sure that the punishment does not destroy the inmate's dignity – first, for dignity's own sake and second, because without dignity, they can't develop a will for improvement. There are countries where the law specifically requires that human dignity has to be protected even in the penal system.'

'And what kind of dignity would that be? These are murderers, rapists and fraudsters who have ruined others' lives. Don't forget what they have *done* – what *suffering* they have caused, *irreversible* suffering.'

'I don't forget that. I also don't forget the rawness and brutality that I felt with some of the inmates I met earlier. But I am going to tell you what I understand as the dignity that I think also needs to be protected in their case. First of all, it means that, just like others, we encounter them as people who are not *determined* by individual actions from their past and cannot be completely defined by them. Leaving them their dignity means encountering them as humans who, even after their horrible deed, can face an open future, which contains the possibility for change, perhaps radically so.'

The director steps to the window and looks out in silence for a while. 'Sounds good', he eventually says. 'Sounds romantic. I can hear myself – twenty years ago – saying similar things. Do you know the reoffending statistics? A few days ago, we released someone who had been here for manslaughter. I watched him go out through the gate from this window. This morning I saw him again, going in the other direction. He had killed a person.'

'What matters is not how *likely* someone is to make *use* of his open future. This is not about a *prognosis*. This is about an *attitude* – *our* attitude. An inmate's dignity lies in the attitude with which we encounter him. This attitude must also find expression in the way we organize prisons. Earlier, one of the guards pointed at the cell doors, saying: "Murderer, child abuser, drug dealer, bank robber." It sounded like a final, complete and unalterable verdict – as if it said *everything* about the man behind that door. It sounded like the names of different *species of humans*. That is what I mean: A person is punished for a specific deed, and the prison is the punishment. He is now part of a total institution that regulates his entire life. This leads us to forget that he also has a life, an identity that cannot be reduced to this deed alone. *This reduction, we could say, constitutes annihilation.* Everything that happens to him is overshadowed by this deed. He has no opportunity to come into his own as a person outside this shadow, outside this guilt. If this is how the punishment is set up – so that there is this annihilation – it is punishment that deprives the inmate of his dignity. His dignity, in so far as it lies in our hands, consists in the recognition that he is more than the perpetrator of a crime – much more. The institution of punishment needs to develop means, forms of expression and rules that allow this recognition to be felt and experienced every single day, without simultaneously losing conscious sight of the punishment. The inmate has a *right* to this recognition.'

'They have a right to make complaints.'

'And? How does this help them?'

The director shrugs and gives a thin smile. 'The guys can keep personal objects in their cells and they're allowed to wear some of their own clothes.'

'Fine. But what would be important is *work* – so they don't have to serve such dead, empty time here. You can see the emptiness of the time in the emptiness of their looks. And I don't mean sticking together plastic bags – I mean *real* work, *valuable* work, that requires training so that they can *develop* their skills and develop a sense of their *worth*. For some of them, this will be the first time they have felt such worth in their lives. Earlier, I saw someone who always mops the same corridor. "That's what I'm here for", he said when I asked him about it. This is also what I meant when I said, "That's not okay." Even inmates, even those who are guilty, must have the chance to experience their time as properly lived, time in which they do something with themselves. They need to be given *perspective* in life.'

'Some of them refuse to work. They prefer to lie in their bunks and stare at the wall all day.'

'I bet this wouldn't be the case if there was work as I imagine it. There is also another dimension to this idea: I can see them making money with their work, real money – and paying most of it to the victims, as compensation. One could also say, as a way to work on their guilt; not in order to get rid of it, but to integrate it into their lives – to slowly win back their lost dignity. Perhaps this would occasionally also make new encounters possible with the victims – who knows?'

'*My God*, and how do you want to organize all that?'

'It would be possible – if only people wanted it. And just to continue spinning my pipe dreams, it would be even better if inmates didn't just work for themselves, but if it was work that allowed them to do something *together*.'

'There are no friendships in prison. One can have buddies perhaps, but no friends.'

'Exactly. Perhaps that would change, too.'

'All that's left now is for you to start talking about their right to therapy.'

I grin. 'Nobody is born a criminal. Every deed that ends a person up in here is also a derailment. It was a human deed, and human deeds always originate in complex emotional events. To work on one's guilt, instead of carrying it around like a rock, also for an inmate means finding out what actually happened with him. And yes, it's a question of our dignity to support him in it. The opposite would be the attitude of pure, raw revenge: Just let him suffocate on his inner chaos! I don't know how you feel in here, but when I walk past a prison, I often think: how little it takes to get off track; how lucky I am that it hasn't happened to me.'

'What would you say to those who shake their heads at your proposals and proclaim that we're already thinking too much about the *perpetrators*? Who's actually thinking about the *victims*?, they ask.'

'I say: When we talk about the perpetrators, we talk about the perpetrators; when we talk about the victims, we talk about the victims. There are very different things to say about them. And there are very different ways to care for them – practically and in terms of their dignity. It is nonsense *playing them off* against each other. It is nonsense of the crudest kind.'

'I don't even want to imagine the headlines if we made prisons into what you're proposing. What an outcry there was when inmates were allowed television. "The gentlemen want *entertainment*! All that's missing are prostitutes!" '

'I know. Those people *don't think*. They can't *imagine* what it's like to be in here, day by day, year by year. They don't think about the fact that you suffocate, waste away when you no longer have a connection to the outside world; that one must sometimes be able to laugh in one's cell. Many cruelties are committed from a lack of imagination. What's clogging the imagination is the blind wish for revenge, as with the cry for the death penalty. It's the state's duty to counter this blind, raw impulse and to defend moral dignity against the emotion-driven wish for punishment. This can only be achieved if society as a whole thinks like that: when dignity, even the dignity of offenders, is a social concern; when it is not an undignified society that only thinks in categories of revenge, punishment and locking people up.'

'You know of Jean-Claude Romand?', asks the director.

I nod.

'I was at the trial. It was unbearable.'

'Yes', I say.

'And still? Even him? Does this also apply to him?'

I nod.

'A romantic', he says, 'a true romantic. I haven't met someone like you in a long time.'

'I have also heard people describe my views as sentimental.'

'Does it bother you?'

'No. It says a lot about the people and nothing about the issue.' We sit together in silence for a while. I didn't mind his irony. There was an element of respect in it.

He stops on his way to the door. 'A bank robber recently sat where you are sitting right now – a hulk with a face like a wall. "You: big asshole with keys", he said. "You: small asshole – without keys", I said. Nothing happened for a while. Then he began to grin. Some time later I met him on the corridor. "How was your holiday, boss?", he asked.

'You see', I say.

We laughed about the story. I was glad about this laughter when I stood outside and looked over to that grey fortress. One of the small, barred windows was covered with a woollen blanket. This was the cell that Julien had been living in for seven years – if *living* is the right word here. He still had six years ahead of him. The blanket was always there. The director had eventually accepted it. When his cell was opened for exercise, Julien remained inside and continued drawing or reading. What he liked best were books about faraway countries. I went to the book shop around the corner and arranged for a pile of such books to be sent to him. The director assured me that the package would be delivered. Then I passed the fortress again. I thought about all the occasions when things could also have gone wrong for me.

Absolute Moral Boundaries?

We know from the earlier conversation about self-respect that Bernard Winter is a man with principles, someone for whom there must be certain rules that cannot be challenged under any circumstances. When he hears about the Aviation Security Act that wants to authorize the military to shoot down aircraft meant to be used as weapons against human life, fury rises up inside him.

'This is how I imagine it', he says to Sarah: 'someone comes up to me and says: "I'm afraid we'll have to kill you in order to save other people's lives."

'What gives you the insane idea to favour others' lives above mine? To sacrifice my life for others? Have you lost your mind? You can't *offset* humans against one another. This violates their dignity.'

'When the plane crashes into the sky-scraper, you are going to die anyway. Then *both* you *and* the people in the building will be dead. If we shoot you down, *only you* will die, the others will live. This is about minimizing the number of victims – choosing the lesser over the greater evil, reducing suffering. Isn't this an *imperative*? A *moral imperative?*'

'As I said before, one can't set humans off against one another; you can't kill them even if this makes the balance look better – the purely numerical balance. *Every individual* and her dignity matter. This is the only moral standard. You simply can't kill innocent human beings – for *no* reason.'

It was a good day for Bernard when the supreme court ruled that this paragraph of the Aviation Security Law was incompatible with the German constitution and therefore void; incompatible with the right to life in connection with the guarantee of human dignity. He triumphantly read to Sarah from the court statement: 'If the state used their killing as a means to save the lives of others', the passengers 'would be used as mere means, disrespecting their worth as human beings in their own right.' It would be 'utterly unimaginable to intentionally kill innocent human beings in such a desperate situation, on the basis of legal authorization...Even the seeming inevitability of their deaths does not in the given situation stop the killing of innocent people from being a violation of their right to dignity. Human life and human dignity enjoy equal constitutional protection independent of the duration of the individual person's physical existence.'

'Utterly *unimaginable*', Winter repeated. 'The court thinks like me: There are things that are not morally permitted *under any circumstances*; that can't be relativized to any situation; they are *absolute*. They are the condition for human dignity. This dignity – it's the last thing that is sacred in our secular society.'

Sarah looked at him. He normally never said such things.

'What I mean by *sacred* is: something that can't be *infringed* under any circumstances – come what may.'

'Imagine you're on board that plane. You hear the terrorists announce the attack on the building and see the plane head for it. You're *certain* that it will happen. Couldn't you imagine saying: "Okay, go ahead and shoot us down!"'

'I can imagine saying: "*As far as I'm concerned*: go ahead and shoot! Save the people in the building." This would be like throwing myself into a bullet's range to save someone. But I can only declare this *for myself* – I can't declare it for others, decide it over their heads. When I declare it for myself, it's an autonomous decision and an expression of my dignity. If I declared it for everyone, without their individual consent, it would be a terribly paternalistic act that would violate their dignity. It's a simple matter: when someone believes that he has to do something that so blatantly infringes on our interests and even on our lives, he has to step in front of us, explain it to us and then respect our decision whatever it may be.'

'And what if there is no opportunity or time to ask? Is it enough if he can justify the planned action to us *in his mind* ? And if beyond, he has very good reasons to assume that we *would* all agree – simply because the issue is so *obvious*? Imagine that all the other passengers are aware of the exact nature of the situation just as you are and imagine that their minds are not clouded by fear. Wouldn't you be fairly certain that they would also react like you? Otherwise you'd have to ascribe a rather insane attitude to them, namely: "My last minutes are more important to me than the lives of hundreds of other people." And don't you think that this is precisely what those who intend to shoot down the plane would base their decision on? If all of this is correct, couldn't you imagine *after all* that you might want to allow them to shoot? Is dignity really in danger here?'

'It's *always* in danger when we take from someone the most important thing he has: authority over his life. No matter what you say, this authority is taken away from the passengers when they aren't consulted. This remains the case when we assume that they would all think like me. This is not because we cannot be completely *certain* that they would think that way, but because through the silent decision to shoot down the plane, we would deprive them of the possibility of *exercising* their authority, even for the last few minutes of their lives. Besides, I wouldn't find it *that* absurd if someone did *not* think as we assumed. "I don't want to be *used* for someone else's protection", she might say. "I simply don't want to be *used*, not even for this." '

'But she isn't simply being used as a human shield.'

' "What I also don't want", she might say, "is to be *eliminated* for someone else's protection." '

'This is not about eliminating *her*, but the *plane*.'

'Pretty subtle, but nice try. She could say: "I don't want them to *accept* my death in order to eliminate the plane. I simply don't want my life to be the subject of reflections on *usefulness*.'

'At first inspection, this appears to be right and understandable. Especially because "usefulness" here has a disparaging, shabby, almost inhumane sound to it. But isn't this too simple, too black and white? Remember: Those who are in favour of shooting down the plane believe that their thinking is *morally* right. It's not just calculation. They consider it *obvious* that the plane must be stopped from crashing into the tower. "Let's assume", they will say, "that we don't shoot it down. In addition to the dead passengers, there would be all the victims in the building. The tower can topple, take down other buildings with it – there would be hundreds of dead in the street, fire and inferno. Are you trying to make us believe that it would be *right* to simply let this happen? That it would be *morally* right? Just to allow the passengers in the aircraft, who are about to die anyway, to live for a few more minutes? Excuse me, but this is *preposterous!*"'

'This is not about living for few more minutes. It is about a violation of dignity. That was the court's argument.'

'Imagine the plane is heading for a nuclear power station. We know that it would destroy it. There's no need to describe the consequences to you: Tens of thousands dead, hundreds of thousands in the long term. A large area would be rendered uninhabitable. Do we really want to say that the passengers' dignity is more significant than the avoidance of this immeasurable damage and the immeasurable *suffering* that would follow from it? After all, morality isn't just about the protection of dignity, but also about the avoidance of suffering. Moral action is also concerned with minimizing suffering. And shooting down the plane *does* without question minimize suffering, compared to the situation after the disaster.'

'Dignity cannot be *offset* against the common good. Not even against suffering. It is *non-negotiable* – inviolable, as the constitution says. This was the court's argument, too. It referred to the first clause of the constitution. The state cannot *manage* human dignity by looking at situations like that created by the terrorists and deciding: "Normally, dignity stands above everything. But not *here*." The end of averting suffering, great suffering, will justify many means – but not *that*.'

'*Offsetting, negotiating, managing*: these are clever expressions, but also tendentious ones. They make one think of business, shiftiness and morally dubious bureaucrats – this is the constantly present background track, damped, barely audible, but still impactful. It provokes the stubborn, insistent reaction: "All comparisons end *here*, with dignity. No questioning is allowed. Its protection is *absolutely* valid. There *must* be this one sacred thing, as you referred to it. This is what the horrors of history have shown us, especially of our history." But isn't this also a rhetorical trick? Is it not a discreet defamation of those who won't allow the towers to crash at any price? For whom the avoidance of suffering stands above everything? It's a deeply *moral* end that justifies the means here after all, they will say. This is not about offsetting something, this is about *sacrificing*: The dignity of some is sacrificed for the common good. This cannot happen in just any situation, it cannot be the rule and become routine. But there are situations in which it is conceivable that this sacrifice must be made – in order to avert terrible suffering. Those who are under no circumstances prepared to sacrifice dignity turn this sanctity into a *fetish*. Imagine a person looking up at the hijacked aircraft and saying, "I see disaster coming, but my hands are tied. You know, it's because I'm committed to the passengers' dignity in the last minutes of their lives." '

'Of course we must not vilify those for whom the common good and the aversion of suffering stand above dignity. In terms of their morality, they are not any less earnest than the others and should be taken just as seriously. I think the others should simply say, "We *prefer* to live in a society where dignity can never be trumped. This is how we want to *live*."'

'And when the price is predictable and inescapable suffering?'

'Then – well, then that's the price: The price for the sanctity of dignity.'

'And what if the suffering affects *you*?'

'That's the price for a culture of dignity.'

'We can also use a less far-fetched example than a plane that must be shot down. The same question also arises with a more likely scenario: when torture would help save others. "Persons in custody may not be subjected to mental or physical mistreatment", says the law. This is why statements extorted under the threat of torture cannot be used in court and why such extortion is a crime, a violation of one's official responsibilities. Again, the principle is the protection of dignity, which the law treats as absolute. But imagine our child is kidnapped. The kidnapper is captured, and there is no doubt that he is the kidnapper. Normal means won't force him to reveal the child's location – our child's. The will behind his refusal can't be broken. Wouldn't your impulse also be: His will must be broken and if it's only possible with torture, so be it? There have always been and always will be police inspectors who think: "To hell with the law! I don't want to hear a word about this monster's dignity: *I have to save the child!*"'

'I'm pretty sure I'd also have this impulse and could imagine yelling at the police inspector: "What are you waiting for? Save my child – whatever the cost!"'

'But?'

'Nevertheless I would prefer to live in a society where this is prohibited. Not just so I can be certain that I will never be tortured, unlike in the United States. No, also for a deeper reason: Torture is the destruction of dignity and often also entails a person's emotional destruction – like in Guantánamo. I don't want to be a member of a community where this is possible. I simply don't *want* it.'

'And what about our child? His fear, his despair?'

'What I'm going to say now is somewhat risky and it might irreversibly alter something between us: Also for our child's sake, I don't want to depart from the absolute protection of dignity.'

'He's a ruthless, brutal criminal! And this is about our child, who suffers because of him!'

'Still.'

'*Still?*'

'Yes. And now we'll have to be honest and specific. You would expect *others*, the police inspectors, to perform the torture. You wouldn't expect to have to watch this cruelty. Yet if your reasons are so *urgent*, they should also be reasons for you to take the torture instruments into *your own* hands. Do you want that? Do you want to be like O'Brien, who makes Winston betray Julia? Of course your *motives* would be completely different from his, but the *mechanism of cruelty* would be the same: You have to *break* the man to get him to talk. You have to let his pain and fear become so immense that even he gives up his resistance. Do you *want* that? Are you *prepared* for this cruelty? You took *Nineteen Eighty-Four* to the rubbish bin all those years ago. I should burn it, you said, so that these ideas cease to exist. We mustn't allow them to exist.'

'I myself am somewhat surprised by what I'm about to say and perhaps this will change something between us, too: Yes, I think I'd do it. For our child. For *any* child in fear and despair. This has nothing to do with Orwell. The motive is *completely* different, and this also changes the *nature* of the cruelty. Of course it's still cruel to torture someone, I won't deny it. But this cruelty isn't the same as O'Brien's cruelty, which serves to enforce ideological submission. Rather, it is cruelty in self-defence: like when I choke an attacker who is on top of me. One could also say that it is self-defence by proxy – I'm acting on the child's behalf.'

'I see an attitude looming here that is dangerous and that I reject: "Dignity is a fine, noble thing that, in principle, we should respect. But when push comes to shove, it has to stand back – when we have to rescue a frightened child, for instance. *Sorry*, but the prohibition of torture and dignity are not *that* important after all." I will also tell you why I'm repulsed and appalled by this, and I am not afraid to repeat myself: Human dignity – this is the highest good, the last thing that is sacred. That's why we mustn't move away from the principles that protect this good – not even to prevent a suffering that we have not caused, but that others are responsible for.'

'Then instead of the kidnapped child, imagine terrorists who are about to commit an attack. Their bomb will blow up a nuclear power station. The police catch one of the terrorists. The bomb is ticking.

They scream at him, threaten him. He isn't intimidated. The officers who are questioning him slap him, knock out his teeth. *"Where's the bomb?"* – Nothing. The bomb is ticking. They make him stand on a chair and put a noose around his neck. "Speak, you dirty bastard, or I'll knock away the chair!", one officer hisses. The others stare at him in shock. "Prohibition of torture, dignity – they can kiss my ass!", he yells. "Half the country will be contaminated! *Half the country!*" He lifts his leg towards the chair. The terrorist talks. The bomb is deactivated.

The officer is tried for violating the prohibition of torture and failing to respect human dignity. He says his closing words in court: "There is something I want to tell the distinguished gentlemen in the judges' robes", he begins. "If we hadn't tortured this terrorist, threatened him with death, none of you would be here right now. You would be dead or contaminated by radiation. You owe your life and health to me and the fact that I got my hands dirty. You will sentence me – in some way. But I don't give a damn about it. I'm telling you: What I did was *right*. Those who would refuse to do what I did in the situation, refuse out of *cowardice*: because they don't want to get their hands dirty. Or because of their moral vanity, their smugness: 'Look at me, even now I respect human dignity. I won't let anyone destroy my culture of dignity! Even when it ruins half the country...' I'm telling you, such a person is a *dignity fetishist* – someone who has lost all sense of proportion. And you, browbeating me with pronouncements about dignity, do you know what you are: ludicrous *dignity bureaucrats*, who would even insist on their laws in a situation that is so exceptional and dangerous that existing legal rules are *obviously* not adequate to it. I will also tell you: The person who would have refused to get his fingers dirty in my position, would have *failed* and been *guilty* – guilty towards the victims. He would have lost his moral integrity. And now I will turn the tables on you: *He would have lost his dignity* – because he failed to show courage, a sense of proportion, autonomy in thought and action and respect for thousands of people who would be dead or contaminated with radiation. *This* is the truth about human dignity here. And now: Please sentence me! Sentence me because I met the standards of my own dignity!"

And? What would you say to him? Would you still say: No matter how great the suffering, this is the price for a culture that keeps dignity sacred? Even when this culture's physical foundation is annihilated in the process?'

'I'm confused. It is hard to discount the officer's arguments. And not just the arguments: It's also hard to discount his emotions. These are strong moral feelings, and no one will be able to shut himself off from them completely, even if he only admits it in secret. If this is how things stood, we would be glad, *very* glad, for him to reach for the noose. We would be *grateful* to him. It would be silly and insincere to deny it. And you know what? I don't *want* to deny it either. But I'm confused: because at the same time, I believe that *I* am still right. Dignity that is *negotiable* and can be *put at someone's disposal* – That's no longer real dignity. "Human dignity is inviolable, except when it is violable" – what kind of dignity would that be? This culture would be completely different from the culture that is outlined in our constitution. I wouldn't want to live in it. But I will never forget the officer's speech either. As I said, I'm confused. There must be a coherent attitude to this issue after all, that does not deny or distort anything, in either direction. It just can't be that we remain without a coherent attitude to this question, which is in a way the most important question of all. Or am I wrong? Is there an irresolvable conflict here between different verdicts and sentiments that are equally justifiable? I don't know what to say any more.'

'This looks like a conflict between two cultures: One is primarily concerned with the common good and the avoidance of suffering, while the other is mainly about the protection of individual dignity. Both claim to be guardians of moral integrity. For the first, moral integrity consists in not letting avoidable suffering happen, for the second in not letting dignity be compromised under any circumstances. And as the officer's words show, the two perspectives not only interpret the dignity of *others* differently, but also one's *own* – the perpetrator's dignity. From your perspective, this dignity lies in protecting the dignity of others even in the face of imminent suffering – not shooting down the plane or torturing the kidnapper or terrorist; bravely bracing oneself against the flood of suffering and perhaps risking being attacked and morally condemned for it. For the officer, by contrast, dignity lies in not allowing a tidal wave of suffering to run over the common dignity of others, that he would usually also hold in high esteem. This indeed looks like an irresolvable conflict between two different moral perspectives.

Yet perhaps we have been thinking in too simple terms so far. Perhaps it is wrong and even absurd to look for a *rank order* between dignity and suffering. We should remind ourselves where the idea and the need for dignity *come* from. They haven't been decreed by divine authority – even if that's what some people try to make us believe. They haven't been decreed *at all*. We have invented the idea and developed the need for dignity in order to *cope* better with life and its threats and challenges: in order to have a standard, a guideline that helps us avoid a certain kind of misfortune. This misfortune would be what we call the loss of dignity. But it of course already existed before the invention of this idea. This invention – and we mustn't forget that that's what it is – was created for what we can call the *ordinary course of events*: for all the circumstances and situations in life that everyone is familiar with and from which no one is spared. These are not just easy and harmless things, but also experiences of loss, loneliness, sickness and death. No matter how powerful these experiences might be, they do not go beyond the regular scope of human life, but simply define the *condition humaine*.

Yet sometimes the world is entirely out of joint – through war, terrorism or natural disasters, for instance. Then the familiar standard of dignity and the limits it draws for our actions might indeed no longer be – how shall I put it – *suitable*. They no longer seem *appropriate*. Those who have this experience will neither *forget* the standard nor *ignore* it. In the case of these emergency actions, they will effectively consider this standard *interrupted*, momentarily *suspended* – like the officer did. The emergency experience that motivated his action was a deeply *moral* emergency: the unconditional desire to prevent suffering. From this perspective, the prohibition he faced seemed like a fetish that erected a barrier in front of the morally obvious. The appeal to dignity that would usually – also for him – be an *expression* of moral integrity, in his view now led to a *loss* of this integrity: Those who did not want to get their hands dirty when dealing with the terrorist became guilty. Afterwards, once the bomb has been deactivated and the menacing abyss of horror recedes, the strict guidelines of dignity become effective again. And they will be as strict as before. Perhaps this is how we can reach a coherent perspective on this?'

Sarah's train of thought must be distinguished from the view that we encountered with Sophie who licks Höss's boots and with Roman Frister who approves when his tormenter is choked to death: that the world is so out of joint that we can neither speak of any moral imperatives any longer, nor of dignity. The suspension of the protection of dignity that Sarah talks about is something completely different: It is a violation of dignity for deeply moral reasons. We therefore stay *within* the framework of moral judgement. Sophie and Frister, by contrast, speak of a desert-like landscape in which such a framework is no longer discernible even in outline.

'The question would then be', says Bernard Winter, 'when is a disaster serious enough to justify the temporary suspension of a strict protection of human dignity – to either avert devastating suffering or to protect one's own moral dignity? Or put differently: How great must the moral despair be for the person to jump over this barrier? Is one kidnapped child enough? Or do we need many victims, like with the plane and the nuclear power station? And, who decides?'

'*We* decide, the members of a society. Who else? Of course, not every single one of us can be consulted and vote on it beforehand. Our voice will usually only be heard in retrospect. But public judgements will be formed that will exert influence and later serve as a reference point. Besides, there will be the legal precedent. And when I say, *We*, I don't mean the We of common pub talk, but the We of wide public discussion, in which the most thoughtful and intelligent people engage with every actual and imaginary violation of dignity. The limits of violations of dignity out of moral need – they must be drawn as narrowly as possible.'

'And what about the strict laws of the constitution? They don't know *any* exceptions. The first sentence of the constitution is moreover protected by the eternity clause: It cannot be altered or abolished by any legislator.'

'And this is how it should be. Such a clause defines an entire outlook, or even a worldview. It is a reaction to the rule of terror and a lack of dignity. It would be absurd to list exceptions to such a clause. But the world can temporarily get out of joint to such an extent that it's not too hard to imagine the clause no longer being helpful in its programmatic strictness. It would then be up to us to reflect autonomously on what moral integrity demands in this situation.'

7

Dignity as a Sense of What Matters

It is a fact of human life that certain things mean more to us than others. These are the things that are *important* to us. This sense of what matters is also a dimension of human dignity, as it helps us discern *meaning* in our lives. By taking care of the things that are important to us we develop a sense of who we are and what we live for. At the same time, this establishes broader standards for what is important: we learn to distinguish between the things that we should take seriously and the things that are only of fleeting, superficial importance. We develop a sense of proportion. This is also something in which human dignity can express itself. Yet these experiences are not all of a piece. When examined closely, they can seem confusing. What elements do they contain, and how are they interconnected?

Meaning of Life

What can it mean to see a meaning in one's life? This idea is easy to grasp with individual actions: their meaning lies in their contribution towards a goal. Browsing dictionaries has a meaning when someone wants to learn a language. Practising has a meaning when someone wants to win a competition. The steps in an apprenticeship gain their meaning in light of a career goal. We pursue goals, and our actions have a meaning because we know those goals.

What about the goals themselves? Reaching a goal can be a step towards still further goals. One can learn languages in order to become an interpreter. One can become an engineer to build a dam or a doctor to fight suffering. We reach a point where we cannot name a further goal. Then we say: this simply is *important* to me. When someone asks me *why* this is important to me, I answer: because my life is the way it is and because I am the person I am.

Is that not enough? Why can it seem as if beyond that, there is another, deeper question about the meaning of life? It has to do with a change of perspective. We can extend our view beyond individual actions and chapters in our life and contemplate life *as a whole*. This gives rise to the question: What actually is the meaning of *all this*? We then no longer view life from the perspective of the person living it, but from the outside and ask: What is the *objective* meaning of this language lover's or devoted doctor's life?

It belongs to the logic of this question that the answer cannot allude to set goals, inner satisfaction or subjective importance. This question seems unavoidable, and yet we do not see a possible answer to it anywhere. This makes it confusing. One way out of the confusion could be to show that, despite initial appearances to the contrary, the question has no real intellectual content. So it is not surprising – and does not actually matter – that we cannot find an answer to it.

Is it possible for the objective meaning of a life to lie in a goal that is extrinsic to that life? Let us assume that we do not know what this goal is but are just told that it exists. This would be pointless because it would lead us to believe that our life has meaning without having the slightest idea what it is. The experience would be indistinguishable from being in a situation where life lacks any objective meaning. Let us by contrast assume that we know what this meaning is. One possibility is that it is unrelated to the life goals that we are familiar with from our inner perspective on our life. Would we then even comprehend it? What could it mean for our life to have a meaning by virtue of being an episode on the way to a greater, yet completely foreign, purpose? The other possibility is that this goal is related to the goals that are known to us. Then it helps give our life meaning, but not because it is an external, objective goal, but because we can internally consider it as a goal for us.

The idea of an objective meaning in life might not therefore withstand scrutiny: it could turn out to be incoherent and thus not a real idea, but merely a rhetorical device without any intellectual content. Then we would end up where we started: with the goals of individual actions and the importance inherent in day-to-day life. We would have to conclude that meaning is something that we *invent* ourselves, rather than something that we *discover*. This is supported by the observation that we are not usually interested in exploring our life's meaning as long as we live safely amidst projects that we identify with. In this situation, raising questions about the meaning of life usually appears forced and sombre. The question only acquires urgency when a project fails or comes to an end. Yet then it is pointless to search for a greater, overarching meaning that is not rooted in our experiences. All that helps is finding new things that matter to us. And here dignity also requires autonomy: the ability to determine for ourselves what we consider important and essential to our lives.

One's Own Voice

In his play, *A Doll's House*, Henrik Ibsen describes a woman's journey towards finding her own voice. Nora Helmer's husband Torvald treats her like a sweet doll, showering her with cutesy pet names. He never takes her seriously as an autonomous person and there has never been a true encounter between them. This is what her life has always been like. 'When I lived at home with Daddy, he fed me all his opinions, until they became my opinions. He used to call me his doll-child and he played with me the way I used to play with my dolls. And then Daddy handed me over to you. You arranged everything according to your taste and I adapted my taste to yours. Now, looking back, I feel as if I've lived a beggar's life – from hand to mouth. Our house has never been anything but a playroom. I've been your doll-wife, just as I was Daddy's doll-child when I was at home. My children as well, they've been my dolls. I used to enjoy it when you played games with me, just as they enjoyed it when I played games with them. That's all our marriage has been, Torvald.'

There was one moment in their eight-year marriage that was different – when Nora did something that she decided completely by herself. Torvald fell seriously ill and the doctor recommended a sojourn in the south. To Nora, this felt like the most important thing that had ever happened between them, and the sense of this importance temporarily liberated her from the doll's house. She told her husband that she could get the money for the trip from her father. In fact, she borrowed it from a corrupt attorney. He requested a promissory note with her father's signature. Nora did something that she was single-handedly responsible for: she forged the signature. Her step into her own life started with a violation of the law. It was her first desperate attempt to speak with her own voice. Yet instead of liberating her, it made her susceptible to blackmail. It also could not change anything between her and Torvald because it happened in secret. Nevertheless, this first step towards liberation released an energy that led, years later, to an explosion. The attorney, disappointed because of a failed extortion attempt, reveals Nora's erstwhile transgression. Torvald's self-righteous reaction shows to Nora that he has not understood anything about her motives and her move towards autonomy and that he is generally a man who would never hear her own voice.

'Sit down', she tells him. 'This is going to take some time. I have a lot of things to say to you. This is a reckoning, Torvald.' She proceeds to recount her enslavement to him, an enslavement that consisted in him never giving her an opportunity for an encounter, in which she could have made herself heard with her own voice. 'We've been married now for eight years. Don't you think it's significant that this is the first time you and I have sat down to have a serious talk?' 'What do you mean, serious?', Torvald asks and those five words perfectly express his inability to grasp her need for autonomy. Nora declares that she will leave him and the children that same evening. 'This is outrageous. It's going back on your most sacred duties', Torvald exclaims. 'I have other duties which are as just as sacred. My duties to myself', Nora responds. 'I know most people would say you were right, Torvald, and I know you'd be backed by all sorts of books. But what most people say and what you find in books just doesn't satisfy me any more. I want to think everything out for myself and make my own decisions.' 'I suppose you do have some sort of moral code? Or perhaps you don't?' 'Well, Torvald, it's not a very easy question to answer. I really don't know. I find it all quite bewildering.'

The bewilderment Nora speaks of is an expression of her dignity: of her need to take charge of her life herself. What does the journey that she has ahead of her look like?

It will partly be a journey towards inner autonomy, as I described in Chapter 1. 'Experience is something I have to find', Nora says, 'I have to educate myself.' This will mean using her own ideas for guidance and forming her own opinion on the things that matter. 'I want to see whether the things Pastor Hansen told me are true, or at any rate whether they are true for me.' Such independent thinking will enable her to shape her wishes and actions with greater clarity and decisiveness in the future. She will become a woman with a free will. Her authority in handling her emotions will also grow. She will learn to examine her old self-image critically, the inner institution that decides which aspects of life may or may not be lived. She will realize how much of this image goes back to internalized authorities, and she will start opposing these external authorities with her own. This will open up new experiences and possibilities for her. All of this will involve a process of self-recognition and of appropriation. Nora will remember her old life as her father's doll: all the cute little skirts, habits, proscriptions, feelings and words that he invested her with and the extent to which she believed that she had to please him. In part, she will still feel this estrangement inside her. In part, she will recognize it when she reflects on how she used to behave. And after leaving Torvald's home, she will start to recall the estrangement in her marriage: episode by episode, prohibition by prohibition, saying by saying, emotional cliché by emotional cliché. Her statement 'this is a reckoning, Torvald' also applies here. Her task will be to discover, both through emotional exploration and through experimenting with deeds, what she thinks and feels once all instilments have ceased. And then, she will have to embrace these ideas, experiences and activities in a clear and persistent manner: appropriate them and internally put them together into a coherent emotional identity.

Nora will search for what she was robbed of by those who treated her like a doll: *authenticity*. This is a word that is easy to utter. But what actually is it: to be authentic? What determines the authenticity of an idea, experience or action? What is its opposite?

A person can betray his authenticity by being *fake*. What he says and does is motivated by a goal. It is just the means to an end: such as pleasing a future employer, a teacher or a woman he is attracted to. He shows an artificial, functional façade that collapses as soon as he is alone with himself and feels the alienation that all of this entails. This alienation turns wicked when he no longer consciously feels it as such: when the act of deception has seeped so far inside that he no longer recognizes it; when he really believes that he thinks and feels what he says. This could, for example, happen to a speechwriter who provides templates for a politician. She learns how the man thinks, feels and talks, and she supplies his sentences. With time they also become her sentences: they slip out of her mouth during meals, on holiday, in bed.

This is not the case with Nora. A doll-child who imitated her father's views and her husband's tastes did not pursue any conscious goal. She soaked things up without realizing it – by osmosis. We therefore cannot say that Nora's lack of authenticity was based on deception: she did not even have it in her to decide to be fake. Her life's falsity was due to the fact that, from the beginning, it never moved under its own steam. It was a life in which she constantly heard silly sentences like this: 'Nearly all young criminals have had dishonest mothers.' And clichés like this: 'Exceptionally lovely, isn't she? Everyone at the party thought so. She's a dear little thing, but she's so terribly stubborn.' It was a life in which Nora also suffocated herself by saying sentences such as: 'Your taste is better than anyone's.'

When someone attempts to shake off an agonizing falsity and to find his own voice, it can release the force and have the severity of an outburst. On seeing this person let through an anger, desire, longing or fear that we never suspected with him, we might think: he is completely genuine now, completely himself. The speechwriter might burn everything one day and start composing pamphlets against those whom she formerly served as a mouthpiece. Nora, a sweet child and adoring wife, gets up and leaves, regardless of conventional morality. But the pure force of a revolt is not necessarily a sign of authenticity. Such an act can also be copied, adopted from a film or novel, for example. Milder spontaneity does not automatically allow us to recognize authenticity either. Alienated reactions and patters of pretence can occur as quickly as lightning.

Authenticity therefore has less to do with causal force than with a person's inner coherence. Someone's political convictions seem authentic when they fit her life-style. We are suspicious when they appear like a foreign body. We judge the genuineness of emotions similarly: can someone's grief be real after all the anger? How does someone's admiration sit with the many disparaging remarks he has made in the past? We sometimes say: being authentic means showing yourself as you really are. Yet the simplicity of this formula is deceiving, as there is no such thing as a smooth, seamless inner world that simply needs to be turned to the outside. Our experiences, thoughts and desires are always full of ambiguity and ambivalence. We are often not sure what actually belongs to us. We live many different lives, depending on whom we live them with.

The question of authenticity can seem even more complicated when we examine the role of self-images. A self-image, for example a Christian faith, can induce and even enforce certain ideas, emotions and actions. As far as they match this self-image, these ideas, emotions and acts appear genuine. Whatever deviates from this self-image seems alien and false. To assure myself of the authenticity of this self-image, I join a monastery. But then I lose my faith. This can either happen in the course of a creeping process of erosion, or through a sudden, wild rebellion at the sight of suffering in the world. I reject my previous self-image, feeling that it obstructed my way to a life that could have been much more genuine, much closer to my actual feelings. The doors of the monastery shut behind me. I step out onto the hot, dusty street of life. What makes this rebelliousness seem genuine and the self-image a source of falsity? What is now the standard of authenticity?

The road that Nora has ahead of her will lead her towards emotional experiences that are just as confusing. 'Experience is something I have to find', she says. These will be experiences that show her a world beyond her bourgeois family home and her husband's bank, the world beyond fancy-dress balls. Yet what will be important on this journey towards her own voice are not just the impressions from this new world. Above all, it will be crucial that she learns to understand her emotional responses to them; that she allows them to be what they are, without paying any attention to the habits, clichés and platitudes that used to rob her of having real experiences. She will claim for herself the emotional right to leave behind her children and will increasingly notice how Pastor Hansen's voice loses its power. For the first time in her life, she will try out self-images that no one else invented for her. She will get lost and confused. Like everyone else, she will from time to time become uncertain whether she is actually being genuine in what she does and feels; whether she has really found what is important to her. Yet by exploring it, she fulfils the obligations towards herself that she was talking about. These obligations express her dignity.

Equanimity as a Sense of Proportion

An insignificant trifle can turn into a tragedy. This is what Gottfried Keller's story *A Village Romeo and Juliet* is about. Two farmers, Manz and Marti, each own a field. Their plots are separated by a strip of vacant waste. For a long time, they both respect the border to the vacant land. Yet one day, they start ploughing furrows into the ownerless plot. Marti goes further than Manz: he drives across the field and cuts off a triangle for himself. Some time later, the land is auctioned off and Manz wins it. 'I noticed the other day', he says to Marti, 'that at the bottom of the field that now belongs to me, you had driven your plough from the side and cut off quite a fair-sided triangular piece. You probably thought that the whole field would soon become yours in any case. But as it now belongs to me, you will realize that I cannot have a crooked edge like that in it, so you can hardly object if I straighten it again. We shan't quarrel over that.' 'I see no cause for quarrel either', Marti replies. 'As far as I am concerned, you have bought the field as it stands now. We all inspected it an hour ago, and since then it hasn't changed in the slightest.'

This is how the drama takes its course. Manz draws a straight line to demarcate the border, incorporating the contested corner into his part and dumps rocks that he has removed from the fallow land in the area that Marti has already ploughed. Marti is furious and calls the mayor to have him confiscate the contentious little piece of land. 'From this moment onwards', writes Keller, 'the two men were locked in continuous legal battle, and did not rest until they had brought about their utter ruin and destruction.' Both men fall into poverty and despair, and their children, who are in love with each other, commit suicide because their parents' battle means that they could never be together.

The two farmers have, as one would say, lost all *sense of proportion*: they jeopardize their entire existence just to be proven right about a trifling piece of land. Keller finds wonderful words for what happens to them: 'Wise and reasonable as they normally were, Manz and Marti were now incapable of seeing beyond their own noses. The most petty legalistic thoughts filled their minds, and neither had the ability or the desire to understand how the other could behave in such a palpably unjust manner and wilfully appropriate this miserable bit of land to himself. Each thus felt his honour peculiarly offended and gave himself up passionately to the quarrel and to the resulting moral corruption.' Manz and Marti have lost their ability to distinguish between what is important and what is not. When we read about them ruining their lives because of a trifle, at first we just find it strange and pathetic. Yet more and more, we also get the feeling that they have lost their balance in life in such a way that it also entails a loss of dignity.

This is an experience that nobody is entirely unfamiliar with. It is easy to get caught up in hostilities with a neighbour because of a mere trifle. It starts innocently – both sides forego a necessary gesture of courtesy – and then there is no turning back. All of a sudden, one's entire existence seems to be at stake. This not only happens with conflicts. People who, for example, get stuck at an airport overnight because of a strike sometimes work themselves into such a rage that it is not merely ridiculous, but also affects their dignity; or someone loses his temper because an expensive watch broke; or someone lies awake at night because of a scratch on his car. In all these cases, a trivial matter unsettles us to a degree that it should not. In retrospect, we always say: 'I completely lost my sense of proportion.' We feel embarrassed about it because it jeopardizes our dignity in the sense of self-respect.

Yet things might be more complicated than this idea of the loss of proportion suggests. It does not have to be the case that we simply *forget* what matters and mistake the unimportant for the important. We may also cling to an insignificant detail because, without realizing it, it *represents* something that actually is important. We could claim that what is actually at stake for Manz and Marti in their fight over a little piece of land is justice, self-assertion and mutual respect. The passenger's rage at the airport might actually be triggered by painful experiences of insecurity haunting her from her past. And who knows – maybe a relationship broke together with the expensive watch. Unless these things secretly stood for something more important, they would not upset us to such an extent. To avert the threat to dignity in such situations, one needs to recognize the importance behind the trifle and let go of the trifle itself. 'Fine', Manz could say to Marti, 'keep that stupid corner. But don't you dare think that you duped me.' The person looking at the broken watch could say: 'Oh well, this makes sense. But the watch was certainly not what caused it.' This is how the loss of proportion can be revoked and the threat to our dignity, caused by obsessing over a substitutional fetish, averted.

The need to preserve a sense of proportion is, however, not limited to what is important in our *own* life. It can also be about not losing sight of the *whole* – of all the other things that are happening in the world. While obsessing over a minor argument or worrying about a small scratch on one's car, we turn on the news programme and see floods, wars and poverty. We might be overcome by a feeling of shame, thinking, 'How can we take our petty problems so seriously!' This is not a moral perception – our pettiness is not to blame for the suffering we see. The feeling of shame also does not necessarily have anything to do with the looks of others. We can feel ashamed while we are completely alone. After such an experience, it feels different to open a well-stocked fridge. But *how* is it different?

There was a photograph on my desk at the university that showed the head of an African man in agony, tears rolling down his bruised face. The image brought to mind all the things that can cause human suffering: heat and dust, injury and pain, loss and disappointment, grief and death. It made one reflect on what it must be like to get through the day hungry, surrounded by heat and dirt; what it means when the climate, poverty and sickness reduce one to the body, and one does not have the chance to read a book, listen to a concert or talk to interesting people; how infinitely difficult it must be to lead a dignified life under such circumstances. Whenever I looked at the photograph, I thought: one would need to reinvent language to find words that can properly express such suffering.

The aim of the picture was to ensure that I did not lose my sense of proportion in the petty excitement of everyday struggles. When

I put it up, I was certain that I knew what I had in mind. But then visitors kept asking insistent questions about it.

'You return to your office from a meeting, feeling annoyed: you were insulted and had to deal with unnecessary obstacles. How does looking at the picture help you? How *exactly* does it help? It cannot simply *extinguish* your irritation and its cause, can it?'

'No, of course it can't. But it helps me develop an inner *distance* to it.'

'What does this consist in? Does it calm your feelings?'

'No, this isn't about helping me calm down. The very idea is repulsive: using other people's suffering as a tranquillizer.'

'Fine, but what happens to you then?'

'It reverses a temporary narrowing of the mind. I was so controlled by my fury it made it seem as if its cause was the only thing that mattered in the world. As far as my thoughts and feelings were concerned, I could, as Gottfried Keller would say, not see beyond my own nose. This is therefore not about calming the mind, but about expanding it.'

'Are you talking about a *distraction*? About the fact that looking at the picture distracts you from your anger? That it – as we tend to say – takes your mind off it?'

'No, this is not what I mean either. The photograph isn't meant to seduce me into *escaping* the anger. What it's meant to do is make me live through it, but without being swallowed by it – to remind me that, when viewed in a larger context, this anger is a very insignificant episode. This is the inner distance I was talking about. This is how it affects our dignity.'

'But how are we supposed to envision this distance? Don't all focused activities and all genuine feelings inevitably involve an inner *identification*, that is, a lack of distance? Wouldn't the ideal that you're talking about involve not *living* life properly, but merely letting it *pass us by*? Viewed from that perspective, isn't the picture on your desk something that actually alienates you from your life?'

'That's a misunderstanding, though you're right in what you say about identification: if we always stayed out of things emotionally, because we didn't consider anything important enough, we would forget to live. But the way I understand it, there are two types of identification. The first, the desired and unpreventable one, simply involves being fully present. It can be in the context of anything, even secondary matters like football. During the game, the players focus on this one thing: playing the ball and winning. Nothing else matters. If they were just carelessly kicking the ball about – given that football is just a subsidiary matter – nothing would come of it and we would laugh at them. But what matters is that the players don't let themselves be completely overwhelmed by this practical identification, so that playing with balls and winning games starts to define their life. When a player misses a crucial penalty shot, he feels upset by it. If he was completely unaffected by it, we would feel as if he wasn't fully present. Yet when one missed shot haunts him for months and years, destroying his entire confidence as a person, we feel that that's identification gone too far. We would say that he has lost his sense of proportion. The loss of dignity thus doesn't lie in the identification, but in the inability to disentangle oneself from it again. This is what it's always like. Whether we are fired or go bankrupt, when this experience haunts us for longer than necessary, we suffer not only because of the failure and the pain, but also because we feel that being so preoccupied with it is undignified. Perhaps we say: I've lost my balance. These are the moments when one should look at the picture on my desk.'

The more I talked to my visitors about the picture, the more I came to discuss a concept that I have always found fascinating: *equanimity*. It seems to combine two distinct needs. On the one hand, the wish not to be the helpless plaything of one's emotions: we do not want to let random things upset us; we want to have authority over what can captivate us and what cannot. On the other hand, we feel that the goal cannot be a stoic ideal of indifference towards all emotions; about always being in the same mood. The sovereignty that we seek must not be confused with indifference and a lack of sensitivity, so that nothing is important to us. Yet how do we combine the two: sensitivity and certainty in our judgement about what matters?

'You see', I used to say, 'this is exactly what the sense of proportion gives us: the ability to be fully present in our experiences, without becoming enslaved by them; the ability to experience emotions without letting them get out of proportion. Put another way: we can distance ourselves from our worries, yet still take them seriously. We sense and know that there are greater and more significant things than what preoccupies us at the moment – and yet we must not deny the fact that it preoccupies us. The sense that I am talking about – I intentionally call it a *sense*: it's not an abstract, purely theoretical knowledge about more important things that helps us keep our balance. It is a very concrete, palpable knowledge, which is present *in the feelings themselves*. Equanimity – this is precisely this balanced state of mind. Sounds a bit mystical, doesn't it? But I can't express it in any other way.'

One of my visitors got out a copy of Kafka's diary and read: '2 August. Germany has declared war on Russia – Swimming in the afternoon.' 'Yes', I said, 'That's what I mean. The outbreak of war can make it seem ridiculous that someone goes swimming despite this knowledge. But it also depends on *how* he does it – whether the swimming session still stands above everything for him, or whether he feels that in a sense how he performs that day is completely irrelevant. When he feels like that, he will still be pleased or disappointed by his results. The knowledge of the war does not make him emotionless. But his feelings will be couched in the awareness that there are other things that matter more. This is why he might sit by the pool with a rather equanimous state of mind, irrespective of how he did in the swimming session.' A bit later, I added: 'A sense of proportion includes the awareness that there are *several dimensions* of importance – the private, professional and political, for instance – and that they can't be *weighed up against one another.*'

We also often ended up talking about how one can take himself seriously without taking himself *too* seriously and found it extremely difficult to make progress with this question. 'I'm six weeks away from finishing my dissertation', the doctoral student said, 'And in a year's time, I'll sit here saying: I'm six weeks away from finishing my dissertation.' We laugh. 'Yes', I say, '*self-irony*. Being able to make fun of oneself. Irony – it takes off the excess importance, without dismissing the entire issue. An essential part of our dignity is being able to keep this kind of balance. Self-irony is generally the ability to question one's own importance; to put all of our judgements on trial – while knowing that we couldn't simply shake them off, because they belong to our identity. And still: we mustn't consider them absolute. We know that there is always an external perspective that can make things look different. Accordingly, blind self-centredness represents a lack of dignity, and offended vanity can stem from lacking a sense of proportion. Humour helps us to avoid pettiness and stick to what is important.'

Another visitor had just returned from the social welfare centre, a place where dignity is always in danger and everyone feels how fragile it is. Someone had vomited in the hallway. It reeked. The others reacted dismissively: not my business. They sat elsewhere or pulled faces. One person, a well-dressed man with a tie and polished shoes, disappeared and returned with a bucket and sponge. He kneeled down and wiped off the sick. He took the bucket back and returned to his seat, with stains on his trousers. He took out his book and continued reading. 'What he did', the visitor said, 'also had to do with dignity. He did what the situation demanded, without taking himself too seriously, without smugness, without expecting applause.

Dignity can lie in our natural willingness to do the *obvious* – without any concern for oneself. Do you understand?'

Through complex detours, the conversation about the picture on my desk sometimes led to another topic: *self-pity*. We are disturbed by self-pity. Why? Its cause could be chronic pain, a terminal illness, an emotional loss – real suffering. But pitying oneself is different from the natural wish for the suffering to go away. This wish is an inherent part of suffering. Self-pity is also different from despair over the fact that the suffering will perhaps never disappear. When others know about our suffering, they are sorry for us and show their regret – they suffer with us. Why is it so offensive when we are sorry for ourselves? Why should a feeling that is considered good and noble in *others* be criticized when we apply it to *ourselves*? Is this not puzzling? In a spontaneous expression of our suffering, we might break down in tears. Later we cry over this again. What is wrong with the second bout of tears? We can cry for the suffering and tears of others, and the sorrow of others can provoke our own, genuine sorrow. Why can we not grieve over our own grief? Is it perhaps because it might give the impression that the suffering is not serious enough – since it leaves us with enough energy to pity ourselves? Or is self-pity perhaps not objectionable as a silent attitude, but as a gesture towards the others? Because we are asking for something with it? But what is wrong with wanting to alleviate one's own suffering with the help of the empathy of others?

Or is it different again: are we perhaps not criticizing the attitude itself, but the fact that this attitude makes us passive, inhibiting us from seeking help, either through external measures or by developing a new inner attitude towards the suffering? The critique of self-pity would then be a critique of a lack of autonomy and thus of a lack of dignity. And is this accusation perhaps also mixed into it: that in focusing on one's own suffering, one loses one's sense of proportion?

The View from the End

If death is the end of all experience, we should not be afraid of it, since we can only fear what we will experience. Nevertheless, we are deeply terrified when we are told that we will die soon. Why? The fear might be a fear of the agony of dying. But it can also be a fear of having *passed oneself by* in life. This is the fear of not having lived what would have actually been important to us, but other things that just arose or imposed themselves on us, without any correspondence with our sense of what actually matters.

A person does not have to wait for the announcement of her death to develop a sense for what matters in her own life. We can fast-forward intellectually and ask ourselves from the perspective of an imaginary end whether we have been weighing things correctly so far in our life. We cannot live every day as if it were the last. Although this is a well-known and attractive turn of phrase, it has not been properly thought through: it would not be possible to live a continuous life like that, since we usually fill our days with things that are intended to fill many more days. When we examine our life from the perspective of the end in order to affirm our choices, it can set a process in motion that is slow, complicated and difficult: it represents a new attempt to understand our own life and weigh it against the new desires that now enter our consciousness.

A discovery that we discussed early in this book is also of relevance here: the fact that in a life, there are many more thoughts, feelings and desires than an external biography reveals; and also more than the inner, conscious biography reveals. Many motives of our actions and also many driving forces behind our experiences remain in the dark. It is the mark of a subject that she knows about the existence of these unconscious, hidden motives, as well as of the possibility of bringing them to light and thus of inwardly expanding the radius of her self-knowledge. The view from the end will make us feel the need to broaden our self-knowledge; to ask how many things we have banned ourselves from living and why; to enquire into the secret guidelines of the important and where they originated from; to ask ourselves what changes in direction are still possible and from where we might draw the courage to make them happen. The answers to these questions will not be the same each time we reflect on our life from the perspective of the end. The process of questioning will be open and vivid, and it will change us. This also represents a form of autonomy and dignity.

8

Dignity as the Acceptance of Finitude

Old age and illness can make us lose our autonomy as subjects. Nobody takes it away. We experience a slow process of decay. We eventually also stop being partners in encounters. We become lonely because we no longer know how to do this: encounter someone. We lose our sense of intimacy and closeness. The loss of autonomy and the end of encounters endanger our dignity. And dignity is also at stake during a person's final decline – death. How can we make sense of the difficult and painful experiences that humans make with their decay and their end?

When Others Lose Themselves

It can happen that people who used to be part of our lives gradually lose their former faculties. Many aspects of this process bring suffering but do not imperil dignity. Going blind or deaf, being paralysed or having a tremor, having to deal with pain, anxiety or dizziness that are so severe that one can no longer leave the house: all of this is horrible and sometimes unbearable, but it is not already in and of itself something that imperils dignity. All of this involves a loss of autonomy, as well as manifold experiences of dependence, and sometimes this dependence is also experienced as powerlessness. Yet we have the power to support the people who go through this in such a way that their powerlessness does not become humiliation and threaten their dignity. We are still engaged in committed encounters with them, and our intellectual and emotional entanglements uphold the intimacy of our relationship. The loss of their faculties does not alter how we relate to them.

This is experienced differently when fading abilities affect a person's emotional identity. He remains a centre of experience until the moment he dies. But such a centre can gradually lose its inner order, creating gaps in the coherence of the person's behaviour. Such gaps make it harder and harder for us to comprehend and anticipate his actions. He is still the author of his deeds. He remains an actor whose actions are expressions of his experiences. Yet his acts are increasingly fragmented and focused on the short term, and the stories he tells us about his motives only hold for brief periods of time and are sometimes inconsistent. We start to doubt how much of his former self-image still remains. His grasp of the past and the present seems to become thinner; there are cracks in it, and the scope of his awareness of the future is also shrinking. There is still internal censorship – it might even have become particularly rigid – but it is more of a reflex than conscious evaluation.

As time passes, we experience something that seems like a fragmentation of the person's mind: thoughts, experiences and desires occur erratically in disjointed sequence. His unity of consciousness seems to dissolve, giving the impression that a *decline* is turning into *decay*. Does he still have convictions?, we ask ourselves. Is there still anything that he *believes* in? Our beliefs are what they are because of their many links to other beliefs. When these links start to crack – can we still be certain that the words coming from this familiar mouth actually express ideas? Or are they just linguistic habits? It is the same with his apparently fragmented experiences: how far does he still have emotions and desires as he used to? Is anything still being *decided* in his inner world? What must life feel like for him, now that the inner cohesion of his emotional events is growing weaker and weaker? More generally: what is it like to be him now?

People who suffer from such a condition sometimes seem to have an air of emptiness in their faces. Their gaze no longer fully reaches us, and there is something lost about their smile. We are unsure whether they are still fully present; whether we can still hope for the intellectual and emotional responses that used to be natural to them; whether we can still become entangled in encounters and communicate with them on the basis of these entanglements. They still exchange basic information with us and give simple answers to simple questions, but more complicated questions, including those about their condition and their desires remain unheard – even when they seem to give a reply to us. Their experiences become harder and harder to re-enact. And because we cannot comprehend them, we are also unsure whether we treat them in the right way – right in the sense of their experience – or whether given our cluelessness, we are stuck in inappropriate, schematic reactions.

Mary Tyrone from O'Neill's play, whom we encountered in Chapter 4, is also about to lose herself because of her morphine addiction. She is a slave to the drug and can no longer be persuaded to change for the better. Her promises and assurances have been worthless for a long time. She has stopped being a partner to James: as she no longer responds to James's appeals to her reason and understanding, commitment has vanished from their relationship. This also taints their emotions, which can only be natural and spontaneous when there is an attitude of commitment. Even being angry at Mary's unreason and stubbornness has become impossible for Tyrone, because such a reaction requires the theoretical possibility for the other person to change. The destruction through the drug takes its course. Her gaze and behaviour seem increasingly alien. Month by month, she becomes harder to approach and seems more and more absent as she walks around the house. James and her sons witness the fragmentation of her mind. All that they can still do is take a distanced attitude towards her and look at her with the objectivity reserved for the sick. The addiction has robbed Mary of her dignity as a partner. The task for the others is now to protect her dignity as a person who is sick and decaying.

What can we do in order to defend the dignity of people who have lost themselves? We must not write them off completely and must not give them the feeling that we no longer recognize them as persons at all. For as long as possible, we must treat them as autonomous beings, insisting that they take charge of their lives – even when this is only possible for a few more hours or days. We must let them *feel* that we are still concerned with their autonomy, even when it is increasingly compromised. Their awareness of our respect for their autonomy will never expire completely. This is why, even for those who have already largely lost themselves, it is terrible to be spoken to and treated like children. Defending their dignity means decisively opposing such treatment. It also means letting them have their say – despite the fact that what they utter seems strange and bizarre. It is also important to contradict them: through contradiction we recognize them as partners in a debate. We can try to show *solidarity* with them by letting them feel: we know that this can also happen to us. This is the solidarity of mortals. And something else also matters in the fight for their dignity: laughing and joking together. Through shared laughter, there can still be wordless encounters between us at a point when all other bridges have collapsed.

Escape

I was visiting my aunt in her care home when I met my old Latin teacher. He had moved there a couple of days before, and one could see why: he was wobbly on his legs, had to hold onto things a lot because of his dizziness and his hands trembled strongly. 'Living at home wasn't working any more. I kept knocking things over', he said. 'Piles of broken glass. And now – well, now I'm here.' It sounded as if his mouth had gone dry. I had to leave and shook his bony, trembling hand. Because I kept thinking about this hand and because he was a man who hated Caesar and loved Horace, I returned next month. He was no longer there. Two days after my visit, his room had been found empty in the morning. He had run away in the middle of the night – to Athens. His sister knew his address. I do not know why, but I went there: a studio that opened up into the backyard, a kitchenette full of broken glass, books on Modern Greek. 'It was that one incident', he told me. 'Five thirty in the afternoon, a hot, bright summer day. The door to the neighbour's room was open, so I could see and hear what was happening. The nurse had put the man with the catheter to bed. "And now let's take this little white sweet to get you to sleep", she said. The glass of water knocked against his teeth. Then she closed the curtains so it was completely dark. "Why are you putting a grown man to bed at such an hour and drugging him in order to make him fall asleep?" My anger was almost suffocating me. She eyed me up and down. "Shift change", she said, "I'm going home." That is when I knew: I'm not staying here. Not in a place where old and lost people are simply *managed*; where the shift schedule is the only rhythm that matters, and people don't even *consider* the fact that every resident has his *own* rhythm and can claim the right to live according to it. Do you understand, Peter?' He had never called me by my first name before. It was a precious moment. Later, we went to a bar. Every now and then, his dizziness forced him hold onto something. He exchanged Greek words with the barman. 'Language class', he said, smiling. 'Homework.' There were other men with trembling hands there. The barman wiped away broken glass every now and then – it was perfectly natural. 'I'll stay here', my old teacher said. 'Here, in Athens.' I nodded. A few months later his sister called me. He had been run over by a bus. An accident, they said.

Losing Oneself: Resistance

Bernard and Sarah Winter get old. The doctor's visits become more frequent. Bernard suffers from dizziness. The attacks remain unexplained and become a threatening tune that constantly accompanies his life.

'When the moment arrives where I start to lose myself, I want to die and I will take the necessary measures for it', he says at the end of a particularly bad day.

'What does that mean: *lose yourself*? What are the criteria?', Sarah asks.

'All the things that have defined me, that have constituted my emotional identity.'

'Such as?'

'The faculties of perception. There are losses that I could live with. It would be terrible to lose music if I went deaf, but otherwise I could get used to a silent world. But I want to be able to read without restriction. Blindness would be the end; as would be the loss of orientation – when I couldn't find my own home any more or no longer knew where I was in space and time. This would mean powerlessness, the loss of autonomy, dependence.'

'I'd help you. I'd do all I can to make the loss bearable for you.'

'You *can't* make such a loss bearable. *Nobody* can.'

'You'd still have your memories. We would have *our* memories – many of them happy ones.'

'That's true – in the beginning. But with time, they would also fade and eventually disappear completely. I wouldn't want to carry on when I would begin to forget important things: defining moments of my life, crucial relationships to other people; precious, vital emotions. When languages that I used to speak and which opened up new areas of the world to me would start to trickle away. In short: I wouldn't want to carry on when I started to lose my past. Why is this so important? Because a nuanced perception of the present requires all these memories. It would be different without them. Without the richness of memories resonating in them, new experiences would just be flat and boring.'

'But what if you didn't notice this loss?'

'It's not that these things are forgotten abruptly and in their entirety. One notices them crumble away bit by bit – one feels the loss, feels it very clearly. One feels the gaps and holes in one's memory. One perceives it as powerlessness, as a helplessness caused by the fading grasp on one's memories, a grasp that used to be so effortless.

One could consider this powerlessness humiliating. It is humiliating despite the fact that nobody is causing, enjoying and letting one feel the enjoyment of this powerlessness.'

'You could still look forward to the future, feel its openness and rejoice in its surprises.'

'The decay would also affect my ability to learn. And you could say that this would be the loss of the future. An active future that is worth living doesn't just consist in always receiving new impressions that simply replace the old ones. One has to *do* something with them. One has to relate them to things one has experienced, compare and comprehend them in the terms of this relation. This constitutes learning – using one's intelligence. I would be overcome with sadness and perhaps also with despair if I realized: I can never learn another language. My verbal memory is no longer good enough. But that wouldn't be the end. I wouldn't have lost the basic ability to learn yet. The end will only come when I feel that I can no longer relate the changes around me – everything that is new – to what I know. I no longer know how to *do* this. Novelty would then be a landslide of confusion, overwhelming me out of nowhere. It would become impossible for me to *orient* myself. Intellectually, I would come to resemble a mindless fossil, increasingly losing my sense of direction and stumbling around. There would come a point when I could no longer *express myself*. I would no longer find the words and feel: I can no longer find the thoughts either. I could no longer say what I think, feel and want. I could no longer articulate myself. How could I possibly still have encounters with others?'

'We can also encounter each other more intuitively – through feelings.'

'The decay I'm talking would also flatten my sensibility. I would notice my growing inability to react sharply and with nuance to the things that I encounter. My reactions would become merely lukewarm emotions that increasingly blend together. And I'm not talking about equanimity or detachment. My experiences would lack in sharpness and clarity. There would be a certain blurriness to them, progressively turning them into a uniform mishmash of sensations. I would find it calming at first, but then I would be all of a sudden startled by the question: What has happened to my complex and ambiguous emotions? They sometimes used to torment me. But feeling their absence is much worse. I'm becoming an emotional simpleton. They sit me down in the garden, then on the sofa; a little bit of music, then food. I'm glad when people are friendly to me and frightened when I'm snapped at. The modes of perception become simpler and fewer. The contours and contrasts of experiences fade. Noticing all this happen: that would be the end.

What would be particularly bad about all this would be losing the self-image that has defined me in the past; the fact that I would, in that sense, start to forget who I am; having to painfully try to recollect each morning what I still wanted to do in life; being astounded and confused by traces of previous ventures and plans, not really knowing what they have to do with me. Perhaps also: feeling uncertain in my internal censorship. It wouldn't need to come to an actual transgression, but I would not be sure: am I – or was I – a person who does such things, who takes such liberties?

And let's not even talk about the fact that such decay will at some point make one lose control over one's bodily functions – also one's excretions. I don't want to experience that either.

You know: I don't want to continue living below the standard that I always strove to achieve and maintain. The standard that gave my life its meaning. I don't want to end up on a slippery slope where I have to keep lowering my standards until nothing is left of them – just in order to keep extending life, biological life. I don't want that. I simply don't want it.'

'You don't have to. Who would force you to? But let's get to the bottom of things – not in order to *reject* your attitude, but to *understand* it even better. We should be relentless in our will for understanding, since everything's at stake here.

You always assume that you will somehow notice the loss: that it might not be a conscious realization, but still a vague sense of incapacity or emptiness. This won't be the case in the more advanced state of decay, but it could happen in the earlier stages, which is when you want to say goodbye. But try to imagine – simply try it – that this is *not* the case: that the slow, creeping decay is always accompanied by oblivion of what is lost, *complete* oblivion, so that, although objectively speaking there is a new restriction, you don't *experience* what is left to you as a loss. Step by step, nuance by nuance, you lose the abilities you speak of, but at the same time, you lose your ability to notice this loss. Try viewing yourself from the outside and from above, from a bird's-eye view, so to speak: you walk a bit slower and more cautiously than before. Many of the things that used to define you are no longer available to you. But you still enjoy taking the bus to the seaside, still enjoy listening to the music you used to listen to, although you can no longer classify it. You still love eating sweet things. Your utterances are somewhat short and sometimes a bit odd, but people like you or, at least, let you be who you are.

216 *Dignity as the Acceptance of Finitude*

You aren't lacking in the essential things in life. *I don't want that!*, you will exclaim. But *why* not? Why *exactly*? Remember: you don't notice what has been lost. According to this assumption, you no longer have an idea of what it would be like to be the person you are today, during this conversation. What's *wrong* with being this slow and forgetful old man? It cannot be your perception of it – we have excluded that. Your reduced sensations are what they are – you no longer know anything else.'

'I don't want *others to see me that way*, given that they used to know me as someone completely different. "He used to be a really smart guy", the neighbour will say, "now look what's become of him. The other day, he picked up an apple in the garden and stood there, starring at it for minutes, as if he had forgotten what it was and what you do with it." *I don't want that!* I want to go *before* that! It's a question of my *dignity*!'

'It's *now* that you don't want them to see you like that. But when you look up from the apple and see the neighbours greet you, it *won't* be a problem any more – because you will have long lost your ability to envision their gaze scrutinizing all that's been lost to you.'

'But I can imagine their future gaze on me *now*. I see the episode with the apple as they will see it. And I decide *now* that I don't want such a gaze to *ever* focus on me. *Ever*!'

'I know. But why not? A gaze that focuses on us can only be good or bad when it is *experienced*. But you will *never* experience the gaze that you're afraid of – that apple gaze. Not now, because it doesn't exist yet and also not then, because you will no longer notice it. Why should the gaze of a neighbour that you will never notice be a reason to exit your life prematurely?'

'Even when I don't notice it, they'll see the loss of my dignity. I know that that's the case. I don't want to lose my dignity in front of anyone, whether I notice it or not.'

'Because according to your understanding, the loss of your abilities undermines your dignity. But perhaps the neighbour sees this differently. "He's no longer his old self", he might say. "But we all change and lose certain things as we get older. It's no wonder: everything in nature decays and eventually decomposes. His gaze might seem empty sometimes, but I still think he's a nice man. Sometimes I even think: nicer than before, when he used to be so rushed and always a bit of a know-all. When I see him sit outside the house in his neat clothes he exudes a certain dignity. I don't know, perhaps this kind of dignity is a little bit sad. But I won't allow myself to be told that, just because he's no longer completely present, this old man has lost his dignity.'

'*That* kind of dignity, Sarah – I don't want to disrespect it. But that's not the dignity that matters to me. It's dignity in the sense of submitting to one's weaknesses and keeping one's composure – without self-pity, without that second bout of tears. Being able to do this is great. It shows admirable maturity and strength. I don't think I could do it. But even if I could: that kind of dignity is not *enough* for me. I don't want to sit outside the house in my neat clothes; not to mention the care home. Not even when you're there and take care of me. *Especially* not then. Because I also don't want *you* to see me like that. I don't want you to see everything that I've lost – how I've lost myself. I also don't want it – don't want it *now* – because I know that you would then look at me, knowing: he never wanted me to see him like that. The fact that I would no longer be aware of this thought – it doesn't make it any better, not a bit. Now I'm certain that you would have that thought. And perhaps also this one: "He should have done it, while he was still able to notice the loss. Not for my sake, but for his." And you would be right to think so.'

'Is that what *you* think when you see someone else who has lost himself like that? Isn't it *cruel* to think that?'

'It would be cruel if the thought was an *accusation*. As if I was saying to him, "You should have gone a long time ago." The thought would also be cruel if it was meant to be *universal*, something that applies to *every* person who is sick like that – without distinction. All of this is completely foreign to me. Yet I can imagine thinking it about a person like me, who I knew never wanted to be seen like that. When I think it about someone like that, it is the opposite of a cruel thought: It is a compassionate thought. A thought that serves to mentally defend and protect him.'

Losing Oneself: Accepting the Journey into Darkness

Sarah tries a fresh argument. As she said earlier, this is about the unrelenting will to understand when everything is at stake.

'It's not the case that I don't understand how you feel. Perhaps I'd also see it that way. Nevertheless, I ask myself: what sort of idea of our worth and dignity lies behind your powerful, almost angry emotions? What are the silent requirements that we are perhaps not even aware of? Perhaps the best way to recognize them would be by envisioning a completely different attitude and perspective, one that we encounter in other cultures. We could call it the *natural* perspective, and this is what it would look like: we are above all biological creatures, *natural beings*, who only acquired their autonomy, skills and their entire sensibility in the course of a long, slow process of maturation, that is principally biological. At the end of this process lies what we perceive as our personal emotional identity. This is the perspective from which you judge all the things that later appear as decay. Yet this identity is of course also dependent on our biological processes: all mental events are inevitably connected to physical events. The identity that rests on physical events thus changes in the course of time through thousands of small changes in our bodies. Then, from a certain age or as a result of an illness other tiny changes occur, changing our perception of ourselves as centres of experience, as subjects. These are the changes that you reject. Why? Because they change your perception in an unwanted way. Because things get lost. Because it would be different to be you. But couldn't we also see it this way: we have to let nature take its course. We mustn't resist being a part of nature, which is subject to the laws of growth and decay. This needn't involve a mystification or idealization of nature. It is completely matter-of-fact, a perspective that you as a scientist could accept.'

'The person who sees it like that: what does she think about the stage of advanced decay, the stage when others don't recognize her any more and when she has also forgotten what it's like to recognize herself? What does she think of it in terms of dignity?'

'I imagine she might think like this: "I sense that I'm about to lose myself. And I feel that it will be a journey into darkness, compared to the light of my life so far. But I'm ready to embark on this journey. I will make sure that I am as little of a burden as possible on others. Aside from that, I will live from moment to moment and take the days as they come. I will smell the sea and listen to the snow fall. What are the others thinking of me? I no longer care. The main thing is that I – somehow – manage to stay myself, even as I lose myself." This attitude exudes the dignity of someone accepting herself as a creature of nature, which like everything in nature grows, develops, blossoms, but ultimately also wilts and decays. It is inevitable. This is the dignity of a person who is not ashamed because of it and is not afraid of how others will look at her decay. She is also not afraid of it because she trusts that the others will not despise her, since they know that this can happen to them, too. It would also belong to her dignity, I think, to make provisions for the time when she is no longer autonomous, but increasingly dependent, and when she no longer takes part in encounters, but is merely grateful for the care that she receives.'

I imagine that Bernard Winter will carry this perspective with him and keep evaluating it against his own perceptions. He will feel that this is a conflict of emotions that is impossible to reconcile. On one hand, there is the desire to stay in control of one's life until the very end. On the other hand, there is the willingness to resign oneself to decay. He will ask himself whether we can call it a *decision* when someone chooses one over the other. If it is not a decision – what is it then? Can we say: it is simply an *expression* of what I am like as a person and of how I have lived my life?

When one day, Winter notices the first signs of his decay, he will ask himself how much he values what he can still experience of the present. The academic books lie in the corner. Sarah is still there, as are music, poetry and the smell of the sea. Yet these things get fewer and they keep fading. Based on what he has said thus far, he will at some point decide: it has been enough.

Dying

Two things happen when someone dies: biological functions stop and the person as a centre of experience ceases to exist. What does it mean to ensure that both events happen with dignity? What can others contribute to a dying person's dignity and what can one do oneself in order for one's death to be compatible with one's personal idea of dignity? What can *dignity* mean here in general, viewed both from within and from without?

I began this book with the following idea: a person's dignity lies in her autonomy as a subject, in her ability to determine her life for herself. Respecting her dignity therefore means respecting this ability. Dying is the event in which a person loses her autonomy. In what sense can we still behave autonomously in relation to this event? Is it not illogical to speak of an autonomous loss of autonomy and of wanting to determine the loss of one's self-determination? Yet it would only be illogical if what we meant was experiencing every moment of this loss as if we were in full possession of the skills that we are about to lose; if I thought I can still exercise my full autonomy in each moment of loss, including the last one. This is conceptually impossible – a paradox. This is not how we can understand the dignity of dying. How else can we make sense of it?

It can mean the following: now, while I am still in possession of my autonomy, I determine what the loss of this autonomy will look like one day – which paths I want it to follow. This only applies to what we call a *natural* death: not death through accident or violent crime, where the suddenness of death forestalls the question of its dignity. How would a person want to configure his natural death?

The process of dying is the last episode of a life – of a very specific, individual life. Part of the idea of dignity is that this episode *fits* the life that it concludes. To put it differently: everyone should have his own individual process of dying and also his own death. Yet what constitutes such a death? How can we understand the individuality, the singularity of a process of dying? What might an individual design for the end of life consist in?

When we see pictures of sick bays or large halls in old hospitals, where people lie and die among many others, we might have the ter-rifying thought: these people not only have to endure pain, fear and loneliness – they are also being denied their own, individual death. We might develop a similar feeling when visiting a dying person in a modern hospital, a place marked by the smell of disinfectant and the squeaking sound of rubber soles on endless linoleum corridors. Afterwards, when we are back outside, we might look up to the window where the patient lies in one of the countless rooms that resemble concrete boxes from the outside. There are reasons – good medical reasons – why he is dying in there. The machines and tubes alleviate his suffering. Viewed that way, it is the right choice.

Yet it might seem the wrong choice in another sense: namely because it precludes him from dying in the environment and sur-rounded by all the things that have defined his life: furniture, dishes, paintings, photographs, souvenirs, books, bric-a-brac that have shaped the atmosphere of his rooms, the lamps with familiar light. It is not just that we think: he misses all those things up there – that must hurt. We might also think: it is not acceptable that a person has to die in one of the unfamiliar, uniformly grey-white rooms, alienated from himself at the end of his life. It is not acceptable for reasons of dignity.

'What is the alternative?', my wife asks. 'Yes', I say, 'I know.' When we arrive at home and walk through our house gate, I stop. I imagine I had spent the last hours packing my suitcase and would now be standing here, ready to drive to the hospital to die. I walked through all the rooms, touched many objects that are heavy with memories for the last time. Now I will shut the gate one final time. 'No', I say, taking the suitcase and returning to the house. 'This will make your life shorter', my wife says. I nod. 'And what about the pain?' 'There is home care. There is morphine', I say. 'Are you okay with it?', I ask. Perhaps I do not even ask her. There are questions of dignity that do not require others' agreement.

One's own death has not only to do with one's own, familiar environment, but also with one's own people – with those who have shaped me and have helped determine my life's tune. I might want them to be with me at the end; or I might want to be alone in my last hours. In either case, it belongs to a dignified death that we have the opportunity to say goodbye to those without whom our life would not have been the same. Saying goodbye will involve looking back: envisioning what we have lived through and dealt with together, which parts have succeeded and which failed. This might be accompanied by the wish to apologize and reconcile. It represents a last attempt to gain clarity on the life that is about to end in its entirety. In that sense, the dignity of the dying encompasses the dignity of truthfulness, as we discussed it in Chapter 4.

Truthfulness also belongs to the possibility of a dignified death from the perspective of others. We should be honest with the sick. This also applies to those who are terminally ill. We have to tell them what is wrong with them, how much time they have left, what kind of suffering lies ahead for them and what can be done about it. Why? Because they must have the chance to *prepare* for their death, both in terms of external measures and their inner attitude. When we leave them in the dark, it is not just outrageously paternalistic. We rob them of nothing less than the chance to conclude their lives. There are doctors and family members who keep the truth from them because they dread a panicked reaction, a sudden irrational act. But what kind of idea is that exactly? There will come a point when they can no longer keep it a secret. If this is a person given to strong emotional reactions, such a response will naturally follow this revelation. What has been won? Undignified weeks in which he was greeted with false solace and dishonest optimism every morning, while death was already raging inside him? Did it really do him any *good* to be robbed of precious time to prepare for death? We can also ask ourselves the following question: when we cannot stop someone from taking his own life in sheer panic after receiving a fatal diagnosis – must we not accept it as her way of dealing with it? Who would claim the authority to prevent it at any cost – even at the cost of dishonesty that robs the sick person of her dignity in the sense of autonomy?

Are there any lies that are justified at the deathbed? Lies that protect the dying person's dignity despite violating the principle of truthfulness? They could be well-meaning lies about the person's abilities, reputation, his moral integrity, about feelings of affection and appreciation that others allegedly have towards him. 'You were a good father, a role model. We'll miss you. And your compositions – everybody knows that they are brilliant and will outlive you.' Those lies would allow him to die with an airbrushed self-image. What do we feel when we witness such lies or are even involved in them ourselves? 'He'll be able to die in greater peace', someone might say. This is not a small good, nothing that could be easily dismissed. After leaving the dying person and reflecting on it outside, we might say to ourselves: 'It was the right thing to do. Who would have benefited from telling him the cruel truth?' Yet there might also be nagging doubts. In this important moment, we avoided a true encounter with this person and did not take him seriously. We could experience this as a violation of our integrity. But not only that: we could also feel as if the lies violated *him*. They prevented him from coming to terms with himself at the end of his life. This would have belonged to his dignity. Even when he did not experience this loss – it *took place*. And we are not blameless, even though we acted out of noble motives.

Letting Someone Die

I might become terminally ill. All that medicine can still do for me is delay death and make the process of dying more bearable. My dignity in the sense of autonomy requires that I, the sick person, determine myself what the doctor may or may not still do with me. I have the final authority over it. I might make a decision that is unreasonable by medical standards: no more interventions, even when they could delay death for some time. No chemotherapy. No other medication that extends my life, just palliative care. No artificial respiration or life support. I forbid resuscitation in the case of sudden cardiac arrest.

This can meet with resistance on behalf of my doctors. 'It's my duty to do everything I can to keep you alive', she might say, 'it is required by the ethics of medicine, the goal of which is the protection of life as the highest good.' I remind her that every medical intervention on a patient who is capable of making decisions requires his consent. In this way, the patient's dignity in the sense of autonomy is anchored in law. 'But this is about your life!', she might say. 'Precisely', I will respond, 'that's why. It's *my* life and *my* death, and I alone decide how it happens. It is not my intention at all to disrespect your ethical principles of care and the protection of life. But you can't simply equate them with the patient's welfare. Your principles reach their limit when they clash with the patient's self-determination. If I consider it crucial to my welfare to be allowed to die, you have to respect that. You have to respect it on legal grounds alone. But what is more important to me: you have to do it out of respect for my dignity. If you succeeded in overriding my will, it would be a presumptuous, paternalistic act with which you would forfeit your own moral dignity.'

It might also happen that I fall into a coma after an accident or an attack. What can this mean in terms of the respect for my will, my dignity and the doctor's actions? The degree of the damage will be decisive: according to the medical assessment, is there a chance that the patient will return to consciousness and will then be able to decide what should happen to him? Or has his brain function completely stopped so that he will never be a centre of experience and volition again? Things are clear in the first scenario: we do everything to keep him alive and thus give him the chance of returning as a subject with experiences and agency. Both the protection of his life and the respect for his dignity demand it. There is no conflict between these two considerations. Even though the patient cannot express his will at that moment we can be sure that we are acting in his interests.

Things are more complicated, both from an intellectual and an emotional perspective, when we are certain that the person lying in front of us under artificial respiration will never return again as a conscious being, because his brain activity, which is indubitably the precondition for any experience, has stopped entirely. We can imagine this happening to Bernard Winter. The accident occurs while Sarah is away. The next day, she is alone with him in the hospital room. It is quiet; the only sound is the gasping of the ventilator. Bernard looks as if he could wake up at any moment. She touches his hand and caresses his hair. She sees the lever that would deactivate the machine. She knows what he used to say and think about this – she knows it exactly. Nevertheless, she would like to imagine him speaking one more time. It does not work here. She cannot hear his voice. So she drives home and sits across from the armchair where he used to talk about these things.

'When we are provided with artificial respiration and nourishment, despite the fact that we will never wake up and experience something again, this artificial survival is nothing but an empty mechanical process – a dependent process on top of that, which no longer sustains itself. As there is no subject any more, it is a life that no longer *belongs* to anyone. It is a completely *alienated* survival. With a person, unlike with a plant, the meaning and significance of biological functions lie in the fact that they produce a centre of experience, a subject. In the case that we are discussing here they have lost this significance. When we continue them nonetheless, they become idle functions without an inner perspective. I imagine feeling my strength fade and sense that my perception will soon become extinguished. I am suddenly overcome by fear: they will continue to keep me alive artificially for years. It will be a process that no longer has anything to do with me, the person I used to be. My body – it will no longer be *my* body. It will be *nobody's* body, but simply a biological system. Where there used to be a body with an inner world of experience, there is now a mere *shell* that will never be anything other than a shell again. But it is not just *any* shell, but *mine* in the sense that it previously sustained me as a living subject. This is why now, while I can still experience and take a position on this, I'm not *indifferent* to the fact that I will continue to be kept alive in this ghostly way. I'd want it to *end*. I don't want to be reduced to *this*. This wish must be respected. It is a respect for the former person, whose integrity was defined by the interaction between physical function and experiences. It is a question of dignity.'

Bernard sometimes used to add: 'Human dignity also consists in the willingness to accept death and dying, not to resist it by any means. Isn't it actually insane that one has to protect oneself against people who want to patronize us on this question? And that it is doctors of all people, who witness human lives ending all the time. Isn't it a strange, even utterly insane idea that the body's survival constitutes the highest goal – no matter if someone still inhabits it or not. The fact that Ariel Sharon was denied a natural death for years: I find it atrocious. I find it *inhumane*. It represented a glaring violation of his dignity.'

The next day, Sarah returns to the hospital with the living will that Bernard had composed, in which he prohibits all life support measures in the case of such a condition. She demands the machines be switched off.

'I won't kill Mr Winter', the doctor says.

'You aren't *killing* him by turning off the machines. You're *letting him die*. Why do you pretend not to know the difference?'

'Our task is to protect lives, not to terminate them.'

'But surely not the lives of inanimate *bodies*, but the lives of *persons*.'

'For me as a doctor, who has taken the Hippocratic Oath, the protection of human life is the highest good.'

'The highest, inviolable good is human dignity. At the core of this dignity lies not the protection of life, but individual self-determination. You are denying my husband the process of a natural death that he has requested for this eventuality. You want to contravene his unambiguous wish and deprive him of self-determination in this last episode of his life. This is presumptuous. It violates his dignity. Given what he has requested, I am not only entitled, but *obligated* to enforce his will. And you know that the law is on my side.'

The doctor looks at her provokingly: 'But you wouldn't be prepared to turn off the machines yourself, would you?'

'Yes, I would', Sarah says.

A woman approaches Sarah in the corridor whose son is in the same condition as Bernard.

'I come here twice a day to check up on things', she says. 'You never know with the hospital staff. Sometimes they don't place the pillows correctly. He should want for nothing.'

'He no longer feels anything', Sarah says to her. 'He will never feel anything again. Why don't you let him die? He has a right to it.'

'But he's *my life*! Coming here and checking on him – that's *my life*!'

'Who is this about? Is it about him or is it mainly about you?'

The woman is left speechless. She looks at Sarah in a disturbed and angry way.

In one of their conversations on this topic, Sarah had said to Bernard: 'Let us imagine the opposite scenario: someone demands to be kept alive despite irreparable damage that has destroyed him as a subject with experiences. Under no circumstances should they let him die. What do we do? Couldn't this person appeal to dignity through self-determination just like you?'

'He can appeal to his right to self-determination and we will listen to him. But there are differences. One of them is: I wish for something *not* to be done to my body. He wants his body to be fed and venti-lated indefinitely. He expects something of the others that I don't. He wants to determine their future actions – I don't. The issue is further complicated by the fact that he demands an unending activity that many of us consider pointless. Self-determination is thus not always self-determination.'

' "Every person is an end in itself", this person might say. "That's why my wish must be granted." '

'People will respond that the idea of an end in itself does not refer to emotionless bodies that are artificially kept alive, but to persons capable of experiencing something. I would describe to him what I have explained to you on previous occasions: how absurd and repul-sive I find the image of a body that used to be inhabited by a subject with experiences, but is now soulless, ownerless and dark, indefinitely attached to a machine.'

'He won't let himself be terrorized by your images, he might say. He is not at all repulsed by the idea. And he will return to the subject of self-determination.'

'Then I will remind him that dignity not only comprises self-determination, but also the willingness to accept our finitude and mortality; that with his wish to endlessly delay death, he violates dignity in that sense. Letting someone die once he has perished as a subject of experiences – this is the natural thing to do, and in this naturalness lies his dignity. Withholding death from someone who is already in darkness – that's unnatural and undignified.'

'When faced with instances of medical paternalism, you always used to stress that you wouldn't let yourself be tyrannized by other people's ideas of dignity. It also belongs to the experience of self-determination that everyone can have his individual understanding of dignity and must be respected in it. What if this person confronted you by saying: "I don't share your idea that dignity lies in dying naturally. You have no right to dismiss my request that is based on a different idea of dignity, just because it does not fit in your conceptual world." It could get even tighter. Perhaps he follows a religion that demands that the body must be kept alive by all available means – indefinitely. "My religious views are no less worthy than your perspective", he will say.'

' "Yes", I would respond, "But your perspective for us involves the tyranny of infinite care, which we consider pointless, not least because you do not experience any of it. You can't expect us to accept this tyranny on behalf of someone who has long ceased to exist as a deciding subject.'

'And what shall we do with someone who permanently falls into a coma without having made a will or left behind any specific instruction for this eventuality?'

'When we are certain that she will never become conscious again, we should grant her her death. Her dignity demands it – according to our criteria. She has not left us with any other criteria after all.'

Ending One's Life

We can imagine that a person concludes one day: I have lived enough. I don't want my life to go on for any longer. It does not need to have been an unhappy life full of deprivation. The feeling is not: I have suffered enough. It might have been an average life, in which happiness and unhappiness were balanced. It can even have been a predominantly joyful life, in which circumstances allowed the person to live in accordance with his desires and abilities. This is not about wanting to terminate suffering. This is about something else: the feeling of no longer being *curious* about what the future might bring. The person no longer expects to be *surprised* by himself.

He has left the job that he enjoyed doing, retired feeling that he had had enough of that activity with its repetitions, its successes and failures, the recognition and the disappointments, the words that had to be exchanged every day, the familiar jokes and rituals performed at the office in the changing light of the seasons. He sometimes still passes by the building and looks up to the window behind which he spent so many years and then sits down at the café across the street to reminisce – the memories are predominantly positive. Every now and then he also waits for a former colleague to walk by on the opposite side of the road. Yet his visits become less frequent. His life increasingly acquires a new rhythm: journeys that he used to have no time for, books, music. He experiences the seasons more consciously. His wife died years ago. He has got used to her absence. Sometimes he wonders whether he has just got used to missing her or whether he does not actually miss her any longer.

What he is most annoyed by is the fact that he no longer has new emotional experiences. That it has become *predictable* what he will feel in the evening, the next day or next month. His feelings are not unpleasant. They are just less and less novel or surprising. More and more, these experiences have the stale taste of repetition. This is also the taste of the things that he says and that are said to him. He sometimes wonders how he endured those countless repetitions for all those years and decades. He is now sometimes so repulsed by them that he prefers to say nothing rather than utter a banality. What is the matter with him, the others then ask him.

He flips through travel brochures. There are still a few countries, a few picturesque streets that he would like to visit. But all the repetition that would precede it: at the station, at the airport, in the car, in the hotel. And all the empty phrases that he would have to hear and say. Is he tired? Perhaps, but not in the sense of exhaustion like after a long suffering. 'My soul is weary of my life', he had read somewhere. Is that it? Perhaps, but not in the sense of an angry rejection. Rather, it is simply the feeling: this is enough. I have had enough.

He reads the relevant literature about depression, but does not recognize himself in it. This is not what this is about. This is not about a psychological disorder in general. He does not suffer. He does not feel that he lacks in anything. Will I be glad when it is over – all this living?, he sometimes asks himself. Then he laughs about the absurdity of the question. Is this perhaps a sign that I want to keep going after all?, he wonders. This reaction expresses a wish for an experience after all: the wish to experience the end of all experience.

He grew up in a family where religious beliefs made ending one's life unthinkable. It was sacrilege, sin. He had never understood or embraced this attitude. Who else should be in control of one's own life if not oneself? If one cannot decide this question by oneself

– the most important question of all: What else could one decide by oneself?

'He must have been in great despair', they would say at his grave. He already contradicts them, calling out to them into his voiceless future: 'Who says that one cannot simply do it because he's had enough? Enough of everything, even of having enough?'

But this is certainly not the most common motive for ending one's life. Those who commit suicide mostly do it because they can no longer endure what their life has become. 'Mere living is not a good, but living well', Seneca wrote to Lucilius. 'You can find men who have gone so far as to profess wisdom and yet maintain that one should not offer violence to one's own life, and hold it accursed for a man to be the means of his own destruction; we should wait, say they, for the end decreed by nature. But one who says this does not see that he is shutting off the path to freedom. Must I await the cruelty either of disease or of man, when I can depart through the midst of torture, and shake off my troubles? This is the one reason why we cannot complain of life; it keeps no one against his will.'

What sorts of reasons can make a life so unbearable that we no longer want to cling to it? And what do they have to do with dignity?

There are suicides that are flight responses or sudden acts committed out of dark, uncontrollable impulses. When it happens this way, one could perhaps say: 'This has nothing to do with dignity.' The entire category does not apply here. In other cases, however, it happens in the clear awareness that dignity is at stake. Seneca writes of a man who is going to be thrown to the wild beasts. 'Lately a gladiator, who had been sent forth to the morning exhibition, was being conveyed in a cart along with the other prisoners; nodding as if he were heavy with sleep, he let his head fall over so far that it was caught in the spokes; then he kept his body in position long enough to break his neck by the revolution of the wheel. So he made his escape by means of the very wagon which was carrying him to his punishment. When a man desires to burst forth and take his departure, nothing stands in his way.' This is suicide in order to pre-empt unbearable torture and humiliation – suicide thus in order to prevent a loss of dignity.

We can imagine different variations of Seneca's example: Winston in Orwell's book hangs himself in his cell to escape torture and to prevent Julia's betrayal. Prisoners in concentration camps throw themselves on the electric fences. A defendant who takes his life in order to avoid being accused of being a henchman of capitalism in a show trial. In all those cases, suicide serves the protection of dignity. We can value our dignity higher than our life.

Willy Loman, the salesman, also eventually takes his life – not with the pipe in the cellar, but with his car. It is a suicide out of despair about ill fortune and failed dreams. This is different from someone killing himself on the way to the torture chamber. The difference lies in that one could attempt to stop Loman from doing it. One could attempt to show him that this is not the only way. 'He had the wrong dreams', his son says. They were dreams of success, of big money and also of popularity. 'That's the wonder, the wonder of this country, that a man can end with diamonds here on the basis of being liked!', Loman had said. The deceptive worldview of the American Dream was the invisible prison cell that Loman inhabited. 'We never told the truth for ten minutes in this house', his son says. Linda, his wife, could have tried to unlock the prison cell of his delusions. She could have enforced truthfulness and its dignity, and she could have made Loman aware that he can still be someone without those lies – someone with a life that is worth living, despite its failures. 'He never knew who he was', his son says at his grave. Had this been different – it would have perhaps never come to that.

Yet perhaps it still would have. In Chapter 3, we encountered a Willy Loman who says to Linda: 'I hid the pipe because I wanted to be alone in my despair. There are certain things you need to deal with alone.' Does such defiant loneliness not also exude a certain dignity? One reason why Loman drove into his death was to allow Linda and his sons to claim the money from his life insurance – his last, his only achievement. Up until the end, money and success are his standards. 'This is how I am, this is how I've lived', he could say to Linda. 'And this is how I'm going to end my life. I don't want you to try and change me. You couldn't anyway. But I don't want you to even try it.'

What might an encounter look like with someone who is preparing for suicide? How could we speak to him, while preserving both his dignity and our own? We can support him in finding an autonomous will. It is important for his dignity that this last, final will is entirely his own: not manipulated, not something he was talked into, not an imitation. There are group suicides and suicides motivated by fear of imminent apocalypse. There are also suicides in consequence of extortion and suicides that happen because of identification with a real or fictitious hero who killed himself and perhaps glorified it. Our dignity in this encounter can consist in questioning the will behind the decision: in investigating where it came from, what kind of foreign influences might be involved and how far it is consistent with this person's previous self-image. If we do this right, the person who has come to find life no longer bearable will gain greater clarity, without feeling pressured or suffocated by us and our commitment to his life. Our plea for his life and our respect for his own will are in balance. Eventually, he will gain a better sense for whether the logic of his life makes this last step inevitable. He will also gain a better idea of why he cannot be stopped even by his relationships to those who want to hold on to him.

His decision will be the lonelier the more it is based on feelings of guilt and lost dignity. We earlier envisioned a Willy Loman who betrayed his friend to McCarthy. We can imagine that he cannot live with this betrayal. His guilt and his loss of moral dignity are too severe. When talking to him, we would need to avoid something that is a danger both to his and our dignity: trivializing the matter. We must recognize the seriousness of the transgression. He would explode if we tried to convince him that he was deceiving himself. 'You have no way of *judging* what this means to me!', he would say.

We saw how Bernard Winter also claimed this final loneliness after he concluded: 'Rather than lose my emotional identity, I prefer to put an end to my life.' This would also be the case if something else happened to him: if he became paralysed from the neck down and, in addition, also lost his eye-sight. Being trapped in such immobility and darkness would be hell for him. From the moment he becomes aware of his condition, he will have only this one – non-negotiable – wish: to die. But he lacks the ability to do it by himself. He needs someone's assistance. He needs that person as a means to realize his wish and put an end to his life – he wants someone to take his life upon his request. The legal term for this is: killing on request. It is prohibited in many countries, yet there are some that allow it. Doctors are the ones who can do it safely and without causing pain. We can imagine Winter talking to two of them. He manages to convince one, but not the other.

'We should be relentless in our will for understanding when everything's at stake', Sarah had said in their previous conversation, and this is also the case here: this is not simply about being *for* or *against* something. This is about gaining as precise an understanding as possible of our thoughts and feelings in such a situation. We can experience this situation as confusing and we will need to get to the bottom of what this confusion consists in. If, in the end, we declare ourselves to be in favour of or against something, it will be the unforced result of such a process of self-questioning and affirmation. This must not become a war of opinions, with opponents accusing each other of unethical motives. The significance of the topic demands that we remain composed and attentive while we explore the conceptual implications of certain assumptions, and then ask the other person, "Do you still agree with it?"

First doctor: I don't want to kill anyone. I won't commit murder. As a doctor, my task is to save and to preserve lives, not to extinguish them.

Winter: As with other important questions, we have to be wary of a seduction through words. Words can stir up feelings and cloud our thinking by evoking pictures and associations that do not actually belong here. In those cases, we do not even notice that we are being carried away by words rather than ideas. This is what's happening here. *Killing, murder, extinguishing lives*: these words carry an aura of cruelty about them, because they belong in the context of crime, war and extermination camps. By using such words, you conjure up cruelties that we *all* reject. What I'm asking you to do, by contrast, is not an act of cruelty that inevitably brings suffering, but in fact the opposite: the release from suffering, the termination of agony. It would therefore be better to use a neutral term for this, such as ending a life. This is what I want you to do: to put an end to my life.

First doctor: Nobody is allowed to end a human life. This would violate the person's dignity.

Winter: Dignity? What do you mean?

First doctor: The dignity of a life lies in being God's gift. We therefore can't dispose of it at will.

Winter: I don't wish to be tyrannized by an idea of dignity that is alien to me and that doesn't even make any sense to me. I will tell you what my dignity consists in: in my autonomous and self-determined will. If you want to respect my dignity, you will have to respect my will and it is: I want you to help me die. When you won't fulfil this wish despite being able to, *that*'s a violation of my dignity.

Second doctor: Invoking divine prohibitions indeed has nothing to do with our role as doctors. This idea of dignity doesn't make any sense to me either. What kind of dignity is it that is indifferent to a person's will, setting itself against it so strictly, as in this case? A *ruthless* dignity? This must sound like *mockery* to Mr Winter in his prison of immobility and darkness. But still, Mr Winter, you cannot expect my colleague to act against her religious conviction. This has to do with *her* dignity, in the sense of her personal consistency.

Winter: I can accept that – at least on an abstract level. But let's take note of the fact that she is thereby disregarding my dignity in the sense of self-determination. She is saying to me, 'Your personal dignity matters less to me than the divine dignity that I believe in.' And that's not a trifle. I wonder: does she actually *understand* what she is doing? Has she ever really tried to *imagine* what it is like not being able to *move*? Not being able to move *ever* again? And being blind on top of it, so that I cannot even connect with the world through seeing and reading? Is she *aware* of what a hell of powerlessness that is? And is she aware of how *cruel* it is of her to tell me: I won't be moved by your suffering because of a divine prohibition?

First doctor: I'm indeed capable of putting aside my religious convictions. I would still never kill anyone on request. And this is because we can never have full knowledge of a person's will. Is he really completely *certain*? Is he really entirely *clear* about the irreversible consequences? Is his wish *genuine*? Is this really *his* will, free of foreign influence? Is it free from self-deceit?

Winter: If I were to legislate on this, I would place strong emphasis on the need to check all these issues – repeatedly and over an extended period of time. And I would demand that every reasonable doubt be taken very seriously. But you know: at some point, you simply *know*; just like you know with other life-determining decisions that someone takes. If you now said to me: 'Mr Winter, I hear what you say about your will to die. I've been hearing it for days and weeks. But how can I be certain that you *really* know and understand your will? How can I be sure that you are not attached to your life in paralysis and darkness *after all*?' If this is what you said to me, I would be overcome by a feeling of anger and powerlessness. What an incredible arrogance, hidden behind the sanctimonious façade of intellectual diligence, I would think. As if I could be wrong about my clear, desperate wish!

Second doctor: But couldn't your will to die still *change* after all? Is this not at least *conceivable*?

Winter: *Any* will can change in theory. But it cannot follow from this that we don't respect it as it is, as a self-determining will. Otherwise there would be no respect for a person's self-determination *at all* and thus no respect for dignity.

Second doctor: Fine. But this is about your *final* wish!

Winter: The fact that it's my final wish that, once executed, will be irreversible doesn't change anything about the fact that it's self-determined and must be respected. Otherwise the absurd principle would apply: *because* it's this life's final wish, it doesn't need to be taken seriously.

First doctor: I will now tell you something that might sound cynical to you, because it doesn't apply to you personally, but that relates to our political responsibility: if we made killing on request legal, it would open the floodgates to abuse. We would have to fear that patients who are in someone's way or whose care is deemed too expensive would be killed under the pretext that it was their wish.

Winter: There's no reason to talk about an opening of the floodgates. This metaphor, just like the metaphor of the slippery slope, means by allowing one thing, we *necessarily* also have to allow the other. Put differently, if we allow this one thing, we can no longer for *any reason* refuse to allow the other. This is not at all the case here. As I said earlier: 'We must apply the strictest standards and gain comprehensive reassurance that someone really wants to die.' The autonomous, genuine and non-manipulated will is the criterion. We could also request an inspection by an independent committee that can rule out dubious or insincere motives. This inspection would represent the new floodgates.

Second doctor: The opening of the floodgates my colleague speaks of is not so much an intellectual one, but one that opens the way for *abuse*.

Winter: As I said: we would have the resources to identify each case of abuse as such and follow it up. The possibility of abuse is *never* a reason not to pass a law that is beneficial when applied properly. You see, your argument effectively involves you saying to me: 'I genuinely feel sorry for your suffering, but I can't fulfil your wish, because in order to do so we would need to be authorized by the law and such a law cannot be passed because it could be abused.' Imagine you were in my position and please imagine it *precisely*: wouldn't you also be foaming with rage?

First doctor: Someone recently murmured 'euthanasia' and 'Holocaust' when we discussed these issues on the ward.

Winter: This is stupid, undignified and irresponsible blather – a sign of intellectual negligence. People who can't distinguish between respect for a self-determined will and a fascist extermination programme do not belong in a hospital.

Second doctor: We indeed shouldn't pay any attention to such crudity. But someone recently said to me: 'It would be conscious, intentional killing. Wouldn't that be *murder?*' Courts also sometimes speak in those terms, when they contest a powerless patient's right to die by another's hand.

Winter: Those people should be forced to read a dictionary. *Murder* – this is when someone is killed against his will and out of base motives. Neither is the case here. What I said at the beginning applies again: people are easily swayed by words and forget to think.

First doctor: Okay, I will try to get as far as I possibly can. What I can accomplish is this: I understand your wish for me to kill you – or, as you prefer to call it, put an end to your life. And I admit: people who don't understand this wish lack imagination and empathy. I'm even prepared to take one further step: I understand if someone did it because she could no longer witness your agony – and because, unlike me, she had no religious objections. But I could never take the final step: inject the poison into you myself. I think I also couldn't do it if I didn't have my faith. I simply *couldn't* do it.

Winter: Given my suffering, it's hard for me to do this, but I can say to you: I accept that. I can't expect anyone to overcome such emotional opposition. Yet I wonder how *coherent* such opposition really is. After all, you don't normally hesitate to relieve someone of his suffering. This is your job as a doctor.

First doctor: But only *within* a life!

Winter: But why? What if continuing to live is exactly what constitutes the suffering?

Second doctor: I'm also terrified at the thought of injecting the lethal poison into you. Could I live with this?

Winter: Imagine you attached me to an IV, which just needed to be activated by pulling a lever. What you do is legal, as long as *I* am the one who pulls it. *But I can't!* I CANNOT do it! I need your hand for it. Couldn't you see it that way: you lend me your hand, as a sort of instrument, so that I can complete my wish?

First doctor: I understand what you mean. But this is *your* perspective on my hand. It can never be *mine*. From my perspective, this is an *action* like any other. And I couldn't live with it.

Winter:	Imagine you sit by my bed for many hours. I beg. I plead. You can also feel that there's nothing I want more than for this lever finally to be pulled. Couldn't you even do it *then*?
First doctor:	I would imagine you lying dead in front of me afterwards and I would have to think: I did this. I think I'd leave the room.
Second doctor:	It would be hard for me to live with that, too. Yet perhaps I could manage to wholly adopt your perspective and say to myself: it would, above all, be liberation. There was an elderly patient at my old clinic whose entire body was paralysed. Aside from his eyes, he could only move a muscle on his chin. He needed a ventilator and a drip-feed. A sensor was installed on his chin that allowed him to send impulses to a computer. The man could see an alphabet on the screen. A light dot slowly moved over the letters. When it stopped on the right letter, he used his chin muscle to make a signal, selecting that letter. The screen was filled with words. The man wrote – an entire book. It took him many years. When he was finished, he wrote: *I'm done. Cremate.* We had an agreement: if I read those words, I'd help him. He died naturally the following night. I stood by his bed for a long time. I was glad that I hadn't had to do it. But I think I'd have been ready to.

Responsibility Towards the Dead

We also take care of a dead person's dignity. He will never know about it. Nevertheless, we feel that this is about *him*. It is of course also about us: about the way we feel towards this dead person and the dead in general. Yet we sense that, beyond that, there is also something that we have to protect *about him*. What is it?

The dead person is not just *any* body: it used to be a person with whom we had encounters by becoming entangled in our thoughts and feelings. The body will disintegrate and cease to exist. This is why we are allowed to burn it. But there are many things that we cannot do with it: for example, eat it, sell it or play with it. These prohibitions are a continuation of the idea that the dead person was once a subject and thus an end in itself: a being that one cannot just use and treat as a mere object.

We also protect the dead against the intruding looks of sensation-seeking voyeurs. We cover the bodies of accident victims. It is as if we wanted to say: he does not want to be seen like that. This is about dignity as the respect for intimacy – even when this intimacy is no longer experienced by the person herself. This is why serious news sources do not publish pictures of mangled corpses, not even when they belong to brutal despots. The disfigurement reduces what was formerly a person to flesh and bones, to an arrangement of matter. It is a brutal dissolution of the person. Here we also want to say: nobody wants to be seen like that. This thought also motivates the impulse to avert our gaze. We feel nothing but contempt for those who make a business out of this. Without noticing it, they gamble away their dignity.

Some dead are laid out. This allows others to say goodbye to them and see them for a final time. We would condemn anyone making fun of this situation. 'But still: I don't want to be put on *display*', I hear Bernard Winter say. 'I don't want my shell, which still carries a pale and hollow version of my features, to be exposed to the looks of others. Looks that I can no longer confront – unlike when I wake up from a sleep. I don't want my dead body to be *arranged* either.' 'But you wouldn't notice it.' 'I don't even want to have to *imagine* it now.' A colleague of Winter had his death filmed – for educational purposes. 'This feels so *alien* to me!', Winter said. 'This *entire person* is so alien to me!'

We not only respect the dignity of the dead by protecting their bodies. We further pay our respects to them by dealing with what they have left behind. 'But she's no longer here – so you no longer have a relationship with her', one might object. Yet the emotions that this relationship gave rise to remain important. They survive. This is why we respect the things that used to define this person's life. This attitude of respect could not be sustained if we simply ignored her wishes and threw everything away. The relationship would then come to an end not simply because the person is dead. The death of our respect for her would entail a change in attitude, a change that would be selfish and that would damage our earlier relationship to this person. One can say that since the other person's death is not a reason for this change in attitude, the cause must lie with us. And this shows that our attitude of commitment to this person was not unquestionable and firm but perhaps a delusion or even a lie.

Lasting respect cannot mean that we do not change anything and pretend as if the person was still there, sitting at the table with us. Her belongings, which we cannot bring ourselves to touch, would become a fetish. But we will also not destroy the things that the person created and that were important to her life. We will not handle them arbitrarily either, not even when it would be to our advantage.

There are authors who could not bring themselves to destroy their texts, yet did not want them to be published either. Many people would still want to read them and their publishers could make a lot of money. 'They are great works that are of public interest', people will say. Yet publishing them would go against the dead person's will. It would violate her dignity as someone who wanted to determine her life, especially in its most important facets: her words, her plays and everything that they express.

There are still other things that we do not do after someone's death: we do not betray the dead person's secrets and we do not waste his money. We have to imagine stepping in front of him and justifying it to him, whatever it is that we want to do. What happens when we know that he would not understand and could not accept this justification – while we are certain that it is the right thing to do, because it would alleviate suffering for instance? What happens to his dignity in this case, to the extent that it depends on us?

And what if a death was a relief? What if we are glad to be able to finally throw all this stuff away? Where lies the difference between an undignified destruction and a liberation that still preserves the dead person's dignity? Does it suffice that I do not just throw the things in the rubbish, but hand them to someone who will use them?

Our dignity towards the dead consists in our respect for their will and the way in which this respect fits the logic of their lives. We can pay this respect in front of others – then it is not actual respect for the dead, but for the expectations others have concerning the demonstration of such respect. Or we respect the will of the dead in silence, when we are alone with them. The respect we show in those situations is very different from all other demonstrations of respect – as it is usually their intended nature to be noted: this is a respect that is unnoticed by anyone but ourselves. One might think that it is the ultimate expression of respect, because it is dependent on nothing but itself.

References and Further Reading

〰️

Where available, English translations of foreign-language works have been cited. Otherwise the translator has provided her own.

Introduction

Human dignity is the inviolable right to be respected, anchored in faith in God. An example of this view is Wilfried Härle's book *Würde – Groß vom Menschen denken (Dignity – Thinking Highly of Humans)*, Munich: Diederichs 2010. Härle writes: 'A fact that can be generalized and that is also not denied by critics of religion and human dignity is that there is *no justification for human dignity that is more comprehensive, firm and convincing than the faith in God as the creator.* The connection between faith and human dignity is so strong that they support and explain each other – without the one, the other would be lost or disappear from life.' (page 79) For non-believers this means having to live with a dignity that they cannot quite make sense of.

Chapter 1

Being an end in itself: This concept as an explanation of the idea of dignity is found prominently in the work of Immanuel Kant. Here are some classic passages: 'Now I say that human being and in general every rational being *exists* as an end in itself, *not merely as a means* to be used by this or that will at its discretion; instead he must in all his actions, whether directed to himself or also to other rational beings, always be regarded *at the same time as an end.*' *Groundwork of the Metaphysics of Morals*, Section II. 'Humanity itself is a dignity; for a man cannot be used merely as a means by any man (either by others or even by himself) but must always be used at the same time as an end. It is just in this that his dignity consists...' *The Metaphysics of Morals, Doctrine of Virtue*, §38.

Dwarf-tossing: The French legal battle took place between 1991 and 1995. It began with Manuel Wackenheim's lawsuit against the mayor of Morsang-sur-Orge, who had prohibited him from letting himself be tossed in a nightclub. The verdict of the UN Human Rights Committee of July 2002 is put down in Communication No. 854/1999. Manuel Wackenheim had claimed that the prohibition violated his right to private life. The committee put a limit to this right, arguing: 'That limit... is justified by higher considerations deriving from the respect due to the dignity of the human person.'

Robert Walser, *Jakob von Gunten*, translated by Christopher Middleton, Austin and London: University of Texas Press 1969. The cited passage is on page 132.

Slaughterhouses: While writing this section, I happened to be reading the book by Michael Hampe: *Tunguska, or the end of nature: A Philosophical Dialogue*, translated by Michael Winkler, Chicago and London: The University of Chicago Press 2015. It was astonishing to see how similarly we think on this subject – even down to the same vocabulary. This is especially obvious on pages 67–9.

George Orwell, *Nineteen Eighty-Four*, Harmondsworth: Penguin 1954 [1983 printing]. The cited passages are on page 227 (book 3, chapter 3).

Wilhelm von Humboldt: This quote is from his 1792 work *The Limits of State Action*. See the English translation by J. W. Burrow, Indianapolis, IN: Liberty Fund 1993, page 19.

A doctor's freedom of conscience as an excuse for an action contravening a declared wish: This is how the Higher Regional Court in Munich ruled in a case where a Jehovah's Witness had refused a blood transfusion. One can read more about the verdict in *Medizinrecht* 2003. I thank Tatjana Hörnle from the Humboldt University in Berlin for this reference.

Arthur Miller, *Death of a Salesman*, London: Penguin Classics 2000. The citations in this chapter are on pages 45 (act one), 59ff (act two), 8f (act one), 62, 64 (act two).

O'Brien's attempt to deprive Winston even of the autonomy of arithmetic thinking: see pages 214ff, 219 (book 3, chapter 2) in Orwell's book.

The subject of inner autonomy is also discussed in my Graz lectures, published as *Wie wollen wir leben?* [*How do we want to live?*] by Residenz-Verlag in 2011. My book *Das Handwerk der Freiheit* [*The Craft of Freedom*] is dedicated to the subject of inner autonomy in our wishes and decisions. It was published by Hanser Verlag in 2001 and as a paperback by Fischer Verlag.

The delegation of inner censorship to an external authority, connected with a complete loss of autonomy. The classic text on this subject is Sigmund Freud, *Group Psychology and the Analysis of the Ego*, translated by James Strachey, London: Hogarth Press 1959.

Humbert Humbert writes in *Lolita*: 'I was weak, my school-girl nymphet had me in thrall. With the human element dwindling, the passion, the tenderness, and the torture only increased; and of this she took advantage... Only very listlessly did she earn her three pennies – or three nickels – per day; and she proved to be a cruel negotiator whenever it was in her power to deny me certain life-wrecking, strange, slow paradisal philters without which I could not live more than a few days in a row. Knowing the magic and might of her own soft mouth, she managed to raise the bonus price of a fancy embrace to three, or even four bucks.' Vladimir Nabokov, *Lolita*, London: Penguin 2000, page 183f.

Heinrich Mann, *Small Town Tyrant*, translated by Ernest Boyd, New York, NY: Creative Age Press 1944. The cited passages are on pages 117f, 129, 176.

Alfred Andersch, *The Redhead*, translated by Michael Bullock, London: William Heinemann 1961. The cited passage is on pages 80–2.

Max Frisch, *Montauk*, translated by Geoffrey Skelton, New York and London: Harcourt Brace Jovanovich 1976, page 125.

Chapter 2

On the connection between intellectual entanglement and communication see: Stephen Schiffer, *Meaning*, Oxford: Clarendon Press 1972, and Paul Watzlawick (with J. H. Beavin and D. D. Jackson), *Pragmatics of Human Communication*, London: Faber 1968.

Loman's anger: page 64 (act two).

Linda's anger: page 44 (act one).

The German Supreme Court's legislation on the peep-show was passed on 15 December 1981. See reference BVerwG I C 232.79.

The women in the Amsterdam shop windows: Their case also makes one think of another definition of dignity by Kant: 'In the kingdom of ends everything has either a *price* or a *dignity*. What has a price can be replaced by something else as its *equivalent*; what on the other hand is raised above all price and therefore admits of no equivalent has a dignity.' *Groundwork of the Metaphysics of Morals*, Section II.

Robert Walser, *Jakob von Gunten*, page 23. The official translation has been slightly modified by the author.

Franz Kafka, *The Trial*, translated by Willa and Edwin Muir, London: Vintage 2008. The cited passages are on pages 3, 14f. The official translation has been slightly modified by the author.

Loman being laughed at: page 28f (act one).

Recognition and authority: I have learned a lot about this connection from René Majer's book *Scham, Schuld und Anerkennung [Shame, Guilt and Recognition]*, Berlin: De Gruyter 2013, especially chapters 2 and 3.

The English title of Claudet Sautet's 1971 film is *Max and the Junkmen*, starring Romy Schneider and Michel Piccoli.

Orwell: The cited passages are on pages 257, 262 and 263 (see Appendix: The Principles of Newspeak).

Chapter 3

What the look of others does to us: Nobody has described this more vividly and powerfully than Jean-Paul Sartre in *L'Être et le Néant*, Paris: Gallimard 1943.

English: *Being and Nothingness: A Phenomenological Essay on Ontology*, translated by Hazel E. Barnes, New York: Washington Square Press 1956, 1992. The key text is in the first chapter of part 3, section IV: The Look.

Per Petterson, *I Curse the River of Time*, translated by Charlotte Barslund with Per Petterson, London: Harvill Secker 2008. The cited passage is on page 30.

On the connection between shame and loss of authority, I have again learned a lot from René Majer's book *Scham, Schuld und Anerkennung* [*Shame, Guilt and Recognition*]. A work that I found very enlightening on the subject of shame in general is K. Schüttauf, E. K. Specht, G. Wachenhausen, *Das Drama der Scham* [*The Drama of Shame*], Göttingen: Vandenhoeck 2003.

The fear of being exposed that undermines an active experience of the present is the topic of my novel *Perlmann's Silence*, translated by Shaun Whiteside, London: Atlantic Books 2012.

Philippe Claudel, *Le Bruit des Trousseaux*, Paris: Stock 2002. The cited passages are on page 36f. English by the translator.

Linda discovers Loman's pipe: page 46f (act one). Miller writes: 'How can I *insult* him that way?' The situation suggests that what she also means is *shame* him.

Christa Wolf, *City of Angels or: The Overcoat of Dr. Freud*, translated by Damion Searls, New York: Farrar, Straus and Giroux 2013. The cited passage is on page 51.

Max Frisch, *Drafts for a Third Sketchbook*, translated by Mike Mitchell, London: Seagull 2013, page 65. The passages from *Montauk* are on pages 76 and 102.

Bernard Lown, *The Lost Art of Healing*, New York: Ballantine Books 1999. The cited passage only appears in the second German edition: *Die verlorene Kunst des Heilens*, Stuttgart: Schattauer 2003, page 59, and has been rendered into English by the translator.

Edward Albee, *Who's Afraid of Virginia Woolf?*, New York: New American Library 2006. The passages cited in this chapter are on pages 40f, 54, 70, 92f (act one); 149–52, 154, 156 (act two); 245ff, 250f (act three); 101f (act two).

Chapter 4

Emmanuel Carrère, *The Adversary: A True Story of Murder and Deception*, translated by Linda Coverdale, London: Bloomsbury 2000. The cited passages are on pages 75, 159 and 151.

Carrère's book also contains an example of the shift from a committed to a distanced relationship, as I describe it in Chapter 2. He talks about how Romand's friends feel after finding out about the fraud and the killings: 'When they spoke of him, late at night, they couldn't manage to call him Jean-Claude any more. They didn't call him Romand either. He was somewhere outside life, outside death, where he no longer had a name.' (page 16)

Loman's life-lie: The cited passages are on pages 10, 24–6, 23 (act one).

Albee: The cited passages are on pages 254–6 (act three).

Christa Wolf, *City of Angels*, page 53.

Eugene O'Neill, *Long Day's Journey into Night*, London: Jonathan Cape 1966, page 74. Emphases by the author.

Howard's blather: page 65 (act two).

Harry G. Frankfurt has published an important essay entitled *On bullshit*, part of the volume *The Importance of What We Care About*, Cambridge and New York: Cambridge University Press 1998. He says on page 125: 'It is just this lack of connection to a concern with truth – this indifference to how things really are – that I regard as the essence of bullshit.'

Chapter 5

Friedrich Dürrenmatt, *The Visit: A Tragi-Comedy*, translated by Patrick Bowles, London: Jonathan Cape, 1962, pages 36, 38f, 81.

Orwell, *Nineteen Eighty-Four*, the passages cited in this chapter are on pages 242, 247, 250, 252 (book 3, chapter 4).

William Styron, *Sophie's Choice*, London: Vintage 2000, pages 272, 328, 346f, 349. The crucial scenes are in chapter 10.

Joseph Conrad, *Lord Jim*, London: Penguin 1986. The cited passages are on pages 88–90.

Friedrich Dürrenmatt, *The Pledge*, translated by Joel Agee, London: Penguin 2001. The passages cited in this chapter are on pages 26, 72, 142.

Bernstein: This episode is recounted in Humphrey Burton's biography of Bernstein. Roy Harris had tried to convince him to change his name. Bernstein writes in a letter: 'Harris was very nice…He also spoke very seriously about my changing my name. Something Anglo-Saxon like Roy Harris, no doubt. He thinks I might ride in on the crest of the wave of reaction against the foreign artist craze, which reaction he thinks is due for the next twenty years.' Humphrey Burton, *Leonard Bernstein*, London: Faber and Faber 1994, page 59.

The original title of Melville's 1970 film is *Le Cercle Rouge*.

Chapter 6

Romand's last words: see page 167 in Carrère's book.

John Burnham Schwartz, *Reservation Road*, London: Phoenix House, 1998. The passages cited in this chapter are on pages 288, 290–2.

Roman Frister, *The Cap Or the Price of a Life*, translated by Hillel Halkin, London: Weidenfeld & Nicolson, 1999. The main episode is described on pages 241–4. The last sentence is on page 385, the episode on the train to Auschwitz on page 271.

The passages in Claudel's book are on pages 30 and 34.

The verdict of the German Supreme Court and its justification can be found in the court's press release of 15 February 2006. The judges could also have argued: the state must not *set* humans *off* against each other, as this makes them *countable* objects that are *replaceable*. This also would have been a justification in the spirit of Kant.

The prohibition of torture: see Article 104, section 1, sentence 2 of the German constitution and §136a of the code of criminal procedure.

Chapter 7

Henrik Ibsen, *Hedda Gabler and A Doll's House*, translated by Christopher Hampton, London: Faber and Faber, 1989. The passages cited in this chapter are on pages 169–73 (act three), 127 (act one), 158 (act three), 126 (act one). Gottfried Keller, *A Village Romeo and Juliet*, translated by Ronald Taylor, Richmond: Oneworld Classics 2008. The cited passages are on pages 15f, 19f. Max Brod (ed.), *The Diaries of Franz Kafka*, translated by Joseph Kresh, Martin Greenberg and Hannah Arendt, Harmondsworth: Penguin 1964 [1982 printing], page 301.

Chapter 8

Seneca: The cited passages are from the 70th letter to Lucilius. See Seneca, *Ad Lucilium Epistulae Morales*, translated by Richard Mott Gummere, London: William Heinemann 1920, volume 2, pages 59, 65, 69, 71.
Loman: see pages 110 (Requiem); 68, 104 (act two); 111 (Requiem).
I have found the following two books particularly instructive on the subject of death: Michael de Ridder, *Wie wollen wir sterben? [How Do We Wish to Die?]*, Munich: Deutsche Verlags-Anstalt 2010; and Christoph Müller-Busch, *Abschied braucht Zeit [Partings Take Time]*, Berlin: Suhrkamp 2012.

Credits

Quotations from George Orwell, *Nineteen Eighty-Four* (Harmondsworth: Penguin 1954 [1983 printing]):

Quotations from Arthur Miller, *Death of a Salesman* (London: Penguin Classics 2000):

Quotations from Edward Albee, *Who's Afraid of Virginia Woolf?* (New York: New American Library 2006):

Quotations from Henrik Ibsen, *Hedda Gabler and A Doll's House*, translated by Christopher Hampton (London: Faber and Faber, 1989):